To Cha

with lo

THE MAN ON THE ICE CAP

Nicholas Wollaston

THE MAN ON THE ICE CAP
The life of August Courtauld

Constable London

First published in Great Britain 1980
by Constable and Company Limited
10 Orange Street London WC2H7EG
Copyright © 1980 by Nicholas Wollaston
ISBN 0 09 462990 0
Set in Monotype Ehrhardt 11 pt
Printed in Great Britain
by Ebenezer Baylis and Son Ltd
The Trinity Press, Worcester, and London

Contents

Illustrations

ERRATUM

The caption to the bottom picture
facing page 181 should read
'The children'.

Acknowledgements

I am grateful to Faber & Faber for permission to quote from
T. S. Eliot's *The Waste Land;* to Martin Secker & Warburg
and Mrs Sonia Brownell Orwell for permission to quote from
George Orwell's *The Road to Wigan Pier;* to Methuen & Co
for permission to quote from Christopher Isherwood's *Lions and
Shadows;* to Sidgwick & Jackson for permission to quote from
Evelyn Waugh's *A Little Learning;* to A. P. Watt for permission
to quote from J. M. Scott's *Gino Watkins* (Hodder & Stoughton)
and his *Portrait of an Ice-cap* (Chatto and Windus); and to
Macmillan and Co. for permission to quote from Christopher
Burney's *Solitary Confinement.*

The pictures of the 1930 Greenland expedition were taken
by Air Commodore Iliffe Cozens, who with August Courtauld
was a member of the team.

Author's Note

I never met August Courtauld, though I had heard the story of the man on the ice cap. Probably he would be puzzled and a little annoyed to be told that a book had been written about him, especially by a stranger. I have come to know him partly through his letters and diaries, mostly through his friends and family. Whether my picture is at all like the man they knew I can't tell, but I should like to acknowledge my debt to them and return my thanks. Without the help of so many people it would have been much more difficult.

Without one person, Lady Butler of Saffron Walden, it would have been impossible. The book was her idea in the beginning, it could never have been written without her encouragement and kindness, and properly it belongs to her. To Mollie, with love, I offer my gratitude.

N.W.

Childhood

On 5 May 1931, high up in the middle of the Greenland ice cap, the dawn opened into a bright spring morning after a spell of gales and drifting snow. Even there, in one of the world's most desperate and sterile places, the new day broke with a distinct sense of hope and life. Anyone straying into that Arctic desert could persuade himself that the possibility of human survival, almost suspended during the winter months, had at last returned.

There were three young men on the frozen surface of the ice cap, searching for a fourth who might be somewhere underneath. They had spent a fortnight dragging their sledges up from the coast across 140 miles of desolation, steering by compass and navigating by sun and stars in a land empty of landmarks. For the first week or so the weather had been ideal, with clear skies and light winds, though the heat of the sun was enough to peel their faces and crack their lips. By the time the wind began blowing hard at thirty degrees below zero, the faces of the three explorers were so sore that it felt like having iodine poured into an open wound.

On 1 May, when they had reckoned they were close to the point they were making for, the weather clamped down and it became impossible to get a proper fix. All they could do was lie in the tent and wait for something better. Their five weeks' rations might be made to last ten weeks if necessary, after which they could eat the sledge dogs, so their impatience was less a matter of discomfort than of their agonizing nearness to the spot where their friend had last been seen, five months before. But on the evening of 4 May the gale died and the sky cleared. At daybreak next morning they were able to plot their position. With theodolite and wireless time-signal it would be accurate to within a few hundred yards.

The calculation put them one mile north-west of their target. Excitement gripped the young men, and apprehension too. They put on skis and spread out to cover a half-mile strip of ground between them, each taking a dog on a lead in the hope that it might pick up human scent if nothing was visible above the snow.

5 May 1931: the most momentous day in one man's life, though he didn't know it yet. He was also unaware that on that same day, halfway round the world and in a very different climate, the first airmail service was on its way from Australia to England—a journey that would take twenty days, knocking two weeks off the sea voyage. And in the previous month a man had flown from London to Cape Town in only six days and ten hours. But these things were not irrelevant. Remotely, it was the idea of an air route from Europe to America that had brought the three young men, now fanning out on skis in search of their friend, to the Greenland ice cap.

The featureless plateau of ice, more than a mile thick, was not absolutely flat. It rather resembled a long and gentle ocean swell, rising and dipping from horizon to horizon, with wide hidden hollows and broad backs not steep enough to form shadows. On topping one of these undulations the three explorers, almost simultaneously, saw a small black speck half a mile ahead of them. They went racing over the snow towards it.

But as they got closer their hopes dropped. For the first time the leader of the three—a man of only twenty-four who was himself to die in Greenland the following year—was frightened. Even in that godforsaken desert the place had an extraordinary air of abandonment. The black speck turned into a ragged piece of cloth sticking a few inches above the snow, but could it be the flag they were looking for? Was it really a Union Jack? If it was, it marked the spot where their friend should be.

On 6 December 1930 he had been marooned with a tent pitched inside a cave built of snow blocks, with food and fuel to keep him till the spring, and a few books, but no wireless. Since then the wind had sometimes blown at force nine for days on end, with a temperature down to forty degrees below zero. The winter's gales and blizzards had spread an immense layer of snow across the landscape, eight feet thick. It must have been a long time since a man could have fought his way out of an ice hole, even if he wanted to; even if he was still alive.

Earlier in the spring another rescue team, after two false starts due to a broken sledge and the awful climate, had spent a month criss-crossing the ice cap in search of this flag. But so appalling was the weather that often they had been unable to leave their tents, and on the rare days when they could get going the visibility was too poor for accurate navigation. They might have passed within a few yards of the man beneath the ice, and never known.

It was less than twenty years since the bodies of Captain Scott and his companions, at the other end of the world, had been found in the tent where they had lain all winter, and the memory of that epic tragedy must have struck the three young explorers as they approached this place. Perhaps remembering that Scott had had St Paul's letter to the Corinthians read over him before being buried in his sleeping-bag, the leader had brought a prayer book with him in case they found the worst: *The last enemy that shall be destroyed is death . . . Death is swallowed up in victory. O death, where is thy sting? O grave, where is thy victory?* The ice prison of their friend could well have become his tomb.

So many things could have happened to him in the five months since he was left here. Though he had then been fit and strong except for frostbite in his toes, and though he couldn't have caught any infectious disease on the lifeless ice cap, he might have fallen to some organic illness and died alone in terrible pain. Or, when he could still go out to make scientific observations before the weather locked him in, he might have strayed too far from the tent (half a dozen paces would be enough in an Arctic storm) and been unable to find his way back, to perish quickly of exposure. Or later, after the tent was submerged but if the ventilator pipe had got blocked with snow, he might have been poisoned by carbon monoxide from his stove.

There was another thought, perhaps the most dreadful of all, that troubled the three rescuers as they raced across the last few yards to the tattered flag: this friend of theirs—a perfectly sane and sensible person when they last saw him, though he had ignored every plea to retreat with the others to the coast in December before it was too late, and had defied the warning of the expedition doctor against being left without communication or hope of relief until the spring, and had insisted on staying behind in a tent soon to be buried in the snow so that, for some private reason of his own which he never quite made clear, he could spend the winter alone on the ice cap, which nobody had ever done before—this friend of theirs might possibly have gone mad. Imprisoned all those months in a tiny cell below the surface where they now stood, a man's body could just have survived. But what of his mind?

They didn't stand there long. The tent in its cave of snow blocks, with two small igloos for stores, had sunk under a snow-drift that rolled to the horizon and hundreds of miles beyond. But rising above the surface near the scrap of flag were the tops of some meteorological instruments and the handle of a spade. More important, an inch or two of brass pipe was visible. If the ventilator was still clear above the drift, there was hope for the man below.

The leader knelt on the snow beside the pipe and shouted down. Then, after an ageless second while three hearts stopped, there came a faint shout in answer from the depths. The voice was tremulous, as one of the explorers wrote later, but it was the voice of a normal man.

That normal man, 'just an ordinary chap' as he called himself, was a quite unremarkable Englishman aged twenty-six at the time of his voluntary Arctic vigil that turned into five months' solitary confinement. His name was Augustine Courtauld, known by his friends as simply August, which was what his rescuers shouted down the ventilator pipe.

Though August Courtauld was far from being an eccentric, his portrait is a study of a slight oddity, peculiar in that he was peculiarly English; partly a typical man of his times, partly a man who didn't quite belong to them or who outlived them, though he died only in middle age. By his own lights, certainly, he was nothing very unusual. It is those lights, the criteria of a man of his particular slot in English history and English society, that now seem extraordinary.

He belonged to a generation, most of them too young to fight in the First World War and some of them almost too old for active service in the Second, that flowered astonishingly in the 1920s and '30s, throwing out a brilliant variety of blooms. The poets, the propagandists, the young men who flirted with Communism and joined the hunger marches or the International Brigade in the Spanish Civil War, are the ones whose conscious quest, or conscience, is best remembered. There were others who searched in the dark corners, not of the mind but of a world where wide unmapped tracts still lay.

The men of intellect and the men of action often came from the same background, even from the same family. W. H. Auden, Stephen Spender and Graham Greene all had brothers who joined expeditions to the Himalayas. Greene, between his novels, wrote books about some very exotic and difficult journeys, and so did Evelyn Waugh. Others—H. W. Tilman, Eric Shipton, Gino Watkins, Freddy Chapman being the most famous—were explorers who, driven by something like the Renaissance spirit of adventure and lured by a passion for any blank on the map, however dangerous or inaccessible but preferably among mountains, practised their art in the way in which they travelled: romantic rather than scientific, and accompanied by the smallest number of friends, if not alone.

The search for a man's character, like the search for the man himself on the Greenland ice cap, can be bewildering. The stranger who never knew him is uncertain what to look for and finds unexpected, puzzling things. Time has dropped a vast blanketing snowdrift over everything and only the tips of a few solid objects still show above the surface. Soon many of them will have disappeared. Meanwhile their evidence varies, they tell different stories of the man underneath; and he, like everyone else, is a bundle of elements, a mixed bag of effects and influences.

The most lasting clues, but not the most telling, are the inanimate ones. In a village church in Essex a painted wooden board says that one Saturday in 1931, in three hours and ten minutes, 'Bob Minor'—a peal of 5,040 changes—was rung on the bells to commemorate the safe return of Mr Augustine Courtauld from the Arctic regions. Those regions themselves honour his name with a mountain, a glacier and a fjord called after him. Less impersonal relics are not numerous, or they lie submerged, which is in keeping with his character. He edited a very good book about polar explorers and wrote a rather bad one about himself. More intimately, he left half a dozen notebooks and a box of letters.

People, his surviving friends and family, remain the best material for a study, but twenty years after his death he is as elusive in their memories as he often was in life. To his sister, though he could be outspoken and argumentative, he was a very private man, shy and reserved: 'It would be quite impossible for anyone who hadn't known him really well to give a true picture of him.' Perhaps nobody did know him well. He had no lack of friends yet seemed to cultivate independence. All the more surprising—or all credit to the power of love—that he fused himself so totally in marriage. 'We were very much one person,' his widow said of their happiest years.

Even during his life it was difficult to pin him down, to the regret of many of his contemporaries: 'I remember feeling that Courtauld was one of the people I would have liked to know better . . . I am very sorry I didn't get to know him well . . . One admired him from a distance . . . I wish I had met him again . . . I wish I had known him—he was one of the most original and creative of our generation . . . I didn't know him—sadly my loss.'

A bishop remembered him more distinctly than most: 'He had the appearance both of an athlete and an artist—medium height, spare, ascetic, with a charming welcoming smile. He had a strong face but a kindly one, with lively eyes . . . He was in no way an intellectual but he had a good store of common sense and his mind was clear and alert.'

The hint of contradiction, already visible in his appearance, grows with each witness. A man who had known him since university days said the point about him was that he was a very complex character, but a man who had known him since school said he was essentially simple and straightforward. For one old friend 'lovable' was the first word that came to mind; for another it suggested a charm that he never had. Yet the bishop mentioned a charming smile and others agreed: 'I have always remembered his great charm . . . How charming, how exceedingly kind and how very English he was . . . A great, courageous, original and charming man . . . Gay, unconventional, brave and charming . . . Quite unconscious of his charm.'

At first sight he is a scientist without a science, but on looking closely more of an artist without an art. He seems to be the epitome of an amateur, outraged by the incompetence of professionals. His name put a label on him which he couldn't escape. 'Being a member of the Courtauld family made him one apart,' an exploring friend wrote. 'To be a Courtauld in the '20s and '30s was quite something,' a sailing friend said. He was remembered by one man as being always thoughtful for others but never for himself, and by another as a kind and cultivated host; by one woman for his pungent personality, and by another for little except his extremely good manners. To many he gave the impression of being unique, of having his eyes set beyond most men's horizon where he saw possibilities outside the limits of ordinary life: 'This unusual man . . . I would say he was a man of great vision . . . A wonderful and a very rare person . . . A

fascinatingly interesting character . . . I think all of us who were
at Cambridge realized that he was in every sense a very special
person, quite different from the normal run and quite clearly
marked to do something out of the ordinary.'

They were unanimous about his courage: 'The bravest man I
have ever known . . . He wasn't physically a strong man but he
had the heart of a lion . . . Outstanding courage—mental tough-
ness, if you will . . . He was courageous in mind and spirit, and
most certainly possessed great physical courage and endurance . . .
My dear and most gallant friend.'

One of them touched on something less obvious: 'Frivolity was
what many will wrongly remember him for, but his great
characteristics were loyalty and integrity to his friends . . . He had
a profound knowledge, backed by remarkable instinct, of many
subjects . . . Casual observers would never grasp the depth of
these virtues. They were often concealed by a light-hearted over-
lay which gave the impression, wrongly, of superficiality and
almost a juvenile outlook.'

For most of his friends he was the richest man they knew,
but to look at, according to the wife of one of them, you would
never have guessed he had two farthings to rub together. Others
were more specific: his clothes were a shambles, his fingernails
were clogged with tobacco ash, he missed trains, he lost things,
he was none too fond of soap and water, he was other-worldly
and casual and sloppy and careless. Alone and snowed up on the
Greenland ice cap, he couldn't dig himself out of the tent because he had left the spade outside. When he was in the navy his
cabin, as someone said, was 'a glorious mess of everything lying
around everywhere—it only needed a few frozen fish to complete
the effect of a floating igloo'. On the contrary, someone else
remembered it as empty and austere with few of the comforts or
private possessions most men needed. But as a rich man there
was another side, hardly glimpsed by friends unless they were in
difficulties: 'Sometimes we guessed but we were never told about
the many fields in which his stealthy, almost surreptitious,
generosity was given rein.'

Other friends turned up other facets: 'He had a rumbustious sense of humour and his anecdotes were often picaresque . . . He really enjoyed being alone . . . Very much the life and soul of the party . . . A doer rather than a talker . . . A natural rebel against social conventions . . . Full of humour, originality and humanity . . . Unaware of class distinctions or ephemeral social values . . . August took rather a delight in saying things to shock people—or perhaps I should say that this was often his way to make a point . . . He treated the world with such derision.' And darker shades are hinted at: 'I found him quiet and somewhat withdrawn . . . His introspective nature . . . It wasn't in the least surprising that he should commune with the spirits . . . Perverse and even solipsist . . . puritanical . . . iconoclastic . . . ruthless . . . Certainly he *could* be very unkind.'

The mixture of conflicting testimony, as his old friends lubricate their memories, reflects the paradox of the man. There was a rift in his character, a split for which a doctor who knew him well used the word 'schizoid' as if his identity was too fully loaded for a single image. It makes him no easier to focus on. A stranger's portrait may turn out unrecognizable to his friends, but they themselves have such a variety of views. Bit by bit a convincing picture forms; though as always, the closer one gets the less one sees of the whole. It is as well to stand back and examine, not just the figure, but aspects of the landscape too, which can help explain why a young man—summed up by a lifelong friend as 'handsome, intelligent and very rich'—came to be buried one winter on the Greenland ice cap. His ancestry is not irrelevant.

The Courtaulds came from Oléron, a low sandy island off the west coast of France known for its vines, melons and oysters. The earliest recorded Courtauld, the direct ancestor of August by eleven generations, lived there in the sixteenth century. His name was Christophe and he called himself *marinier*—not merely skipper but shipper, a merchant who sailed his own trading vessel up and down the Atlantic coast between Brittany and Spain.

Almost certainly Christophe was born a Catholic, but of all Frenchmen the tough independent people of the west coast were among the most susceptible to the ideas of Calvin. The principles were harsh, the Bible was the law. Man was damned by the fall of Adam, indeed the old Adam survived within every man, his potential vice. Only God's grace could save him from damnation, and the only proof of grace was in man's own good works. It was a severely practical dogma, a recourse to a life of action rather than one of contemplation or intellectual theorizing which appealed to a number of the French middle class. While the peasants remained loyal to their Catholic traditions, Protestantism became the religion of a small liberal élite. Along with many of his fellow islanders, Christophe Courtauld was probably a convert to the Reformation. Certainly his children were brought up in the reformed church, dissenting Huguenots in a Catholic state.

The existence of a well-organized, well-armed minority— almost a state within the state, efficient, articulate and denying the king's absolute power—was intolerable. Huguenots were treated to consistent persecution throughout the sixteenth century, culminating in the massacre on Saint Bartholomew's Day in 1572 when several thousand were slaughtered in Paris. Reaction followed the obvious pattern. Elizabeth of England went into mourning, but the Pope had a *Te Deum* of thanksgiving sung, and Philip of Spain sent his congratulations. A truce of sorts came in 1598 when Henry IV of France, himself a Protestant who was obliged to turn Catholic on becoming king, signed the Edict of Nantes granting basic rights to the Huguenots. His successors were less generous, though for nearly a hundred years the Protestants, harried and hamstrung, held their own against the Catholic establishment. It needed Louis XIV, the Sun King himself, to finish them off in 1685 by revoking the Edict.

Many Huguenots were forced to renounce their faith. Many were hung, burnt, strangled, imprisoned, tortured or driven off to the galleys. Many, managing to flee from the cruelty of a vindictive nation that forbade their escape, somehow got away. Hundreds of thousands reached England, Holland, Germany and America; among them a large number of merchants and artisans who took valuable skills and methods to their new country. If their hosts' welcome was sometimes tinged with envy of such quick success, it was soothed by religious sympathy for the refugees and by the general prosperity they brought.

On the island of Oléron the terror of 1685 was accompanied by wholesale renunciations and conversions. In a solemn document Augustin Courtauld, great-great-grandson of Christophe, swore to abandon the heresies of Calvin and embrace the true and apostolic Catholic creed. It was an oath he couldn't keep. The only way out of a false position was flight. Soon he had set himself up in London as a wine merchant, and in time he apprenticed his two sons to a Huguenot silversmith there.

In the early eighteenth century there were thirty-five French Protestant churches in London with congregations of merchants, manufacturers and craftsmen who were rapidly earning respect and riches, and turning into Englishmen at the same time. As with Jews who have also found sanctuary in England the names of Huguenot families are now familiar—Olivier, Martineau, Cazenove, Romilly, Bosanquet, D'Arcy, Delamere, Du Pré, Chenevix, Portal, Colville and many more. Among them Courtauld is one of the best known and most distinguished.

The family craft of silversmith lasted barely three generations. In that time Courtauld silver found its way to the Inner Temple, the Mansion House, Trinity House, Windsor Castle and the Russian Imperial Palace where the Empress had a silver table to put her samovar on. But in 1771 George Courtauld, whose mother was the daughter of a Huguenot silk weaver, was apprenticed to a silk throwster in Spitalfields. The line of silversmiths ended as a new one in textiles, far more prosperous and enduring, began.

George himself was a hopelessly incompetent businessman, moving from one job to another, dabbling in republicanism and making seven Atlantic crossings in his search for success, almost ruining his family in the process. But failure was redeemed by an

idealism that converted him from the Calvinism of his ancestors
to the still more rigorous principles of Unitarianism, a creed that
has attracted several of England's most successful industrialists.
It was George's son Samuel—Samuel Courtauld III on the
family tree and great-great-uncle of August, the polar explorer—
who built the family business and dominated it for most of the
nineteenth century. Borrowing money from a friend, he began
with a small mill in the village of Bocking in Essex. When he died
in 1881, a self-made magnate aged eighty-seven, he left a fortune
of £700,000 made almost entirely from the profits of black silk
crêpe.

Success stories tend to spawn hypothetical questions. Nobody
can say how much of Samuel's vast wealth was due to his own
ambition, his autocratic methods, his faint paranoia, his
symptoms of a manic-depressive, and how much to the rules of
fashionable society by which any widow claiming to be a lady
must cover herself with black crêpe for a year and a day after her
husband's death. Not just widows but sisters, aunts, cousins and
even servants, who all had their allotted period of mourning.
And, to the great advantage of the trade, it was thought unlucky
to keep a piece of crêpe in the house, so that at each death more
supplies of it had to be bought.

Samuel Courtauld III kept to the strict Unitarianism of his
father. He reconciled the practices of a *nouveau riche* tycoon with
the principles of a radical dissenter. He built a chapel and
supported it generously. He waged a long and successful war
against the levying of church rates on non-Anglicans. In a
business where mill hands worked sixty hours a week and were
lucky to be paid £15 a year, he acquired a reputation as an
enlightened employer truly concerned with the welfare of his
people. He also acquired a yacht and an enormous house and
several thousand acres of land. As one of those splendid, energetic,
intolerant and rather unloved Victorians who built a gigantic
industry from nothing, his success worked to the benefit of many
others, not least the members of his family.

By the time of Queen Victoria's death, twenty years after

Samuel III's, the boom in mourning was also dead. Another profitable commodity had to be found. Artificial silk, or rayon, was first made by the Courtaulds in 1905. Within one generation fashion had so totally accepted the new material for women's underwear and stockings, and demand was so much more universal than it had been for crêpe, that the success was repeated on an even bigger scale. The first family fortune had its roots in bereavement and woe, the second in sex appeal.

As often happened in dissenting families after winning great riches, the nonconformity of early generations turned into a predictable conformity among their descendants. The process didn't take long. George Courtauld III, nephew of Samuel III and grandfather of August of the ice cap, was brought up in a Unitarian home, but as a young man he started attending the Anglican church. He was elected to Parliament as a Liberal, but later became a Unionist and finally a full-blown Conservative. He ended up in the proper convention as a justice of the peace, chairman of the bench and sheriff of the county of Essex. From being originally Calvinist refugees and Huguenot silversmiths, briefly republican and latterly merely dissident Victorian industrialists, the Courtaulds became orthodox Edwardian squires.

Orthodoxy, so far as it appears on people's faces, can generally be seen in the Courtauld portraits. There is a distinctive family look: strong, serious, confident, practical, implacable, responsible, handsome. They have tended to stick together, perhaps at first because of the needs of an immigrant family in an alien land, perhaps later because of their common interest as shareholders in the Courtauld business, though few members have worked in it recently and their control ended long ago. Family feeling, where modesty has often over-shadowed pride, is typified in the opinion of Samuel Augustine Courtauld, father of August, who said that they had always been an undistinguished family, of little interest to themselves and of none to the general public—'a very hum-drum lot'.

Yet orthodoxy, in the case of that same Samuel Augustine

Courtauld, was spiced with a faint but happy touch of individualism. When he was sixteen, the year that the great Samuel Courtauld III died, he left school at Charterhouse to go into the family business, riding to the factory every morning on his pony. For the next seventy years he epitomized the old order of things. When black mourning crêpe was doomed and only a switch to rayon, which might have been invented for the purpose, could save the firm, Samuel Augustine opposed the new venture—the new fortune—though in time it brought him immense wealth. He chose to spend most of his business life in the little Essex silk factory where he began, always to be identified with the past, weaving silk in the tradition of his ancestors, presiding over the old trade's decline while the rest of the firm moved on to fresh conquests round the world. Expansion was the dominant, strident note that sounded from the boardroom and echoed round the factories. But for one elderly director, week by week entering by hand in his private ledger the number of packets woven and sold, it was reward enough to be still manufacturing something beautiful, which he understood and loved.

Probably he was content to see the chairmanship pass him by and settle on his younger cousin, Samuel Courtauld IV, who became a far more recognizable tycoon, a public figure famous not only as a great industrialist but also as a collector of Impressionist paintings, benefactor of the Tate Gallery and creator of the Courtauld Institute of Art. The two were very different men. At a summer tea-party, according to a family story, they sat under separate trees with the whole lawn between them. In years to come, when both cousins had died, the widower of Samuel IV's daughter—R. A. Butler, later Lord Butler of Saffron Walden—was to marry the widow of Samuel Augustine's explorer son, August. Family unity could be preserved even by members who joined it from outside.

August's own description of his father—'a gentle, kindly man'—is convincing: worthy, prosperous, bookish, slightly dull, possibly surprised at the riches brought to him by rayon with so little effort of his own. 'He didn't make his money—it came to him, as it were, from the sky. He used to say that the thing about having money is that you don't have to think about it.' And probably Samuel Augustine Courtauld very seldom did.

In Essex he liked to walk from his home to his factory at the other end of the village, and when business required him in London he walked to his office in the City from his house in Palace Green—'millionaires' row'—now the Dutch embassy. Literature was his passion, particularly Horace's odes; he once collected and published his own anthology of translations. When he had a lot of slum cottages knocked down and fifty new houses built to replace them he named them after characters from Jane Austen. His works of philanthropy—a biochemistry institute for a London hospital, a science block for an Essex school, two village halls and a sports field—were subdued and discreet. He indulged only mildly in the pastimes expected of a rich country gentleman. Though he rented a grouse moor in Scotland, he liked best to sit in the heather or beside a stream, eating a good lunch with his friends; the sight of all the dead birds rather appalled him. He didn't care for grand living or ostentation, he didn't go in for yachts or the acquisition of great treasures apart from his books. His pleasures were benign, scholarly, reclusive. 'I'm like the cat,' he used to say, 'I prefer my own fireside.' In fact he was fond of cats and usually kept a blue Persian which was allowed to play on his desk or on the dinner table. He liked port too, and old Courtauld silver. He admired tidiness, he hated fidgeting. Best of all, more than either his business or his books, he loved his family and in return was loved by them.

His eldest child, August—Augustine IX on the family tree— was born at Bocking on 26 August 1904. He was followed two years later by a sister, Betty, and in 1910 by a brother, Peter.

August's childhood was comfortable, secure and well tended by servants. There were no surprises, no magic, no fantasy, unless they were invented by himself. Like other rich and loving Edwardian fathers, Samuel Augustine Courtauld took little part in his children's lives beyond walking two miles to church with them every Sunday. He and his wife left the daily matter of up-bringing to a succession of nannies and nurserymaids, paying occasional visits to the nursery and only allowing the children to come downstairs for lunch, and perhaps for an hour after tea when they were old enough to behave. Health, food, entertain-ment and discipline were the nanny's job. She put them to bed and got them up, she ordered their meals and administered their medicines, she took them for endless walks, she locked them up in cupboards or got the gardener to cut canes for her when they needed punishment. If they went out in the pony trap and August was naughty, she turned him out on to the road and made him run along behind. It was in the nanny's interest as well as her employers' to maintain an untroubled routine—a boring one, for a lively spirit. Any excitement or diversion from the smooth tedium of nursery life generally had to be devised by the children themselves. August rubbed plasticine into his sister Betty's hair to turn her into a monk, and when he couldn't get the plasticine out he cut off her hair with scissors. Another time, with a new crane given to him for a birthday present, he lowered Betty out of an upstairs window, to the neighbours' surprise.

Many of the Courtauld relations lived not far away. Thus the children, already inhabiting a world of butlers and maids and nannies, dwelt in another of uncles and aunts and cousins. But visitors were not popular with the children, who were told they must disappear from sight after being produced for a quick inspection. They got their revenge by hiding in the bushes before the invaders arrived and attacking with bows and arrows; or, when the enemy were safely shut in the drawing-room, by spitting and stamping on their hats.

For a special treat they were taken out for a drive in the car. Though August's father employed a chauffeur he also drove him-self, in a style of his own. Hills were taken in top gear, without changing down. In fog he handed over the wheel to the chauffeur while he walked in front to find the way. The roads were empty, the ditch was usually soft. For a seaside holiday the whole family piled into the car, complete with cat and canary and tortoise, and set off for Frinton-on-Sea, thirty miles from home. Life was easy and sunlit and, on rare occasions, fun.

Mostly it was dull. The Courtauld parents led an unruffled life, their activities were hardly unusual, their friends were not very interesting. They held no strong feelings for the arts or politics, and though they might go up to London for the Royal Academy summer exhibition and stay in their town house for the Season, they didn't belong to high society. They did the proper thing—they would have felt disappointed otherwise—and were content. Nothing was expected of them, by relations or friends or neighbours, that they didn't expect of themselves. A momentum of behaviour, enlivened by only the mildest domestic excitement, was established and couldn't easily be upset. An appointed distance was kept between parents and children, preserving the distinction of each generation; their lives hardly connected. There was no struggle, no anxiety at home, or at least nothing overt. If there was a brooding family passion it was locked within, and not to be exposed.

August's education was begun at home by a governess. At the age of nine, in a bowler hat, he was put on a train and sent to school at Eastbourne. His parents had probably never seen it. Like many other prep schools on the south coast it was run as a commercial business by a clergyman, hearty and versatile but not unkind, who took his boys for runs along the top of the cliffs and made them pull their trousers down to be beaten when they misbehaved. In chapel he conducted the service, read the lesson, played the organ and preached the sermon. 'You needn't worry yourselves about the Trinity,' he told them. 'It's quite simple, just the same as the cricket wicket. Off stump Jesus Christ, middle stump God the Father, leg stump the Holy Ghost—three in one and one in three.'

At the end of his first year when he came home for the summer holidays August found, as he put it afterwards, 'there was a bit of a flap on'. It was 1914 and his mother said there was going to be a war. But the Courtaulds were too removed from world events to be much concerned, still less alarmed. In their pleasant corner of Essex, protected by their own indifference to outside affairs and supported by their healthy profits, they had little to worry about. The prospect of sudden cataclysm, the threat of the comfortable cycle being cracked at last, hardly penetrated the family scene.

The First World War was a new experience for the people of Britain—bigger, bloodier, more wasteful, more nearly total than any war before. Far from being a distant campaign engaging only the armed forces, it involved everyone in the country. For a boy of August's age, ten in the month it broke out, the war dominated an important phase of childhood. Consciousness of the world grew during those four years of war, and though there were bleak times ahead the outbreak was an exciting event. The first thing that happened was the arrival of a column of soldiers marching in khaki down the road past the Courtauld home, band playing and officers on horseback. The people of Bocking came out with food and cups of tea. August ran to the gate to watch.

The troops had come to dig trenches and defend the country against the Germans, and it was all very thrilling. Eventually the general and his staff were billeted on the Courtaulds—'an iron-grey man as hard as nails' in August's memory, who read Kipling aloud to the children in a fine deep voice. Once August was taken on a route march, riding on his pony beside the general at the head of the troops with the band playing behind them. The maids were just as excited; they had the officers' batmen living in the house.

During the war the Courtaulds moved to a bigger house at Halstead, only a few miles from Bocking. It was better for the growing family, with a park and a pond where August could launch his model destroyer. Ships were already a passion. He built a harbour and drew a chart of the pond which was framed and hung on the schoolroom wall. The real war also impinged, but not very seriously. Though it was the time of the Zeppelin raids, in Essex the pheasants were usually the first to give warning of the enemy and nobody else took much notice.

For convention more than safety, an air-raid shelter was dug in the park, which August and his sister and brother put to their own use. With the help of the gardener's boy, they installed a stove in it and entertained their parents to lunch, getting the French governess to cook the food. But nobody considered going into the shelter during an air raid. The Zeppelins, if they had a purpose at all, were just good sport. One came so low over the gamekeeper's cottage that he said he could have hit it with his shotgun. Another landed on the marshes near Frinton-on-Sea while the Courtaulds were there on holiday, as if for their benefit. The German crew got out and set fire to their machine before surrendering. Also at Frinton, standing on the sea wall, August saw his first real aeroplane taking off from the golf course. It went out of control, crashed through a hedge, turned over on its back, and he got a piece of the propeller as a souvenir.

At school the war passed peacefully enough, the normal routine of cold baths and canes and milk puddings being scarcely ruffled except that the masters went off to join the army and had to be replaced by mistresses, to the boys' disgust. Irked by the limits of sixpence a week pocket money, August would catch an early train to Eastbourne at the beginning of term, giving him time to open a £5 credit in a local shop which would keep him supplied with strawberries and cake. British airships flew over on their way to bomb U-boats in the Channel; and the boys, out for a run on the cliffs, once saw a ship sinking off Beachy Head. Destroyers in clouds of smoke came rushing over the horizon to rescue her, but she sank.

A shipwreck on the south coast of England is the climax of *Moonfleet*, the story that was August's favourite reading at the time and for many years afterwards. It is a splendid book, told in straightforward prose without rhetoric or sentimentality and all the more moving for its simplicity. No wonder August liked it. The tang of sea spray and hemp, as much as the tale of danger and courage, are irresistible and it wouldn't have been hard to transpose the Dorset fishing village of Moonfleet, beset by salt marshes and an inlet where seabirds and oysters breed, to the familiar Essex coast. Possibly the author's language had a lasting effect on August's own writing, where short words and short sentences prevailed. Certainly one episode of the story had an uncanny echo in his life. The hero, a boy of fifteen, climbs at night down through a cracked grave in a country churchyard and finds his way along a passage into a tomb underneath the church. Smugglers arrive, bringing casks of brandy to be stored in the tomb, and the boy hides in terror behind a coffin, but when at last the smugglers go away he finds they have blocked up the entrance crack with an old gravestone. Now he can't get out. He is trapped in an underground prison, his candle goes out, his tinder is too wet to light, he screams and wails and hammers on the walls, before falling senseless to the floor.

The war, the dominant background to August's growing-up, must have helped form the first idea of a possible career—the first and only such idea in his life. He never again came so near to settling for a regular profession as he did in the summer of 1918. The news of naval warfare and his own love of ships, as much as his reluctance to follow his father in the family business, drew him to a life at sea. It was something quite novel among the Courtaulds; it was his own intense desire; and it was a failure. Years later he could dismiss it as 'the episode of entering for the navy' without saying how deeply it must have hurt. The disappointment was painful and enduring.

Aged thirteen, he walked one day with his father to the Admiralty, summoned for an interview. The medical test was simple enough, and as he already knew the name and armament of every ship in the fleet, also the names of all the lighthouses round the coast of Britain, he was still confident when he was called in to face the board. Even when questioned about the military campaign in Mesopotamia and the crops grown by Essex farmers, his answers seemed to satisfy the old gentlemen across the table. But when he was asked to write an essay and saw the subject—*The Public School System*—his mind went blank, and his paper remained so.

It should have been no surprise, back at school, when the headmaster came in one morning and handed him a curt note to say that their lordships of the Admiralty had no use for his services. But August had gone on hoping. Now, in front of the class and the mistress, he burst into tears.

Instead, a few weeks before the armistice, he was sent to Charterhouse where his father had been at school. He went to his father's old house and his father took him there on the first day, as if to emphasize the continuity that August had tried to break. Though he might not admit it to himself, let alone aloud, Charterhouse was always a second best. Being a public-school boy was a poor alternative to being a naval cadet, and he could hardly be enthusiastic. But all through his life, except for rare and light-hearted mentions of the navy episode, he never talked about it to his friends and kept the disappointment to himself.

'From my first moment at Charterhouse I suffered an oppression of spirit that I hesitate to recall in its full intensity.' So wrote Robert Graves who was in the school, in the same house, a few years before August Courtauld.

Charterhouse was typical of its kind—conventional, narrow-minded, complacent, a stronghold of orthodoxy and philistinism with a rigid hierarchical system that it was dangerous to challenge. Conformity and caste were the essence of the social code. A boy who broke the rules had to be very wilful or very lucky to survive. For a sensitive spirit even the buildings exuded the tyranny of the place. 'Tradition was so strong that to break it one would have to dismiss the whole school and staff, and start all over again.' It is a wonder that not only Robert Graves but also Vaughan Williams, Max Beerbohm and Richard Hughes had been through the same remorseless process.

August's years at Charterhouse fell in a period of recovery after the kindly but lax reign of a previous headmaster and the disruptions of the First World War. Things had got out of hand, in the opinion of the present headmaster, Fletcher, who set out to retrieve the virtue most beloved of such men—a healthy tone.

2

An application of severity, which he believed the boys would accept and eventually appreciate, was the proper cure. Offenders were to be repressed, which meant flogged, or if necessary eliminated, which meant expelled. 'In spite of some modern theories,' Fletcher declared, 'I have no doubt that the fear of the headmaster has a salutary effect in a big school.' Though he took pride in being able to see the other person's point of view it simply meant that his usual reply to a boy asking for permission to do something out of the ordinary was, 'I quite see your point but I don't see why you should.' He was hasty, insensitive to the susceptibilities of young people (he had no children of his own) and unconscious of the wounds he inflicted. August kept away from the headmaster as much as possible and afterwards remembered speaking to him on only two occasions in the five years he was at the school.

His housemaster had hardly more influence. Known as 'the Duke', he was famous not only for his dressy suits and superior manner but for his gloomy prophecies on the boys' careers. They wouldn't pass their exams, they would fail everything else in life, they were doomed to disaster. Later he was remembered chiefly for the phrase, 'What abysmal ignorance,' uttered with despair. Possibly he never asked himself the reason for that ignorance. With an unconcealed preference for games players, and as master in charge of the army class for aspiring officers, his interest in August was slight. A boy who seemed heedless of the need to win silver cups for the house and indifferent to the rest of life's normal conventions, who showed by the way he dressed that he cared nothing for his own appearance, who didn't go out of his way to please the housemaster or pay respect when he didn't feel it, wasn't likely to be a favourite.

Between them the headmaster and the housemaster were the fount of authority, and authority in one form or another was the blight of August's life. At the back of his mind was the feeling that he shouldn't be at Charterhouse at all, he belonged to the navy, and his resentment turned to hatred of authority. It was authority that had wrecked his plans in the first place and now it was authority, in its triumph, that made school so odious. The wound of failure might have been more bearable if authority hadn't seemed to gloat so much.

The chief apostles of authority were the monitors and the 'bloods', members of the cricket and football teams, who ruled the school, an honour which entitled them to wear grey trousers and butterfly collars, cross the grass, walk arm-in-arm with each other and march up the aisle in chapel last, after lesser boys were already in their places. Having themselves once been persecuted by their seniors it was now their duty—not an unpleasant one— to exercise the same privilege on the next generation.

Though August avoided being bullied, he was tormented by conformists for whom the disapproval of others was part of conformity. Also he got at least his share of official justice, dispensed by boys on boys with all the pleasure of self-important youth. A monitor's beating could be a painful affair especially when delivered by an expert racquets player with an unerring eye who could land six strokes in quick succession on the same spot: 'After one such beating you didn't want another that term.' Appeal to the housemaster was futile—authority at all levels had to be upheld—and anyway to August the alternative, a moral lecture, was worse. 'I never used to mind being beaten at school,' he wrote long afterwards to the girl he wanted to marry, 'but I could never abide being "talked to".'

Things might have gone better if he had been good at games, but he didn't even like them: 'Football was mostly a matter of being knocked about. Cricket was worse because it lasted longer. I was never put on to bowl and used to spend most of my time fielding, chewing a piece of grass at the edge of the field. Generally I was near the bottom of the batting order and the game was over before I could go in.'

To avoid playing games he took up rifle shooting, a more individual sport and useful practice for holidays at home. Eventually he got into the school team, which was as near to being a blood as he ever reached. But fancy clothes, or any other kind of conspicuousness, were no more to his taste than organized games. All his life he shunned flamboyant behaviour. Modesty was natural, arrogance quite alien. The joys of bloodhood would have left him cold.

Ironically it was this one success that brought him his first encounter with the headmaster, in his last term, aged nearly nineteen. For setting off an explosion during a chemistry class he had been punished with extra work on Saturday afternoon. It conflicted with a shooting match against Marlborough, so he went to the headmaster to explain that if he didn't shoot with the team the match might be lost. Fletcher, incapable of risking defeat by another school or relaxing discipline in his own, offered him the choice of a beating. August took it. Next day in the bus going to Marlborough he was too sore to sit down, but it didn't stop him making top score of the day, and Charterhouse won the match. The only other time he met Fletcher was a few weeks later when he went to say good-bye on leaving school and the headmaster merely said, 'Well good-bye, you scoundrel'—a terse dismissal from a man who was to be praised after his death for his kindliness, high ideals and true humility, though better remembered by the boys for his ambition and conceit.

One state of war existed between small boys and big boys, another between all boys and masters. Everybody was somebody else's enemy; traitors weren't tolerated. Among the younger masters in August's time was George Mallory, who later died on Mount Everest. One of his old pupils, when he read of the climber last seen disappearing into the mist close to the summit, couldn't believe it was the pale and weedy man he remembered at school. Mallory was unconventional enough to care neither for strict discipline and the accepted routine nor for cricket and football. He tried to make real contact with the boys, but though he was often on their side against authority they no more approved of him than his older colleagues on the staff did. His efforts to make friends puzzled and offended them, and he couldn't control his class properly, or didn't want to, which was considered weak and therefore contemptible.

Work was scorned and a boy who was keen on it was likely to

be given a rough time; games were ritualized and a boy who shone at them was a hero. In this atmosphere August—neither scholar nor athlete but keeping carefully to the mainstream of school life, treading somewhere between meek surrender and open rebellion—spent his adolescence. It didn't help matters that he cared nothing for the figure he cut, and he was teased for being casual and untidy where he might be expected to be elegant and fashionable. Schoolboys being alert to every kind of snobbery, any of August's friends who didn't know of the rapidly growing wealth of the Courtaulds must have noticed when his grandfather died leaving a fortune of more than £2 million. Few boys could boast a family as rich as August's, but so far from splashing Courtauld money around he never mentioned that there was any —not so much from tact as from a feeling that it wasn't worth talking about.

'My dear friends,' he wrote at the age of sixteen when he was set an essay in the form of a letter from a Chinese boy at school in England. 'Since my parents have sent me to one of the great English public schools I write to you endeavouring to give my impressions of this admirable system which nevertheless has many drawbacks. The first thing which struck me on entering the school was the extraordinary competition, which amounts almost to hostility, in games.' The stilted language may have been an attempt to strike an authentic Chinese note. 'The English spare no expense in the advancement of all branches of sport, particularly football and cricket. The boys at these schools play some game every day and are continuously having matches against one another. There is far keener interest, strange though it may seem, in matches between the houses inside the school than in inter-school matches or even in international ones.' August warned against a clever boy being sent to the school in the belief that he would be admired for his brains: 'He will be despised. For if a boy is not interested in the crude battlings after a ball he will be nothing among his fellows.' Yet that didn't mean that a boy got any credit for being a fool: 'If he is not clever he will never learn much, for they have as few teachers as they can and a boy mostly teaches himself. If he is clever others will profit by it, for he will be made to share his knowledge.' After explaining the house system and remarking that 'the moral tone of the houses varies to a great extent,' and after crossing out a sentence deploring that in some houses 'the fellows don't seem the gentlemen that these schools profess to keep,' he summed up his Anglo-Chinese feelings: 'The tone of the school seems to breed unselfishness and a wish to do as well as you can for your side, whatever it is; honour of a sort, though to cheat in work is not by many considered dishonourable; and a general ambition to do something for the school which deigns to have you in it. Farewell.'

The master wrote 'Good' at the bottom of the essay and gave him full marks. In it August had touched on a fact of Charterhouse life that Robert Graves also remembered: 'We considered it no shame to cheat, lie or deceive where a master was concerned, though the same treatment of a school-fellow would have been immoral.'

Another time August was given *A Gentleman* for his subject and had trouble sorting out various definitions: 'One hears people speak of a man being a perfect gentleman. How different are these perfect gentlemen from one another! Some mean a man with greasy hair, a monocle and exaggerated manners, who gets taken to people's at homes, partly to show him off like a dog with his tricks, and partly to extract all the scandal possible out of him. Others mean a man who will be a slave to them, and go wherever or do whatever they want him to do, whether he likes it or not.' After touching on knight errantry and the growth of a gentlemanly spirit he came out with his own version: 'A gentleman should be chivalrous and kind, especially to the opposite sex; unselfish and always ready to do anything reasonable for anybody. He may have pride in his family or in his ancestors, but never so much as to be overbearing to those round him; never self-satisfied or proud in his own doings. His manners are always with him, because they are natural.' The master wrote, 'Not bad —don't be too long-winded.'

The title *The Irishman* was a chance to air some opinions which don't sound as if they came from August's own experience: 'The Irishman's temperament is a strange mixture. He is whimsical and kind-hearted, but always on the look-out for some sort of a row. His patriotism is intense and he puts it before anything else . . . He, like the British workman, will fight tooth and nail for what he thinks will be his liberty, without stopping to consider what state he will get himself into if he wins. He has a great sense of humour and a habit of mixing things up . . . He is a delightful man except when roused, when he becomes a dangerous lunatic.'

An eye-witness account of a South American earthquake gave him scope for vivid details and perhaps showed more of his private feelings than he realized. Obviously he enjoyed describing the amazement and horror that creeps into the faces round a dinner table. The meal is nearly over and people are telling strange stories over the dessert when the first tremors are felt. Conversation stops, the table tilts violently, a plate of oranges begins to slide, but everyone is too paralysed, clinging to their chairs, to stop it dashing to the floor. Next, the sideboard goes over with a crash and a terrible scream is heard from far away across the town. The men stagger to their feet and help the ladies to the door. A little girl is thrown down by a sudden jerk and crushed by falling furniture; her yells, as the servants try to save her, are only silenced by death. Outside, it seems the world is coming to an end. Houses are lifted, rocked and felled. Gaping cracks open in the ground and swallow the shrieking population. Some flee howling to high ground outside the town, pursued by an ever-widening crevasse. Others stand and watch petrified, as their friends are caught and devoured. Who will win—man or nature? There is a worse monster still to come. As the tremors die away a vast wall of water comes rushing up from the sea, sweeps across the harbour, lifts ships and men on to its crest and deposits them half a mile inland. All that remains is a handful of miserable survivors, homeless and half demented, wailing amid the wreckage of their town. August's tone leaves no doubt whose side he was on. His pity for the people was perfunctory; he was much more excited by the monstrous phenomenon of nature.

The Officers' Training Corps was compulsory, but August no more liked playing soldiers than football. The war ended during his first term. Drilling and make-believe tactics had prepared boys for the brief glory of the trenches and, too often, for a place on the roll of honour in the school chapel. Nearly 700 from Charterhouse had been killed. But going on parade three times a week, for the post-war generation, seemed pointless now. The standard joke was that the Corps, founded in 1907, was part of Britain's preparation for the Boer War, which finished in 1901, and the sense of tardiness and futility must have survived in August's day. The need for heroism was gone, the first reaction against soldiering had set in. It was hard to be serious about military training that wasn't going to end up in Flanders mud or on the war memorial; and for August this schoolboy army stuff was a bitter comparison with the navy where he should have been. When he wasn't attending to his uniform, worrying over a button-stick or polishing boots and belt and bayonet frog, he was marching and forming fours and sloping arms. It was unpleasant as well as unnecessary, and he was constantly being punished with extra drill.

Slightly less objectionable were the field days out in the country and the annual camp on Salisbury Plain in the summer holidays, when the boys slept on straw palliasses in army bell-tents; though even there, instead of squad drill, they were given fatigues. Later the sharpest memories of camp were likely to be of peeling potatoes, of washing up, and of a liquid that was dished up, labelled tea or soup or cocoa according to the time of day, but always tasting the same. But the battles against other schools could be fun. Charterhouse attacked a hill and captured the Harrow lunch, and another time they stuffed date stones into their rifles on top of blank cartridges and shot the umpire's horse.

Spoilt yet spartan, sheltered yet worldly, totalitarian, intolerant, philistine—the infliction of a Charterhouse education on a boy for five impressionable years was a queer preparation for life. For some it was fatal; they never grew up but continued through their lives in a state of suspended adolescence, caricatured as overgrown schoolboys, preserving and hardly modifying the system. For others it was a negative experience; nothing in life afterwards could ever be so unpleasant. For a few it was a period of golden happiness, to be looked back on with nostalgia. For a few more it was a bad dream, a memory of hell that could never quite be lost. For August Courtauld it was an episode to be endured which quickly became irrelevant. Whatever fine legacy he was supposed to take from school, his chief impressions were of extra work, extra drill in the Corps and beatings. Luckily he had resources to support him and during the holidays at home in Essex, riding and shooting and walking, he stored enough fuel to last him through the bleak terms in between. Instinctively he knew that the spirit of Charterhouse didn't fit his own opinion of what mattered in life and, if he could only hold out long enough, time would bring release. Unable to defeat the system or support it, he settled for a detached position, neither complying nor suffering more than he could help. He showed, then as later, that he was a natural and talented survivor.

Five years after failing to pass the navy exam, with Charterhouse behind him, he would have had no trouble writing an essay on *The Public School System*. The chief effect of it on himself was a deep dislike of the kind of mindless tyranny he lived under at school, inflicted by people he knew to be in no way better than himself, who assumed power on the strength of seniority. He never went back, he didn't attend old boys' dinners or wear the old school tie, he seldom spoke about his time there, and he sent his own four sons to Eton.

But however much he hated it he wasn't wretchedly unhappy, as was General Orde Wingate who was at Charterhouse at the same time. Certainly there are points of similarity in the experiences and attitudes of the two men. As boys, neither of them excelled in any part of school life and neither left much mark on the place or impression on their contemporaries. As reluctant conformists, each of them nurtured a natural rebelliousness that grew into a lifelong conflict between himself and the mass, between the needs of the individual imagination and the demands of the majority. But their later careers pointed up the differences. Wingate, who believed he had been terribly wronged and humiliated by school persecution, held an abiding bitterness towards Charterhouse. 'I was looked down on and made to feel that I was a failure and not wanted in the world,' he said, which might explain some of the extraordinary events in a life that swung from the depression of an attempted suicide to the elation of a brilliantly successful commander. August Courtauld, a more stable character, showed his defiance of authority and convention in less violent, but equally stubborn ways.

He left Charterhouse in the summer of 1923. By way of celebration he went off on a bicycle tour of the Highlands with two friends. Their brakes didn't work properly so they had to push downhill as well as up, but the glens and lochs and mountains were a fitting antidote to school. And after several days on the road, when they arrived at a smart hotel full of dinner jackets and stuffed shirts and were turned away because of their appearance, it only reinforced August's contempt for the pretentiousness and prejudices of most people in authority.

Three years later, aboard a small Norwegian sealer on his way to the Arctic for the first time, he found that another member of the expedition had been to Marlborough. They agreed that it would be better to go to prison than back to school.

Chapter 2

Cambridge

IN OCTOBER 1923, aged nineteen, August went up to Trinity College, Cambridge. At first he lived outside college, on the top floor of a lodging-house—in the best tradition of its kind, with a landlady in the basement who sustained a smell of boiled cabbage at all hours and a church next door which seemed, also constantly, to be ringing its bells. For relief, living in the same house, were two other Trinity men, Bill Corbett and Goose Gosling, like-minded and friends for life. But it took time for the friendship to get started. Corbett and Gosling had been at Eton together, so knew each other already; and as Gosling said, anyone who hadn't been to Eton hardly existed.

August, not for the last time in his life, was the odd man out. To emphasize it he appeared aloof and shy, too independent to seek other company and too self-sufficient to need it. Then, as later in life, he was inclined to meet his friends only for a specific purpose—to pursue some undergraduate adventure or to go shooting or sailing—rather than for mere sociability.

Partly because he loved mechanical things (as a small boy he had discussed model steam engines with his father on their way to church) and partly to avoid anything that reminded him of Charterhouse, he decided to read engineering, which was new to him. But he hadn't done enough mathematics at school for the honours course so he had to settle for an ordinary degree, though being practical rather than academic it suited him better. Besides, studying was not the only object of university life, or even the most important. 'In those days,' he wrote thirty years later, 'there wasn't the emphasis on work there is now,' and he remembered with admiration the young men who avoided lectures altogether. Unfortunately the engineering faculty required its students at nine o'clock every morning: 'But there was no work in the afternoons; then we would take our dogs out or go beagling.'

A faintly self-disparaging, even frivolous, tone sometimes crept into August's remarks about his own behaviour. Understatement was not enough, he also had to puncture any vestige of earnestness in case it sounded pompous and therefore too like the voice of authority. Thus, writing about Cambridge long afterwards, he could hardly bring himself to mention his studies. It was easier to stick to sport, dogs, rag days and the social side of life. There was plenty of material.

Other Cambridge men of the period have spoken of the ghost of war, with its fondness for tragedy and bitter wit, that still haunted the place. Christopher Isherwood, an exact contemporary of August's (they were born on the same day), wrote, 'Like most of my generation, I was obsessed by a complex of terrors and longings connected with the idea "war". War, in this purely neurotic sense, meant the Test. The test of your courage, of your maturity, of your sexual prowess: "Are you really a man?" ' It was a sentiment shared by George Orwell, who was a year older: 'As the war fell back into the past my particular generation, those who had been "just too young", became conscious of the vastness of the experience they had missed. You felt yourself a little less than a man because you had missed it.' Recently at Trinity, not long before August went there, undergraduate life had practically stopped for four years while officer cadets moved into one part of the college and another part became a hospital. Six hundred Trinity men had been killed, and old college servants were sometimes careful to remind undergraduates of the legendary heroes who had gone before. Feelings about the war, for anyone of August's age, could be confused: disgust at the incompetence yet admiration of the bravery; horror at the slaughter yet relief at having missed it; guilt at not having been old enough to fight yet envy of those who had. Meanwhile the reality of war, as the years receded, faded into childhood.

Under the rule of 'the Old Men' the generation gap was deeper than usual. The historian of the 1920s, A. J. P. Taylor, said,

> Older men looked back to the years before the war and hoped for their return. Their minds were pre-war . . . For whose who had grown up after 1918 the war was a memory, and soon hardly that. They aspired to make new standards, not to restore old ones . . . Traditional values ran thin. The young began to steer without a chart. Even the praetorian guard of the established order turned traitor. Products of the public schools could no longer be relied on to remain conventional.

To young men the view of Edwardian complacency across the gap of missing years—across the entire missing generation— compared scandalously with the present scene, with the desolation they now saw and the isolation they now felt. This was the time of *The Waste Land*, Eliot's searing vision of futility and anarchy: 'And the dead tree gives no shelter, the cricket no relief, and the dry stone no sound of water.' The mood couldn't have failed to touch August whose hatred of authority, in the shape of the old gentlemen at the Admiralty and the agents of orthodoxy at Charterhouse, fitted the general atmosphere. Even his instinct for suppressing emotions caught a common attitude, though there could be variations in style of doing it and in awareness that it was being done at all.

Cambridge in the mid-'20s was a preserve of the privileged élite. Though about a third of the students came from grammar schools, only one in a hundred came from a working-class family. But after the confines of Charterhouse it was a paradise of liberty and August made the most of it. At last he could do more or less as he pleased, without heed to the demands of someone else, and in his wealth he had a special advantage. Henceforth he was to be free. Subordination, obligation, the conventional hierarchy that most people's careers were committed to—such things were behind him. The future held no stern prospects, not even the ordinary anxieties of a livelihood. Life beyond Cambridge was whatever he cared to make of it, and if he couldn't see quite what he was going to do afterwards, he knew exactly what he wasn't going to do.

Isherwood, writing about that Cambridge era, said that during the first few weeks at the university he worried a good deal about the future:

> I even made some feverish attempts to pull myself together, to cover the lost ground in my spare time, to copy out other people's notes. Then, by degrees, I ceased to bother at all. Nobody else bothered, why should I? . . . And in Cambridge there was so much to distract you from the sordid subject of work. There were the bookshops, where you could read for hours without being disturbed; the curiosity shops which no undergraduate can resist; the teashops full of sickly but delicious cakes. There were comic games of squash with a boy from my old preparatory school, and wild night-rides in Sargent's car. There were the flicks with the films which were, even in those days, not silent, because the audience supplied the popping of champagne corks, the puffing of trains, the sound of horses' hooves and the kisses.

Looking back, he decided that his first terms at Cambridge were among the most enjoyable part of his life: 'I had sufficient money and no worries . . . The word boredom didn't exist.'

The same for August. For a rich undergraduate with sporting habits and no great ambition to get a good degree there were endless ways of spending time and money. It was fashionable to go to the races at Newmarket or to a local point-to-point, and smart men who kept their own horses at Cambridge went out with the Fitzwilliam foxhounds. But though August occasionally hired a horse for a day's hunting and followed the beagles on foot, he had little patience with organized sport, still less with the company he met on the hunting field. He preferred to take a gun out wildfowling on the Cambridgeshire fens, or to go home for a day's shooting with his father. Once, out after duck and geese, he walked over the salt marshes between the estuaries of the Blackwater and the Crouch and found it didn't matter that the weather was too fine for shooting; it was enough to be out under the gigantic Essex sky, in the wide limbo between sea and land. Another time he went as far as Brightlingsea at the mouth of the Blackwater and persuaded the skipper of an old sailing-smack, putting to sea to catch sprats, to take him on board. Following the Fitzwilliam pack was nothing to this; it was hunting of another, altogether better kind. Nine o'clock lectures and weekly tutorials and tiresome college regulations seemed remote and trivial as August watched the fishermen work their nets and the quicksilver cascade of fish slip into the hold.

Social life, for many young men, was the beginning and end of their three years at Cambridge. Never mind work; there were so many other things to learn—to smoke a pipe, to drive a motor-bike, to drink beer, to mix cocktails, to wear plus-fours, to break into hearty laughter, to dance a foxtrot, to wield a punt pole on the river without falling in. The smart set was in and out of the Pitt Club all day but August, who had no use for conventional society for its own sake and no skill in empty chatter, didn't belong. Such clubs were too stuffy or too rarefied. He once asked what the members did. 'Oh,' he was told, 'they scratch their dogs.'

Dogs were an important part of life and it was annoying, when August moved from the lodging-house into rooms in Trinity, to be told that they were not allowed in college. Byron, more than a century earlier, had noted that the rule was only against dogs, so instead he kept a bear. He took it for walks on a chain to annoy the Fellows, and said it should sit for a fellowship of its own and teach the others proper manners. But the rule didn't stop August. He could avoid taking his dog past the porter's lodge simply by hauling it up to his window from the street outside. He even arranged a dogs' tea party in his rooms and his friends' dogs arrived the same way, in suitcases and cricket bags.

It was the period of the great Cambridge rags and of elaborate jokes played by men who had money, wit and leisure. Someone sent invitations to all the black men in the university to have breakfast with the Master of Trinity, dressed in white surplices. Someone, when the midsummer fair came to town, let the grazing on the college lawns to the elephants. On Guy Fawkes' day the market place was given up to the sport of putting out gaslamps. Bangs and breaking glass filled the night, squibs cracked about the feet of proctors and policemen. August tied a firework to the top of a lamp-post and climbed down into the arms of the law, to be summoned before the magistrates and fined £1. On Armistice Day the riot broke out again, more extravagantly but to better use. Poppies in all sizes burst out everywhere. A tide of outrage overtook the town in aid of Earl Haig's fund for soldiers. The streets became a tumult of floats and tableaux and jazz bands and buffoons. Performing undergraduates, whatever the act, assailed the public and demanded money. Collecting boxes were lifted on poles to upstairs windows, pavements were lined with pennies. For the sons and younger brothers of the lost generation it was a poignant revel. Only the gun at eleven o'clock in the morning, freezing the whole nation for two minutes' silence, could stop it.

Surprisingly for someone so unsuited to army drill, August joined the cavalry squadron of the university Officers' Training Corps—for the chance of riding and the early parades on horse-back. A solid morning of lectures was just bearable if there had been a bout of tent-pegging, with sword and lance, before breakfast. But to most of the new generation soldiering was a joke—rather a bad one—and the Corps couldn't escape its dose of ridicule from young men who vied at being the most un-military. When a visiting general, a relic of the First World War who embodied the attitudes of 'the Old Men' still ruling the country, came to inspect the cadets he found that a telegram had arrived ahead of him to say that his car had broken down on the way; the parade had been dismissed and there was nobody for him to look at. It was an unreal, twilit period of British history, when the Empire stretched as far as it ever did, and the shadows of the General Strike and the Depression and the rise of Nazi Germany hadn't darkened the future of privileged young Englishmen.

With few academic pretensions, with a preference for the wide open spaces rather than the introversions of college life, August found that the best parts of his university time were the vacations. 'There were people who stayed up at Cambridge and worked,' he wrote, not with much pity, 'but most of us went off where the spirit moved.' Staying in one place unnecessarily, let alone staying indoors, never became a habit. Any excuse could be made for a journey and North Uist in the Hebrides—a suitable mixture of mountain and loch and rocky shore, full of wild life—was a good place for a winter party. One of the friends, a zoology student, showed interest in the local mouse, but the rest were there for the sport. They lived at a hotel on what they shot—wild geese, duck, woodcock—and on Christmas Day they killed sixty-five snipe.

Perhaps it was curious that intelligent young men should be so self-absorbed, so unaware of the outer world, so apparently indifferent to events. It was a common Cambridge attitude of the time. Even at the Union, the nursery for politicians, the debates had an escapist flavour, as if anything serious was too precious for public handling: this house would like to go back to Methuselah; this house has grave doubts about the rising generation; this house would rather be a three-bottle man than a total abstainer; woman has come into more than her own and this house regrets it.

Afterwards Christopher Isherwood thought it odd 'when one remembers that this was the winter of Hitler's Munich *putsch*, of Mussolini's final campaign against the democrats, of the first English Labour government, of Lenin's death. Hitler's name was, I suppose, hardly known to a dozen people in all Cambridge. Mussolini was enjoying a certain popularity: rugger and rowing

men frequently named their terriers Musso. The Labour government and all its works were comprehended in the withering word
"politics" and therefore automatically dismissed as boring and
vile.'

Briefly, at the end of his first year, August faced reality and
didn't like it. For his degree course he had to spend part of the
summer vacation as an apprentice in an engineering works. He
went to a factory at Rugby where he was paid eighteen shillings
a week to turn out small pieces of gas pipe on a lathe. At the end
of a fortnight, when he had got through the quantity of pipe he
was given, he asked the foreman what to do next and was told
to fetch more pipe. It must have seemed like school again and
probably helped settle his mind, if that ever needed doing, about
a lifetime in industry.

He didn't make the same mistake again. In 1925, when the
summer camp with the cavalry squadron was over, he disappeared
to Lapland with another undergraduate, his cousin George
Courtauld. Fortified with a bottle of pineapple rum, they took a
ship from Hull to Helsinki and after staying at a Russian
monastery on an island in Lake Ladoga they travelled by boat
and bus up through Finland to the Arctic Circle.

August's account of the monks 'in their tall hats and long
beards, manning the little steamer which took us out to the
island', and of the monastery services, 'most impressive with a
wonderful hidden choir', conveys the feelings of a traveller who
was sensitive to the exotic and the beautiful but uneasy as a
tourist. The knack of travel-writing escaped him. Dismissive
little sentences on the verge of boredom, tokens of description,
were the best he could do. But they show that on the journey
north, through lakes and forests towards the midnight sun, there
was plenty to relish and remember: a dip in a cold lake; a day's
fishing for trout and grayling: a stolen night in an empty hut, to
be woken at dawn by the owner returning to cook breakfast,
cheerful and unsurprised; and a sauna bath complete with an
old woman who threw water over hot stones and whipped the
two Englishmen with birch twigs afterwards—'quite the best

bath I have ever had'. And if there were discomforts—food so covered in flies that it was invisible, and a plague of mosquitoes which they only repelled by smearing themselves with olive oil and Stockholm tar—August welcomed them as ingredients of hard travel.

It was only right, before the journey ended, that he should spend his twenty-first birthday at sea off the North Cape, inside the Arctic Circle. But it was no time for wasting words: 'This was the first real travelling I had done . . . I enjoyed it.'

After two years of engineering—after his spell in a factory and his early journeys had shown that a life of travel was the one for him—August switched to geography for his final year at Cambridge. He must have done more work than he admitted, for after getting only a third in the first year's exams he got seconds for engineering the next year and for geography in the last.

But even if he took life more seriously than some of his friends, academic subjects hardly filled his mind. There was so much else to do. While he was still at Cambridge he was given a racing yacht by his father, a twenty-four-footer called *Duet* which he kept at Burnham-on-Crouch and sailed on Saturday afternoons. She was the first boat of his own and marked the start of a passion that lasted all his life.

His thoughts must have been drifting to exploration, but though the geography course would make him useful on an expedition his inclination was for adventure rather than scientific discovery. He was too much of a soloist to find fulfilment in a big team. Travel was to be a private matter, an inner experience. He was as vague about where to go as how to arrange it, but his first journey to the north gave him an appetite for high latitudes and he began preparing for the rigours he was likely to meet. Perhaps the effects of privation—or self-deprivation—could be learnt by practice. With a friend he starved for three days to see what would happen, and then ordered a huge dinner from the

Trinity kitchens, ending with a treacle pudding. Soon they were rolling on the floor in pain.

It was the kind of experiment that was being made by another undergraduate in the same college, one of the most extraordinary men of his generation, who dreamed of polar exploration and was hardening his body with violent punishment—running and roof climbing and sleeping under an open window with almost nothing on, to get used to the cold. This was Gino Watkins, two years younger than August, who arrived at Trinity in 1925. Strangely, though they overlapped at Cambridge and shared many of the same enthusiasms, they didn't meet for several years. Watkins was mercurial, gay, clever, debonair, a dandy. He dressed immaculately, he flourished on a mixture of hard work and parties, he loved bright society, dancing, jazz—things that August avoided.

The conventional social graces hardly existed in August's equipment. Dancing came as awkwardly as small talk. He couldn't see the point of either, so didn't trouble with them. Though in May Week he was roped into a party for the Trinity College ball, it was a painful occasion. Done up in evening clothes, strolling by the river on a summer night with a girl in a ball dress, he could only wish he was anywhere else—best of all, lying in wait for wildfowl on the cold marshes or steering his boat through the night watches. 'This is too awful,' his partner said at last, 'can't you think of anything to say?' But August couldn't. Next morning, instead of punting her up the river for breakfast at Grantchester in the proper romantic way, he somehow ditched her and drove across England with his friend Bill Corbett, reaching Bill's home in Shropshire in time for lunch, still in white tie and tails.

It was the same when August's parents gave a dance for their daughter Betty at their London house—untypically, for though they were rich they had no taste for a grand social life. Betty and the rest of the débutantes were abandoned in the drawing-room, wondering why their partners had disappeared, while August and his friends, who had fixed up a bar in the cellar, were drinking beer.

As to sex, on his own admission he wasn't interested: 'I had no use for girls at this time and thought them a nuisance. I never really saw one at close quarters until I became engaged some years later.' It was a casual, offhand remark made in the idiom he might use for stalking deer in Scotland or avoiding a near-collision at sea, but it conveys a hint of the attitude which so many young Englishmen have held for women—somewhere between contempt and timidity, a sexual innocence close to destitution, fused with impeccable good manners and occasionally touched with gallantry. At close quarters, even after his marriage, August was often uncomfortable with a woman. He was always scrupulously polite, and though he could sometimes appear bluff and even intimidating he was never heard to swear or tell a dirty joke in female company. But all his friends were men.

In the summer of 1926 he took his degree and left Cambridge. Just as after Charterhouse the first thing he did was to go on a bicycle tour of the Highlands, on leaving Cambridge he took three friends on a sailing cruise. He had had a new thirty-foot boat built—*Hallowe'en*, bigger than *Duet* and better for long voyages. With Bill Corbett and Charles de Bunsen he sailed across the Thames estuary from Burnham-on-Crouch and picked up Goose Gosling from the end of Ramsgate pier. Fifteen years later, at Ramsgate during the war, he remembered the joys of buying his own food for the first time, going round the bakers and butchers and stocking up with the things he liked best. Then they put to sea and headed vaguely for the Continent: 'Ostend sounded a good place as it had a casino.'

With no charts and not much experience on board it was an exciting passage, even if August's light-hearted account conceals his own seamanship: 'The wind was fair, but halfway over it came on to blow.' Somehow they got the mainsail down and ran before the storm under the jib alone. Off the Belgian coast a lightship reported an English yacht out of control and a passenger steamer came alongside to ask if they needed help, but the four friends made rude signs with empty beer bottles and sailed on. When they reached the other side they saw only endless stretches of sand dunes where they hoped to find Ostend. Tossing up which way to turn and steering north for a few more miles, they hit the harbour entrance. August made it sound more like a stroke of luck than a piece of good navigation. The Belgian customs man came aboard and asked for *Hallowe'en*'s papers, but was told there weren't any and given sherry instead, which set the tone for the trip ashore. They shopped hilariously 'to get some grub', in best schoolboy French with odd results, and spent their evenings in the casino, also with surprises. Coming back to the boat late one night—to complete the traditions of four young English yachtsmen abroad—de Bunsen fell off the quay into the harbour.

Chapter 3

The First Expedition

WITH A CAMBRIDGE degree but no clear vocation or certain idea what career to start—with no great wish to start a career at all—August might have kicked around indefinitely, waiting for something to turn up or someone to offer him a job. Some of his friends, until they knew him better, expected him to join his father in the Courtauld firm and thought he would be foolish not to. 'In those days it was the done thing,' Goose Gosling said, 'to go into the family business if you had one, especially if it was one like theirs.' It was a chance not many men had, but August never considered it and his father put no pressure on him. He now had time for anything and money for anywhere. He could afford to do what he liked, or nothing at all. And he knew precisely what he was going to do next: 'I decided I must go to the Arctic.'

Decisions all his life were simple things. 'I decided' or more rarely 'I thought I would' was the straightforward announcement of a new course. It was a compulsion, almost an obligation, as if in obedience to his own command. The rules were set and the moves controlled by an inner discipline that allowed no refusal. 'A man with a high morale,' Lord Moran wrote in *The Anatomy of Courage*, 'does things because in his own mind he has decided to do them without any suggestion from outside.' Neither doubting nor hesitating nor consulting anyone else, August decided he must go to the Arctic.

At about the same time, in more or less the same way, Gino Watkins came to the same decision. Walking back to his college after a lecture with a friend he said, 'I think we'd better go to the Arctic,' and it was settled.

How to set about it was more difficult. A hunting party to Spitzbergen was a possibility, but August wanted something less sporting and more serious, though he wasn't qualified, or keen, for a professional part in any big scientific expedition. Eventually he found the answer at Cambridge itself, next door to Trinity: 'I discovered a tower in St John's College,' he wrote in his best laconic style, 'surmounted by James Wordie.'

Wordie, a dry diminutive Scot then aged thirty-seven, was a fellow of St John's and a veteran polar explorer. As a young geologist he had spent three years in the Antarctic with Shackleton, first trapped in a sinking ship, later drifting on the ice in conditions of appalling discomfort and danger. Finally, with twenty-one others, he was marooned on Elephant Island while Shackleton took five men and sailed in an open boat across 800 miles of the Antarctic Ocean, through almost constant gales, and then crossed a frozen mountain range to get help. For more than four months the men on Elephant Island lived under two upturned boats, frozen by cold or lying soaked by melted ice or choked by smoke from their blubber stove. None of them had washed for nearly a year. One man had to have five frostbitten toes amputated. As the weather became colder, the seals and penguins which they relied on for food migrated and there was nothing to eat but old bones dug up and stewed in seawater with a few limpets and shreds of seaweed. Wordie, with his wit and equanimity, did more than most to keep up the party's spirits while they waited for the rescue which they couldn't be certain would ever come. It was recorded that he made his tobacco last longer than anybody else's, but could always be persuaded to trade it for geological specimens.

At St John's, entering his room was like going into something that was part explorer's tent, part Eskimo's igloo, part polar museum, while being always the headquarters of an imminent expedition. Wordie inspired new generations of Cambridge explorers and led them to Spitzbergen, Jan Mayen Island and

Greenland. He was remembered by one of his companions as a
leader who seemed never to give an order but only made
suggestions. That was the kind to appeal to August.

Wordie invited him to go on his expedition to East Greenland
in the summer of 1926, at a cost of £100 for expenses. The object,
among other scientific work, was to chart a stretch of coast that
had only been partially explored before. There were to be eight
members, including August and his friend Charles de Bunsen,
but when Gino Watkins applied to join he found that the
expedition was already filled. He and August had still not met.

They sailed from Aberdeen on the last day of June in a small coal-
burning Norwegian sealer, the *Heimland*. To August, who was
one of the few not to be seasick, the sausages were one of the best
things of the voyage. He also liked climbing the mast and watching the world from the crow's nest. On 5 July they reached Jan
Mayen Island, 300 miles north of Iceland, and on the 8th they
entered the pack ice.

Suddenly they found themselves in another element, no
longer ocean but not quite land. The surface of the sea flattened
mysteriously, filled with floating ice. Mists wafted over them,
great white floes edged by blue water surrounded them. The day
never turned to night. Far ahead stretched the brilliant mountain
skyline of Greenland. It was a new world, infinite and alluring,
in which August recognized that a large part of his future was
locked.

The captain, in the crow's nest with his telescope, shouted
commands to the helmsman in the wheelhouse. The little ship
twisted and turned, searching for a passage, sometimes colliding
heavily with a floe or striking the ice with her propeller. Occasionally, overtaken by a patch of fog and unable to find a way
through the pack, they moored to the ice with grapnels and went
off hunting seals, polar bears and walrus. Some of those drifting
floes, broken from the Arctic mass and carried by a southerly
current or blown by the wind, covered a hundred square miles;

and a ship that sailed into one of the long narrow channels between them could be trapped and crushed before she had time to escape.

Three years earlier, in 1923, Wordie had led an expedition to Greenland which never reached it and nearly came to grief. Though they got to within sight of land, their ship, squeezed as if by jaws, was lifted bodily on to the ice and only saved by good seamanship. After a week of fog and another attempt to get through, they gave up and sailed home.

This time the *Heimland* pushed for three days through the pack ice before finding open water again, then steamed for another forty miles towards Greenland. Sausages and mash gave way to seal steak and onions. In the little deckhouse, where the pipe smoke was impenetrable and the gramophone played non-stop until the spring broke, Wordie prepared his plans while his seven men discussed the great questions of life, some greater than others; the expedition doctor found that when they picked up the BBC news on the wireless he alone was more interested in the miners' strike than in Henley regatta. On the evening of 11 July, in thick mist, they reached land-fast ice and anchored in a sheltered bay, not knowing where they were. Next day the mist rolled away across inshore waters littered with ice, and lifted like a curtain to reveal bare volcanic hills.

In a spell of bright weather Wordie put two scientists ashore on Sabine Island with tents and instruments, including a set of pendulums to measure 'g', the value of gravity. The weight of an object, governed by the pull of the earth, is heavier towards the poles than at the equator, due to the weakening of centrifugal force from the earth's rotation, which is greatest at the equator, and to the flattening of the earth at the poles, which are closer to the centre of attraction. The variation of 'g' is so small that an extremely sensitive apparatus is needed to measure it. Gilt pendulums, swinging at right angles to each other from agate plates and corrected for atmospheric pressure and temperature, are timed by a chronometer that has to be often checked with the sun and stars, and after a long series of readings an accurate measurement is made. The pendulums that were set up in tents on Sabine Island off the Greenland coast had once done the same job in an ice cave for Captain Scott, 10,000 miles away at the other end of the world.

For a hundred years Sabine Island, a cheerless place composed mostly of scree, had been used by other expeditions and their traces still showed—rusty bits of iron, broken wooden crates, unfinished coal dumps and the general debris of camp life. 'My God!' August exclaimed. 'We come all this way and the mess is worse than Southend. It only needs a few banana skins and orange peel . . .' But they found a use for some big acid bottles which fizzed nicely as targets for revolver practice.

For a week the scientists on Sabine Island busied themselves with 'g' while the rest of the expedition, working from the *Heimland*, began a survey of the coast. It was August's introduction to the use of plane tables, theodolite observations, sextant determinations, azimuth calculations, circum-meridian altitudes, telescopic alidades, micrometer transit instruments, clinometers, psychrometers, hypsometers and the rest of an explorer's tools; and he could say as he had said about his first Arctic journey a year earlier—he enjoyed it. Though the sun was often obscured by sea mists it never dropped below the horizon, and with endless light they worked six hours on, six hours off, throughout the day and night. In a month they mapped 150 miles of coast, with countless islands and fjords.

The season of navigation on the east coast of Greenland, between the melting of land-fast ice and the arrival of pack ice from the open sea, is usually only six weeks. Nineteen twenty-six promised and proved to be a good year, but there was no knowing when the weather might break and the coast become blocked. The worst danger was a north or easterly wind, driving immense floes from the polar region and packing them so densely that no passage could be forced through. In 1923, while Wordie's earlier expedition was trying to reach the coast, a Danish ship and a Norwegian ship had been caught in the pack and spent ten weeks drifting helplessly southward in the moving ice. The Norwegian, badly damaged, eventually got away; the Dane was abandoned by her crew who were forced to camp on the ice beside the wreck and in the end were lucky, after a trek with sledges across twenty miles of frozen sea, to reach an island. That same summer another small Norwegian ship, after wintering on the Greenland coast, had tried to sail out through the pack ice and was never heard of again—presumed crushed with the loss of all five men on board.

Making the most of their luck, the *Heimland* party explored and surveyed. Wordie indulged in what someone called 'his singular delight in running up mountains', often carrying the rucksack of a man fifteen years younger as well as his own. On one mountain they discovered fossilized tree trunks in the volcanic ash, evidence of rich temperate vegetation that had once covered this barren land; and on the summit of another mountain August found a note left by a German professor on the same day and month fifty-six years earlier. They also examined the remains of abandoned settlements. Eskimos no longer lived north of Angmagssalik, 600 miles away, but traces of old huts, tent sites and graves survived.

An Eskimo skeleton was brought on board the *Heimland*, to August's discomfort. He felt the ship was cursed. Superstition in such a rational man surprised his friends, but he could justify it. They were attacked by a sudden gale blowing up with force ten squalls and rain, sleet and snow. For three days the *Heimland* rode it out at anchor in the lee of a headland, but the scientists on Sabine Island had a rough time; the pendulum tents were blown down and the whole camp was wrecked.

Fine weather returned and the *Heimland* sailed up the Franz Josef Fjord, a magnificent inlet that twisted into the interior of Greenland for more than a hundred miles. Leaving behind the sea fogs they had endless sunshine, day and night, for a week; and as they passed up the fjord they found the bleak coastal landscape turning into something altogether pleasanter. Harsh monotones gave way to soft reds and greys, the scenery became almost luxuriant by Greenland standards, and August wrote of

the brightly banded cliffs above the fjord, of alternate limestone
and sandstone like great wedges of chocolate and cream cake.
Even Wordie, the disciple of Shackleton who acknowledged his
master's poetic feeling, was moved to near-lyricism at the sight
of willow trees and birches 'as much as twelve to eighteen inches
high'. Whenever he could, tireless and enthusiastic in tartan kilt
and tam-o'-shanter, and brandishing his geological hammer, he
led a party ashore. And there was local food to brighten the diet
of pemmican and baked beans: scrambled eider duck eggs for
breakfast and stewed Arctic hare for dinner. But the Norwegian
crew killed for the fun of it, not just for the pot. To August's
horror they shot at everything they saw—seals, bears, walrus,
birds—and once an entire herd of musk oxen, forming a ring to
defend their calves, was butchered.

On 5 August they reached the head of the Franz Josef Fjord. A
previous explorer, from the top of a mountain, had seen 'a
monstrous pyramid of ice' to the west and named it Petermann
Peak. Wordie meant to investigate this unknown giant and hoped
to be the first to climb it. With August and four others he landed
at the foot of a valley and camped 3,000 feet up on a mountain
slope, pitching tents on a springy turf of heather full of crowberries and bilberries. Ahead lay vast snowfields rising to the
west and leading, they hoped, to a plateau where they would
find their mountain. Below they could see the little *Heimland* in
the fjord, beset by icebergs, some of them eighty feet high. Many
were aground, but they made it a perilous anchorage. A massing
of bergs could trap the ship in the fjord for the winter, and,
though Wordie was prepared for almost anything, he decided on
a limit of five days in the mountains and an immediate return to
the *Heimland* if the weather broke.

The second day's climb was harder. They carried their camp
four miles further west and 4,000 feet higher—tough going, made
worse by paraffin leaking into their rucksacks and spoiling the
food. Late in the evening when they reached a ridge and had their
first sight of Petermann Peak the view was both splendid and fate-
ful. It was certainly the right mountain and probably 10,000 feet

high, but it was still twenty miles away across two more mountain ridges. To get there and back would take six, even eight, days. Instead they had to settle for lesser but still unclimbed mountains.

It was all unexplored, untrodden country and no young man could fail to be struck by the privilege of being there. Once August climbed a small peak alone and stood contemplating the jagged, desolate, black and white wilderness around him. No bird or animal stirred, the silence wrapped the land. But his fondness for solitude hadn't yet matured and he felt horribly lonely. Five minutes up there were enough. He stumbled down the loose stones and back to camp.

For Wordie there was a special excitement. He had expected to see the edge of the vast Greenland ice cap stretching away and disappearing over the world. Instead, for the next eighty miles and perhaps beyond if the eye could only follow, lay endless mountain ranges and valleys—a feast for any explorer. Petermann Peak didn't stand alone. Among its rivals were Mount Shackleton, named by Wordie after his own leader, and Gog and Magog, after the little hills near Cambridge. One day some lucky man would climb them.

They returned to the *Heimland* and started back down the fjord under a cloudless sky. For August, as for Wordie, the departure was a time for sadness. The westward view over unknown mountains to Petermann Peak had been tantalizing, the impatience to return would become intolerable.

The coastal survey continued for a fortnight. They rounded new capes, picked their way among new islands, felt for the shallows, plotted the inlets. Whenever the ship anchored a team was put ashore with the plane table. Sometimes at sea level they were smothered in low fog while all was bright up on the mountains, but usually the weather stayed good and the work went on by day and night. The night shift, though very cold, was often cheered by the visit of a bear. And other Arctic treats occurred—celestial haloes, strange auroras, twilight phenomena and extraordinary mirage effects. Once, through refraction, they saw an island from the *Heimland*'s deck 150 miles away.

The first dipping sunset was the signal for the end of summer and by 21 August it was no longer possible to read at midnight without a lamp. Wordie and August climbed one last mountain and were given a grand view of undiscovered country, but clouds were thickening and the long fine spell seemed about to break. Next day it began to drizzle. With ice floes drifting in from the north-east, the expedition turned south before it was too late and sailed away. Wordie's young explorers were taking fixes and filling gaps on their new map to the last moment, as the curtain that had lifted for them on their first morning came rolling down the hills.

One task remained, but a forlorn one. The crew of the little Norwegian ship lost in the disastrous summer of 1923 might just possibly have escaped over the ice and reached land. The five men could have spent three years marooned on the Greenland coast, hoping to be rescued by a passing ship. But though the *Heimland* steamed for 200 miles, keeping inshore and searching every bay, they saw no trace. They left Greenland after calling at the settlement in Scoresby Sound—where August persuaded the Danish governor to take his rifle in exchange for a beautiful Eskimo harpoon—and set course for Iceland to pick up coal. The pack ice was passed in a few hours, but they still had three bad gales to get through, and everyone was sick except August— revenge, perhaps, on behalf of the skeleton on board.

August's superstition was noted by the doctor as one of the tiny quirks which, in each of them towards the end, tested the nervous toleration of the others. The work was over, the weather raged. Cooped up in the deckhouse for a fortnight, they began to feel the strain of their own company. The old topics—war, evolution, sex, religion, sport, politics—were worn to bursting point. Flaws which they had concealed in themselves and ignored in others grew out of proportion. The rasp of personalities, the rumble of tempers—under control or unnoticed till then—began to show. 'To say that we got fed up with each other,' the doctor wrote, 'would be less than the truth.' A little older than the rest, he watched the conflict, felt the tension. For a good explorer, he decided, no physical quality was worth more than a steady character and a restrained, equable temperament. August Courtauld had all the qualifications.

He spent his twenty-second birthday, like his twenty-first, at sea beyond the Arctic Circle. The ship's cook baked a cake. Two days later they reached Reykjavik and learnt that in England the miners' strike was still unsettled but in Scotland the grouse-shooting had got off to a good start. They had hot showers and dinner at a hotel and went to a cinema. Next day, stormbound and unable to leave, they hired a car to visit the hot springs and were given tea by the British consul: 'Very good tea, no women,' August wrote in his diary. At last they got away, but north of Shetland they were hit by a final gale. One of the boats and much gear was smashed when a sea broke over the *Heimland*'s stern—pooped, to August's delight. In Lerwick he had his first shave since June and on 8 September, ten weeks after leaving, they were back in Aberdeen.

His account of that first Greenland journey written thirty years later is bare and unadorned, but he could no more describe his inner feelings in print than he could bring himself to use more fancy words. Without doubt he was sensitive to a wider range of influences, emotional and aesthetic, than he could reveal in public. Just as surely, like a ship in pack ice, his imagination was caught.

Peter, August and Betty Courtauld

August (back, left) was a member of the Charterhouse shooting team

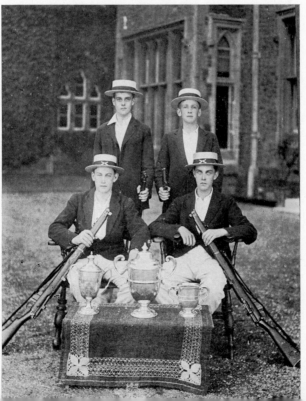

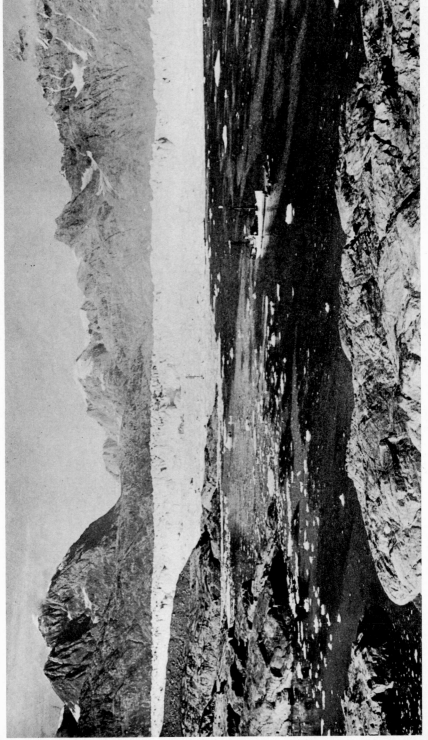

Chapter 4

The Sahara

EARLY IN 1927 August heard that the Royal Geographical Society was sending an expedition to Honduras and needed a surveyor capable of taking star latitudes and wireless longitudes. He wrote to say that he had assisted in that kind of work and with some cramming could possibly take it on. It came to nothing; the job was filled. Perhaps anyway Central America wasn't the country for a man already in love with wide empty places.

But it was a quite different desert, six months after returning from Greenland, that he next went off to explore; and the very sophisticated company, the brothers Francis and Peter Rodd, was unlike anything on Wordie's expedition.

Francis Rodd was nine years older than August. He had fought in France at the beginning of the war, aged nineteen, and later had been an intelligence officer in Italy, North Africa and the Middle East. After the war he went into the diplomatic service but spent much of his time on leave, exploring. For nine months in 1922 he had travelled in the mountains of Air in the middle of the southern Sahara, mapping the country and studying the Tuareg, the legendary, nomadic, aristocratic race living there. The book he wrote after that journey, *People of the Veil*, is a classic of desert literature. There is a small but distinguished band of English travellers who, by their scholarship and bravery and love of its wild people, have made the desert their own; Francis Rodd had joined them. One of his other distinctions— rare for a British diplomat—was to have once led an armed band of Tuareg in defence of the French empire. Another was to be an honorary sergeant of the French Camel Corps. He resigned

3

from the diplomatic service and became a London stockbroker, but the stock exchange could detain him no better than the foreign office. In 1927 he returned with a second expedition to Air.

His brother Peter Rodd was August's age. Later he became known as the original from whom Evelyn Waugh drew much of the character of Basil Seal in his novels *Black Mischief* and *Put Out More Flags*. In his autobiography Waugh described him as someone

> whom I did not greatly like but whom, in my innocence, I was proud to know . . . Peter Rodd had the sulky, arrogant looks of the young Rimbaud. As an ambassador's son he was highly cosmopolitan, but without taste for conventional high society. Nor had he any artistic interests. He was a man of action with his thoughts on the high seas and the desert.

To be not greatly liked by Evelyn Waugh could sometimes be a compliment. Waugh's own biographer said that Peter Rodd's intellectual abilities could be compared with those of the greatest minds, but 'were matched by an irresponsibility which would have been remarkable in a criminal. He had no ambition but instead a ceaseless thirst for adventure . . . He was like a man who prefers to admire his talents as works of art, rather than to use them.' If the character of Basil Seal is anything to go by, Peter Rodd was also a useful companion in a tight corner.

Thus they were an unlikely trio of explorers who sailed from Liverpool at the end of May 1927 bound for Lagos and the Sahara.

> It seems rather mad [August said in a last letter to his father, written in his cabin and sent ashore by the pilot]. It is most awfully good of you to let me go. Not one in a hundred people could see any point in it at all. It costs a lot of money, spends a lot of time and there can be no possible material gain. On the other hand we have spared neither time nor, thanks to you

and the Rodds' people, money in equipping ourselves with the very best and latest tools for our needs. I don't think any small expedition has ever been so well equipped . . . With any luck we ought to be able to do something for the advancement of knowledge. Perhaps add a bit to the map. Possibly be of some use to our Country.

The capital C was important; though August often fumed at the stupidity and ignorance of the British government he was a patriot all his life. '*But* it may take time.' In the rush of departure he hadn't warned his parents how long he might be away: 'Provided we could feed ourselves, seven years might be spent in the region and still we shouldn't know everything. So that although a year is the time we are aiming at, it may be necessary to stay longer, and I'm sure you would rather we made a good job of it while we're about it than come back with nothing much done . . . Well, goodbye till the Canaries.'

As last letters were being collected from the passengers he had time to scribble one more: 'Just off . . . Thanks awfully for wire. Best of luck in Venice . . . Will write from Canaries. Love to all family.' He addressed it to Mollie Montgomerie, who lived a few miles from his home in Essex.

Mollie was three years younger. They had known each other since meeting, aged fifteen and twelve, at a children's fancy-dress party in the Courtaulds' house. August gave her a water ice which she didn't like, so she hid it behind a vase of flowers. Lately they had spent much time together, going to parties and restaurants and theatres and sailing in *Hallowe'en* from Burnham-on-Crouch. Once they ran aground on Foulness Sands and stuck, getting home early next morning to the dismay of Mollie's parents who were only partly consoled by their younger daughter having also been on board. 'I was the first girl friend he ever had,' Mollie said long afterwards. And without doubt there was never any other.

The ship was comfortable, the food eatable, the weather magnificent, but August was never a man to be happy doing nothing. He found the voyage dull and his fellow passengers mostly boring—fat and liverish old 'Coasters', mining people and traders and government officers going out to rule the natives. Life would have been insufferable if he and the Rodds hadn't managed to keep busy. They arranged with the captain to test their special new sandproof long-wave Marconi set in the wireless room, they were up early each morning to get time signals for rating their chronometers, they skipped on deck or played with a medicine ball to keep fit. At last they reached Lagos.

When they disembarked with their eighty pieces of baggage, the Rodds' influence opened all doors. The Governor of Nigeria made them his guests at Government House and supplied cars, horses and whatever else they wanted. 'Everyone bows, salutes, presents arms and lays red carpets as we go along,' August wrote to Mollie, in haste before dressing for dinner. But to a man so recently in the Arctic, it was intolerably hot and a game of squash with the Governor reduced him almost to a puddle. Being a reluctant conformer, he found that colonial life on the west coast of Africa, proverbially the white man's grave, could be another kind of death. It didn't go down too well when he turned up late for a Government House tennis-party; it was no better when he told the Governor that the Union Jack on his car was upside down. After a few days of suffocation, social and climatic, he was glad to board a train for Kano in the north.

The 700-mile rail journey took three days. From Kano they went a further hundred miles by car to Katsina, close to the border of Nigeria and French West Africa. There the British resident took the three English explorers to watch a polo match, lent them ponies to ride, and entertained them twice to dinner. In gratitude August wrote to his mother asking her to send out a present of tennis balls. The Emir was useful too. With his help they bought camels and stores, and engaged camel men and servants. (One of the men, a Tuareg, so distinguished himself by his intelligence that Francis Rodd suggested all he lacked was an education at Balliol—his own college at Oxford.) They would be carrying food for eight months as well as scientific instruments, tents, goatskins for water, tools and presents; also an armoury of eleven rifles and two shot-guns. The caravan was to vary in size but was never less than twelve men in all, and thirty-two camels. It was the end of a very dry season, after five dry years, and the country was brown and parched. They left Katsina on 31 May, the day the summer rains broke.

August, who had never ridden a camel before, found that getting on was the hardest part. He sat in the saddle trying to stir the kneeling animal to its feet, but nothing happened for a long time. At last there was an awful roar beneath him, and an earthquake, and he found himself twenty feet in the air, if he had managed to hang on at all. Getting off was also tricky. He coaxed and tickled until there was a sudden great lurch and the camel folded up like a deckchair. But he loved the early morning rides, though by eleven o'clock the sun was scorching. His bare legs were burnt, he was rubbed sore by the saddle. Around him hung saddlebags full of notebooks, almanacs and photographic things; behind were two water bottles and a rifle; strapped about him were a prismatic compass, a knife and a spare camera; and on his head he wore a solar topi. They travelled slowly but grandly, as he told his mother, like a very rich funeral.

After two days they left the British Empire and entered the French—not that it made much difference to the landscape. It was the hottest season of the year, the sun was right overhead and there was no shade; no wind and no view either. The scrub, which kept visibility down to a few yards, was just too high for them to see over the top. Thorn branches hung across the path to catch them on camel-back; prickly burr-grass didn't encourage them to dismount and walk. Francis Rodd spoke of his belief that the private hell in store for him one day was to wander for eternity through the bush in search of the open desert. They often saw wild game, which vanished before they could shoot. There were scorpions, snakes, centipedes, tarantulas and bushmen with poisoned arrows. Soon the rains began in earnest. Their camp was stunned by lightning, or wrecked by a revolving wind squall, when it wasn't flooded by a tropical downpour.

Although tiny blades of grass and shoots of vegetation, watered by the first rain, began to grow, it was still too thin to feed the camels. After the long dry season they were weak and needed nursing. They made terrible stomach noises all night, or strayed while grazing and got lost. Loading up before dawn for the day's trek was a trying business. A hobble rope was tied round a camel's knee and the baggage piled on its back while it roared and struggled to bite. When it was untied it often threw off its load. By the time the last camel was ready there were several that had to be reloaded. Tempers were short in the early morning.

It continued for more than a month. The Englishmen would start the day on foot, walking beside the caravan until it got too hot; then mount their camels and rock in the saddle for hour after hour. Francis Rodd and August sat reading books and occasionally taking compass bearings; Peter Rodd did needlework as he rode. Sometimes they went three days without fresh water, and what they carried in goatskins wasn't always good to drink. The skins had been peeled from a carcase, greased with goat fat and sewn up to make a bag. Water from an old skin was almost tasteless and always cool from evaporation, but from a new skin it could be grey and reeking of goat. Usually there was nothing else to wash down the roast gazelle or guinea-fowl.

In camp August acted as foil to the brilliant brothers. Afterwards he claimed that he did little but keep the peace: 'Conversations round the camp table in the evening were too erudite for me. Mostly they seemed to be about personalities in London I had never heard of, or Greek history or the origin of words.' Francis Rodd remembered him more favourably: 'He kept everyone amused and devoted to himself by his unending fund of incongruities and idiosyncracies.'

In early July they reached the end of the bush and the beginning of the desert. The stifling feeling was left behind, they could see a horizon again. But the Sahara summer was at its height and even the camels suffered. Wells and pools were at their lowest and fewest, not yet filled by the rains. They found one well, famous for the pasture growing round it and for a thirsty lioness that had once drowned in it, now silted up with sand. It needed nineteen hours' digging before the camels were all watered and the goatskins filled; hard work, but even then they couldn't rest. The promised pasture didn't exist, they were forced to move on in the blaze of the afternoon. Two hours later, struck by a sandstorm, they had to pitch camp hastily. During the night the sand turned to rain. Then the hungry camels began to wander off, looking for food.

But the weather improved and before long they were camped in a gorge among low hills, a watering-place for the tribes which ranged over the desert with their camels and flocks. In the stream bed, in a cleft of sandstone, lay a deep swimming-pool with a sandy bottom and a perfect rock for diving off. Below were smaller pools carved from the red and black rock, beset with arches and buttresses and caves. For anyone recently in Greenland it must have stirred odd memories of Franz Josef Fjord. On the walls of the gorge were ancient inscriptions of the tribes that had camped there, with names and messages between friends and lovers. All around grew green bushes and tall palms. Mountain sheep lived in the hills, with gazelle and sand grouse.

While the camels recovered their health, serious geographical work began. The Rodd brothers studied the rock inscriptions and found drawings of people, camels and horses which they copied or photographed. August got out his instruments, set up his plane table and started mapping.

Francis Rodd's plan was to reach the village of Auderas in the mountains of Air before the worst of the rains came. In 1922 he had lived there for two months, making many Tuareg friends, and he knew it to be a good place for exploration. Their road lay through Agades, one of the great cities of the desert whose fort had been the scene of a heroic defence by the French garrison against a Tuareg revolt. Now the tricolour fluttered in peace, and the officers, with little else to do, detained the English travellers longer than they wished. August hardly took to military life and the Rodds too became impatient, but French

hospitality was imperative; the Fourteenth of July was at hand
and it was more than a week before they got away.

Air is one of the three mountain groups of the Sahara, a huge but
thinly inhabited oasis more than 200 miles across. An ancient
desert trade route passes through it and for centuries caravans
have stopped to recuperate there before travelling on. Though it
lies within the tropics surrounded by immense stretches of
desert, the climate is far from harsh. The hillsides are rocky and
windswept but the valleys could be better cultivated if the people
chose. Instead, apart from keeping small gardens and palm
groves, the Tuareg prefer to wander over the country, nomads by
instinct.

They lived in North Africa, roaming and ruling the Sahara,
long before the Arabs came. Possibly they were Christians before
becoming Muslims. As caravan drivers they carried elements of
Mediterranean civilization deep into Central Africa, but they
never came to like Europeans very much. By force of tradition
and a knightly code of honour they survived French colonialism
in a fairly pure state, with their own language and a script used
by nobody else. They were a unique race, fair-skinned and of
magnificent physique, with the bearing and behaviour of an
aristocracy. Descent and inheritance were counted through the
women, who were the equals of men and had the same reputation
for bravery. But the men alone, on reaching manhood, assumed
the veil and wore it day and night—a band of cloth wound round
the head to form a hood, and over the face to cover mouth and
nostrils with only a slit for the eyes.

Francis Rodd, living among the Tuareg in 1922, had surrendered to their spell: 'The men are born to walk and move as
kings,' he wrote.

They stride along swiftly and easily like princes of the earth,
fearing no man, cringing before none and consciously superior
to other people. Grace and mystery are added to their

appearance by the veil over the face and by their long black robes . . . I thought of how very happy these nomads were. They have no possessions to speak of: a few mats, the clothes they wear, some water-skins, some camel trappings, a few weapons, some gourds and bowls, a cooking-pot or two and their camels. They have no routine of life, and no cares except to wonder if a raiding party will or will not happen on them . . . I hope the gods will be good to them. They were my good friends and I was pleased to live with them, for they were very agreeable. Perhaps we shall meet again and travel once more.

Now, five years later, he was back in the village of Auderas and the Tuareg made him and his companions welcome. The chief had built a palm leaf hut for their camp, set on a rocky knoll among high mountains with a valley winding below. Not far away, beside its patch of irrigated gardens, was the little straw-hutted village. While their camels were taken off to the new rain-grown pastures, the Englishmen feasted on melons, tomatoes, cucumbers, pumpkins, dates and camel's milk cheese.

Then without warning Tekhmedin turned up: Tekhmedin the proud, the independent, the greatest of the guides of Air, famous all over the Sahara, one of the hardest travellers of the world who had done the journey to Ghat in Libya across 400 miles of terrible desert more than eighty times. He knew each stone and bush and fold in the ground as a Londoner knows the streets. He knew the stars—the Great Bear which he called the Cow Camel, and the Pleiades, the Chickens. Tekhmedin belonged to the Tuareg élite. He had fought the French and been imprisoned, and would bear the fetter-marks on his ankles all his life. After he had lost his property and been reduced to poverty he was asked by his conquerors to join the Camel Corps as a guide, but he would have nothing to do with them, he would rather starve. He was in rags in 1922 when Francis Rodd first met him. Slowly his suspicion thawed and he agreed to travel with the young Englishman: 'I will come with you for a month or for a year, but only because I want to come and not for pay. If I come, I will go anywhere you want, but I will not come as your servant. You may give me a present if you like. You must feed me because I am poor and give me a camel to ride, but I will not be paid for any service. I will come only as your friend.' They had done some tough journeys together and Francis Rodd had nursed him when he had fever; he was one of the few men of the Tuareg whom Rodd had seen without his veil. Now, hearing that his English friend was back in Air, Tekhmedin had come 150 miles on foot, walking for a week, to see him again. Soon he was riding with the caravan, in charge of men and camels, through country unknown to him, refusing all payment except something to keep his wife while he was away.

To August the weeks they spent at Auderas were pure idyll. It hardly fitted the common idea of the Sahara, as he told Mollie: 'One thinks of it as flat and sandy, but here the scenery is more mountainous than Scotland. Great crags and precipices go up all round.' The season lent enchantment to the scene. Stony plateaux were laid with a sudden cloth of green, the scent of acacias drifted in the air, great trees shook with their awakening. As the leaves and plants grew after the first rains it was a delight to watch nature's annual rebirth, and a relief, after the long desert trek, to be among mountains. Morning and evening shadows played on the sandstone and foaming clouds sailed on the wind, casting endless patterns on the red rock. At nightfall the cliffs turned blue.

Nearly every afternoon a deluge struck Auderas, but by sunset it was over and the travellers could put their camp-beds out in the open. In the hut, set up with tables and chairs and book-shelves and skins laid on the floor, they wrote up their notes or sheltered from the squalls of rain and wind. Life was full of pleasure and much of it was due to Peter Rodd's control of the kitchen. August sent a menu to his mother: the day began with bacon and eggs and ended with a full-blown supper—melon, soup, a bird they had shot or goat rissoles with rice and beans, salads, pancakes and jam, maize savouries, with cocoa and dates for dessert. Two French officers passing on their way to a remote desert post, who were entertained to dinner, were much impressed by the style of the English camp.

August's thoughts often turned elsewhere, and though the mail by camel was slow and irregular he kept in touch with home; with his boat *Hallowe'en* too. A painting of her racing at Ramsgate was hanging in the Royal Academy that summer and he wrote urgently to his parents asking for it to be bought before somebody snapped it up: 'A real painting of one's own boat will indeed be worth having.' To Mollie he verged on rhapsody:

> I don't know when I shall be back, but we must have another evening at the Café de P. when I do. We will go for some marvellous sails in *Hallowe'en* and get beyond, we hope, Foulness Sands . . . By the time you get this they will have folded her white wings and put her to bed in some dusty shed with nothing but her memories of breathless sailing to tide her through the winter. Perhaps I shall be back by next summer. I hope so and I'll take her out beyond the muddy creeks to where she belongs, the sea . . . I hope you have all had a ripping time in Venice.

News of the family in Essex was welcomed in the Sahara; other events at home were wistfully observed: 'Today being the Twelfth I suppose everyone is banging away at the old grouse in Scotland. We shall do our bit by having a go at the guinea-fowl.'

They got on with as much work as the rains allowed, measuring the daily rainfall, mapping what they could and making hunting trips. As well as winding and checking the chronometers by wireless, August's job was to climb the peaks round Auderas and take sights with a theodolite. The loose rock, split and shattered and slippery at the best of times, was made no easier by the rain, but the views made up for the difficulties. To the east lay the Todra range, nearly 6,000 feet above sea level, which had stirred Francis Rodd's interest before:

The rounded sides rose out of a bed of green and yellow to a crest of bare red rock at the top. The mountain used to change colour all day, a whitish gleam off the rocks at high noon giving place to blue-black shadows under storm clouds and in the evening. At sunset it seemed to glow vivid red from within. It is one of the most beautiful mountains in the world.

Peter Rodd and August set off to climb it. With a Tuareg guide and two porters they left camp one afternoon after the usual thunderstorm, travelling light over the rough ground. The guide's technique was to choose a point in the distance and make straight for it, ignoring obstacles and moving very fast. At sunset they reached a ruined village beneath a precipice and settled for the night, with sore feet and no bedding or spare clothes except a single mackintosh between them. Peter Rodd wrote, 'A full moon and racing clouds, some black with the menace of rain and some all silver, played with the shadows of the hills, making mysteries in the ravines and wonders on the heights. There were several ghosts in the ruined houses of the village.' Next morning they scrambled up a vast gulley that split the mountain, only to find they were cut off from the highest peak by deep clefts and a ridge of unclimbable blocks of rock. They tried to shoot a mountain sheep for food but missed, and they set up their theodolite but were rained on: 'So we sat in a bush all afternoon and let it rain, for as a matter of fact we couldn't stop it.' They slept the next night in the rain, high up in a little glen. 'Our dreams were not sweet, since we were using wet haversacks for beds, only because they were better than biscuit tins. Next day we saw some mutton (potential) and converted it into mutton (actual).' They made a second attempt on the summit but were defeated by another deep gulley. More rain was coming, their feet were sore beyond endurance, they retreated to Auderas. A few days later, alone, August climbed the mountain from the other side and carried the theodolite to the top.

By early September they had mapped 400 square miles of unknown country, the rains were almost spent and it was time to move on. Francis Rodd hoped to travel right across the Sahara to the Mediterranean, but first they would explore the mountains of northern Aïr.

The camel men, even more reluctant than their masters to leave Auderas, staged a near-mutiny. Some had to be dismissed and new ones found. At last they got away and followed an old abandoned track where the country, uninhabited and unexplored, had had little rain, and water was too scarce to let them linger. During a halt for lunch one day August 'had rather a narrow squeak' when a sand viper slipped under his foot; luckily Peter Rodd yelled in time and they killed it. After ten days' march, with another four to go, they ran out of food, which might have been serious if they hadn't met goatherds who supplied them with excellent cream cheese. A fortnight after leaving Auderas they reached Iféruan, 150 miles north, and camped once more among irrigated gardens where bullocks pulled buckets up the wells all day. For the next week the three Englishmen and the two French-men in the fort, a lieutenant and a sergeant, happily exchanged hospitality.

Permission to cross the Sahara northwards had still to be given. The French authorities showed no interest; the expedition might be held up for weeks. Meanwhile the camels needed rest and good pasture to make them fit for the long desert journey ahead. But soon they were beset with troubles. First, Tekhmedin was arrested for sedition, put in the fort and had to be bailed out for a high price. Then another man made off with someone else's money and trousers. The cook also vanished, taking his slave boy with him, which set off a bout of food thefts. All the men had to be fined a week's pay and threatened with a French prison. Finally the explorers themselves were overtaken by a fit of dissension on a minor domestic point.

Francis Rodd, known by August as the C-in-C, said that as they were no longer on the march their breakfast should be advanced from six o'clock to eight. Peter Rodd said that without a proper cook it was impossible to have it before ten-thirty and anyone who didn't like it at that time needn't eat it. August said nothing. The brothers boiled in defiance, while the odd man out watched with interest and mild astonishment. The C-in-C, announcing that breakfast was to be at eight and anyone who disagreed could go the same way as the cook, disappeared into the fort to have lunch with the Frenchmen and stayed there for the rest of the day. The Frenchmen, no doubt, hardly had breakfast at all.

August, who hated a quarrel, walked off alone into the landscape to smoke his pipe and write to Mollie. The only paper was the backs of used navigation forms and the only ink, because supplies were running out, had been diluted with tea, but there was enough to say:

It really is awfully jolly here doing nothing in particular . . . One sleeps in the open on a comfortable camp-bed which one can have where one likes without disturbing any furniture or knocking down any walls. One gets up with the sun, or rather the flies, and dodders about in pyjamas doing odd jobs with thermometers and things . . . A lazy day interspersed with bits of work and cups of tea. Then the marvellous cool of the evening. The sun pops behind the hills, the same old stars come out, the good old supper comes along . . . No, I haven't got a beard but the other two have . . . The C-in-C's is a vast black affair that sticks out in a cave-man sort of fashion, while Peter's is a pale wavy structure . . . No, I haven't picked up any bugs or things, except septic sores. Every scratch, burn or bite turns septic and then one is worried by flies for a month. I have even avoided scorpion bites.

He added that the battle about breakfast, to nobody's surprise, had been won by the C-in-C.

Now that the rains were over, short mapping trips were more comfortable. August would take a camel with a water-skin and a blanket, and hope to meet someone who might give him cheese or a drink of milk. Sometimes he was lucky, sometimes not. There was no need of shelter, he simply rolled up in his blanket and slept anywhere, however stony. It was near to a nomad's life and after four months in the desert he must have been as tough as he could get. But never quite like a Tuareg; a man walking barefoot all day on the sharp ground, with an open crack in his skin that wouldn't heal, could take a needle and thread and sew his own sole as if he were mending a sandal.

Permission to cross the Sahara to the Mediterranean never came. Unless they returned south to Nigeria the only way out of Air was westward across 500 miles of desert to the River Niger, then on to Timbuktu and eventually to Senegal on the Atlantic coast. Anything was better than going back the way they had come, but the western route had other attractions too. Francis Rodd wanted to see the desert pastures where many of the nomadic Tuareg lived, as far from European contact as possible—passing through country that hadn't been visited for a long time by any European traveller, or ever seen at all.

But they were still held up. Some of the camel men demanded to be given a camel each at the end of a month's work, some were frightened of the desert or the tribes in it, others refused to leave Air in any direction, and there was talk of rebellion in the west—not the best news for a foreign caravan.

The Rodds and August didn't waste time. They put the delay to good use, to the benefit of the French authorities as much as to themselves.

Every autumn an immense caravan left Air for the eastern desert to bring back dates and salt. It was the most important event in the annual cycle of Sahara trade, and the largest enterprise of its kind in the world. In recent years it had numbered about 4,000 camels, but before the First World War 30,000 had been counted. For nearly a week they would cross the waterless, pastureless desert, carrying their fodder with them and dropping bales of grass for the return journey. Such a rich caravan was a tempting prize to raiders and under the French occupation it had been escorted by a platoon of the Camel Corps. Mobile troops and any irregular Tuareg bands that could be trusted were sent on patrol to look for suspicious tracks in the desert or watch outlying water-holes where a raiding party might wait. This year one such patrol, ordered to occupy the Tarazit district seventy-five miles north of Iféruan, had failed to report for duty. An important route to Air was thus left unguarded, open to possible raiders. Hearing of it, the three Englishmen volunteered to mount a patrol in Tarazit themselves.

They picked six men and nine good camels, loaded up with a blanket each and water-skins and food for fifteen days, armed themselves with their own rifles and started for Tarazit. They travelled according to Francis Rodd's dictum, as far as possible like the Tuareg, trusting in their own health and knowledge and ingenuity. On the third day they entered the Tarazit gorge, avoiding the normal track in case of raiders and coming over the mountains, down a sheer rock-strewn slope into the most romantic defile any of them had imagined; just the place for a desert skirmish.

There they camped in a cave near a pool, pastured their camels and kept watch for four days, living off wheat, rough-ground between granite stones, and fresh antelope meat roasted on the cleaning-rods of their rifles. By night they stayed awake in turn, one at a time. August wrote, 'It was an eerie job sitting on the rocks, rifle on knees, listening to the sounds of the desert. The hyenas screamed, the jackals howled.' By day they swam in the pool. They even did a little mild geographical work and discovered some rock inscriptions. But no raiders turned up.

They returned to Iféruan through a wilderness of rock and sand where for seventy miles they saw no living animal or plant—good practice for the long desert journey they were soon to make. The rains had entirely failed, the camels were very hungry long before they got back to Iféruan and the nights were already bitterly cold. But an English patrol had performed a friendly service on behalf of France.

Within four days they had packed up their camp at Iféruan and were off again, westward on their way out of Air. Suddenly their labour troubles vanished and they were embarrassed not so much by the men who didn't want to travel with them as by the number who did.

On the second day's march they passed the camp of a Tuareg named Ahmed, an old friend. Letting the caravan go on ahead, the Englishmen stopped to drink milk with him and talk of their journey while Ahmed's wife played to them on a one-stringed violin. Francis Rodd asked if he would go with them to Timbuktu. Instantly Ahmed agreed, and went to fetch a camel. He would drop everything and ride with them at ten minutes' notice, 500 miles each way, without discussing payment or reward and without any man to leave in charge of his women and property. Such impulsive friendliness was typical of Ahmed. Francis Rodd said of him, 'We remember him as one of the greatest gentlemen it has ever been our good fortune to meet in any land.'

In a few days they reached the pools of Arli where the last hills of Air, dropping in gentle steps, slipped into the vast sea of sand that lay ahead. Francis Rodd, while his brother and August investigated more rock drawings, watered and pastured the camels in preparation for the desert and paid off the superfluous men. He also looked for a guide, for this was a part of the Sahara new even to Tekhmedin, and engaged a disreputable old man called Khayar who claimed to know the route. As Khayar owned no blanket, vital now that the nights were so cold, August gave him an old khaki shirt which he wore by day and night to supplement his veil and network of rags tied on by pieces of hide.

On 12 November the caravan left the pools of Arli and launched into the sand. Beyond the last outcrop of rock, in a small depression called the Belly of the Carrion Eagle, there were no landmarks ahead at all. Khayar had heard that the first well they would reach was dry but there was a new one at Battal, one day's march beyond. He had never been there; from its description he thought he could find it.

They carried forty water-skins, more than a ton of water, ample to ensure against evaporation and the danger of a camel throwing its load or bursting precious skins by trying to roll. Pasture for the camels was a far worse problem. For the first five days, across a hundred miles of small pebbles lying on hard sand, they found only two thin patches of *hadd*—a rare desert fodder, something between grass and gorse.

Khayar rode at the head of the string of camels. They started before dawn each day and marched till late in the afternoon, wandering a little off course at the end of the day to look for a chance piece of *hadd* or some sticks of dry *alwat*—another desert vegetable, half vetch, half degenerated cabbage—that could be used for firewood. It froze at night but soon after sunrise it became very hot, and by six in the morning a mirage had formed round them, so they appeared to be travelling on an island afloat in a sea of milk. The shore was always a quarter of a mile away, they never reached it and it closed behind them. Peter Rodd knitted as they went.

August was supposed to be plotting their route with compass and chronometer, but he could find nothing to take a sight on. The least tuft or rock ahead dissolved in the mirage or else swelled and stood on end above the horizon like a tottering piano. It was impossible to get a bearing. In the end he took to riding at the tail of the caravan and sighting on Khayar at the head. He found after five days, when plotting the true position by sun and stars, that although Khayar had neither compass nor marks to steer by he led the caravan for a hundred miles without deviating one mile.

In camp on the third night, Francis Rodd overheard Khayar and some of the men, on their haunches round a fire, arguing about geography. He went over to squat with them, to ask where they were. Khayar said he didn't exactly know, they might be in a place called the Valley of Maggots or they might not have got so far. Valleys in the desert were so shallow as to be hardly perceptible. Next evening they saw five small trees near a line of sand dunes—Khayar's landfall. On the fifth day they passed the promised dry well and after a few hours came to Battal at precisely the point where Khayar expected it.

There they spent a day watering and feeding their camels, resting and making friends with another Tuareg caravan at the well. There was scientific work to do also. On arrival the instrument cases were opened and wireless, batteries and aerial set up. During the day's march August had selected his evening stars from the nautical almanac and tabulated them in a notebook. Now he tuned the wireless for a time signal and checked the chronometers. At sunset, while Francis Rodd sighted the theodolite on the chosen stars as they came out and Peter noted his brother's readings, August recorded the time.

It was a drill they had developed in Air and now used for fixing the water-holes across the western desert. With practice they could take two star sights within seventy seconds, and the mathematics for a series of four sights were worked out in an hour and a half. The result of their observations was that the whole of Air had to be moved on the map several miles east of the previous French position, which had been fixed without wireless time signals. The Tuareg were neither interested nor impressed by this celestial navigation. They understood perfectly well that anyone could find his way about the desert at night by measuring the stars, but they failed to see the point of plotting the water-holes when everybody knew exactly where they were.

The night's rest at Battal was spoilt by the camels who tried to drink at a puddle left by the rains. The water was foul and they had to be driven off—difficult in the dark when the ferocity of a thirsty camel was intensified. In the morning they finished watering with leather buckets pulled up the well by hand, then started for the next water-hole two days' march away.

Now the country became more interesting, with low limestone escarpments breaking the monotony. But Khayar's reputation as a guide, impeccable in an empty landscape, began to fall. It was as if he was confused by the slightest solid feature beyond the mirage. One day Francis Rodd, who had left the caravan to inspect a small hill, had trouble catching up again. The wind had wiped out the camel tracks and he had nobody with him who knew the way. When he rejoined the others he found they were heading north-west instead of west. Khayar confessed that he was lost, that he hadn't known where he was since the last water-hole three days ago, and that he had only struck that water-hole by mistake, never having been there before. It wasn't auspicious for the 200 miles they still had to travel.

Luckily they came to a camp of nomads and persuaded them to lend a boy who could guide them to the next water-hole, the Hyena Well. It proved to be twenty miles from where Khayar thought. The pools lay in a ravine leading to a broad valley hemmed in by white cliffs cut from the surrounding desert and containing plentiful green *alwat* for the camels. They stayed for a day and a night, to rest and take observations.

By threats and cajolings they induced the boy to lead them as far as another water-hole, but he wasn't sure of the way and had never been beyond. Next day, hearing from nomads that there was no more pasture before reaching the Ifoghas hills at the end of the journey, Francis Rodd sent one of his men to borrow a guide from the chiefs of a tribe camped a few miles away. After many hours the man came back to report hostility and refusal. By now Khayar was useless, so ashamed at having lost his way that he had collapsed. But they were far from Air and couldn't abandon him to return alone. Either they turned round and followed their tracks all the way back, or went on marching westward across unknown country where there was no pasture, no encampments and so no chance of a new guide.

They pushed on, at the risk of having to secure a guide by force. After sending the caravan on ahead, Francis Rodd took four armed men and rode off to visit the unfriendly chiefs, ready to make trouble if he had to. But soon the English explorer, late diplomat turned stockbroker, had made friends with an old patriarch who lived in a group of tents with his flocks and children and grandchildren round him. They got on so well that instead of hostility the old man offered his younger son as guide. It was just as well; when they rejoined the caravan they found it travelling in the wrong direction. Khayar, having recovered his confidence, had taken the lead again and was heading into space.

The next stage of the journey, across a stretch of desert called the Belly of the Negresses, passed without event. The low hills of Ifoghas, though providing pasture and water, were nothing to travellers who had lived among the magnificent scenery of Air; the approaching end was not a cheerful prospect; and they failed to find men, as they had hoped, to join them for the last stage to the River Niger. Ahmed, their impulsive companion of the desert, was out of his element here and wanted to go home; but no Tuareg would abandon three Englishmen in a strange country. They marched on through the bush.

After six days, suddenly at sunset, they found the great river in front of them—a brilliant sheet of blue, two miles wide between banks of yellow sand and bright green reeds. The tricolour flying over Burem, with rest-houses and telegraph office and the promise of France borne by the remotest colonial outpost, marked the end of the road.

Having led them to the banks of the Niger their Tuareg friends stopped only a few hours. The water everywhere made them uneasy; they were sure that they and their camels would die unless they went back to the desert immediately. Only Tekhmedin offered to go further—wherever they wanted. They gave him a camel, though he was almost too proud to accept, and money to buy another, hoping he could set himself up in the style he deserved, but which his principles made so difficult. The rest of the camels were sold and the offer of a lift to Timbuktu in a French trader's motor boat was accepted. Gazelle and antelope were exchanged for hippo and crocodile.

It was Christmas, six weeks since they had launched into the desert from Air, but nothing had been so strenuous as the four days' hospitality in Timbuktu. When it was over they boarded a small river steamer, smothered with native passengers, and set up their camp in the tiny dining-cabin. It was a grilling voyage. The boat burned wood and had to stop every few hours to pick up fuel; if there were no logs in sight somebody's house was knocked down and fed into the furnace. The boiler raged, the sun blazed. Eight days later they reached Bamako, only to find that they must wait another week for a train to the coast. At Dakar, where the entertaining was relentless, they bought smart new clothes for all the dinner-parties.

August wrote to his mother to warn her that they were sailing for Liverpool in a cargo boat and he would soon be home: 'I hope I shall find you all well.' He had had no news for seven months.

In London the president of the Royal Geographical Society congratulated the three members of the expedition. They had explored new country and drawn seventeen map sheets; had fixed altitudes, taken thermometer and barometer readings, rainfall measurements and the water temperature of deep wells; noted wind direction and cloud formation, also sunrise and sunset effects; copied or photographed rock drawings and inscriptions; measured the skulls of fifty Tuareg and collected anthropological, ethnological, archaeological, historical, geological and botanical material. They could compliment themselves on a great success; not that any of them ever would, but they might confess to having had a very good time.

In return Francis Rodd had some harsh things to say about travellers who came back from foreign lands with thoughtless, superficial judgements on the people who lived there. He took Spinoza for his model—neither mock nor mourn nor condemn men's deeds, but try to understand:

> Even a race so blamed as the Tuareg has qualities which are worth knowing. Although they live in a manner differing vastly from our own, I have found them to have much in common with ourselves, much that was pleasant and much that was more worthy of admiration than among many people nearer home.

His affection for those proud men, and theirs for him, smoothed the rougher passages through a cruel land and eased the hardship. His old relations with many of them, shared by Peter and August, were among the happiest aspects of the entire journey. Perhaps there was an element beyond simple friendship. Perhaps, to three such Englishmen, the Tuareg were an élite who stirred sympathies deeper than they would admit. Perhaps, in the courage and courtesy and fierce disdain of that desert tribe, they recognized something—a quality of anachronism, even a hint of doom —that touched them sharply.

Without doubt Francis Rodd's own courage, his imagination, his understanding, his energy, his philosophy of travel—the features of his character that infused the expedition—were not lost on August, who caught the message and responded keenly. In a discussion after Rodd had given a lecture at the Royal Geographical Society, August stood up and filled some of the gaps left by his leader's modesty. It was Francis Rodd, he said, who made the preparations and foresaw the disasters, who drew the map and stayed up all one night watering the camels at an almost dry well: 'There are many of the simple people there who count the days to his return.'

Thirty years after their Sahara journey together, August dedicated his own book of memoirs to the man 'whose leadership inspired my life'.

Chapter 5

The Second Expedition

IN THE SPRING of 1928, soon after getting back from Africa, August and his sister Betty were carted off, as he put it, by their parents to the French Riviera: 'The idea was that I should become civilized.' Though the Sahara Desert had been enough of a contrast after Greenland, the lingering grandeur and effete snobberies of the Côte d'Azur were an even severer shock.

The family stayed in a hotel totally English, whose only merit to August was that Rudyard Kipling was also staying in it. No fellow-guest could have given more pleasure to August's father. Old Mr Courtauld and old Mr Kipling could spend an entire Mediterranean spring discussing literature in their hotel. It would be hard to believe that the great writer didn't also have much to tell and ask the young explorer; and it would be nice to know what they said. After all, this was the author whose stories had been read aloud to the Courtauld children during the war by the general who was billeted on them. But the Riviera couldn't keep August for long. After a week of trying to find something to do he gave up, got on a train and went home to sail *Hallowe'en*.

He was now nearly twenty-four and it was decided—probably the last decision in his life that he didn't make entirely on his own—that it was time he settled down to a sensible job. It wasn't hard to find one. His father got him into Buckmaster and Moore, stockbrokers, with the help of Francis Rodd who was one of the partners. A smart City firm would like to take on a young man who would one day be very rich, and though August couldn't have thought seriously about a career in an office he may have enjoyed the idea of learning about finance. He was made a 'red button' with an enamel badge in his lapel to prove it, and was paid £150 a year. He lived at the Courtauld house in Palace Green and generally spent weekends at home in Essex.

At first his duties as apprentice stockbroker were to carry messages from his own office to other people's and check the day's transactions between brokers and jobbers. Later, on promotion, he was put into the 'box' inside the sacred Stock Exchange itself, where he took down clients' orders on the telephone. But the excitements of boom and slump left him cold. The fluctuations of the stock market were nothing to the transformations of light and colour on a mountain or the changing moods at sea. A year ago he had been in Air, two years ago in Greenland; now he was sitting in a box.

It made him no happier to think how other people might be spending their summer. 'Everybody now seems to be on holiday,' he wrote to Mollie who was in Scotland. 'I suppose you are having a perfectly marvellous time at Glenisla . . . I suppose everybody is very busy killing grouse, stags and other denizens of the highlands. Have you been eloped with to the hut yet? You get a divine view over all the hills of Scotland from up there.' The panorama in the City was limited: 'I am here in this minute box at the door of the Stock Exchange surrounded by telephones, buying and selling stocks and shares, feeling rather mauve.' He changed colour before the end of the letter and signed himself 'yours beigely'.

He kept sane by taking flying lessons after office hours, shuddering through the air above the London suburbs at a breathless eighty miles an hour in the open cockpit of a Gypsy Moth. There can't have been many young stockbrokers learning to fly. After three hours with an instructor he felt he could do anything except loop-the-loop, but what he longed for was to fly solo, which was forbidden until he had flown eight hours. Even worse, he would have to do fifty hours before being allowed more than three miles from the aerodrome. He wanted to fly over

Mollie's home in Essex: 'The only thing will be to have a kite of one's own and not insure it.'

His love for Mollie, growing quietly since his return from the Sahara, lit his life in a way that had never happened before. They spent more and more time together, but never enough for August, though he was no more comfortable as man-about-town than as stockbroker. He was shy with women, he felt helpless among them, he couldn't be bothered with the punctilios of dress and decorum, he didn't seem to do the proper things on the dance floor. Mollie was clever, gay, pretty, also restless and unconfident. She had no lack of suitors but no wish to become anybody's wife yet. Life was a whirl of weekend house-parties, hunt balls, point-to-point dances, theatres, concerts. August, spending his days in the box, tried to keep up. When he couldn't see her, he wrote to her. She didn't write back often enough. He tried to console himself with *Hallowe'en* or on shooting parties with his friends, but it didn't work. Nothing worked unless Mollie was there. Except for a passion for a governess in his nursery days, he had never in his life, as he told her, gone so completely loopy over anyone.

Early in 1929, in a fit of gloom, he wrote the first of many declarations:

> It is a marvellous day and here I am in this office with all the shares going down and nothing worth doing to do . . . I suppose because I only see you once in a blue moon you don't think I really love you. You can't know the effort it takes to get through five days of London before I can come down to see you. Monday is the most frightful day.

Mollie had spoken about a rival admirer, somebody more serious than the others, but August said it would make no difference: 'Do let me be fond of you as well. I know I am only one of thousands but you are one of one, the only one I have ever been in this stupid state about.' If she left him the sun would go out, there would be nothing left, he would have to go into a monastery:

'I know this all sounds very funny, especially as you think I am a complete misogynist. So I was, till lately.'

Sailing was the best escape, until he could go on another expedition. His friend Frank Carr owned an old Bristol Channel pilot cutter, *Cariad*, nearly fifty feet long—much bigger than *Hallowe'en*. Carr had meant to sail round the world, writing books to pay for the voyage, but he had had to give up the plan and now found *Cariad* an extravagance he couldn't afford. He and August agreed on a sailing partnership, sharing costs and cruising together or separately as they chose. It was a happy arrangement, not least because of the thorough seamanship of both young men. They were expert amateurs, good sailors and good friends, with ideas of how to run a boat that exactly tallied. Frank Carr reported that he had found the perfect sailing partner. August took Mollie to see *Cariad*.

The effect was encouraging. August suggested a sailing holiday on the west coast of Scotland in the early summer, if Mollie's parents would allow it and a chaperone could be found. The whole point of having a share in *Cariad*, he said, was to give Mollie a really jolly time. If she couldn't go sailing with him it would all be a waste: 'So *do* try and persuade your Ma. After all we *have* known each other all our lives.' Much later he admitted to another motive: to see how Mollie would take to the kind of life he liked. At some stage he had made one of his quiet, irrevocable decisions.

Then good news came from Cambridge. Wordie was planning to go back to East Greenland in the summer with an expedition to climb Petermann Peak, the mountain they had failed to reach in 1926. August would go with him, it was just what he had been hoping for. His career on the Stock Exchange, never very secure, was doomed. With Mollie and *Cariad* and Greenland to think about, his mind couldn't settle on scrip issues or market prices. Once, in the hateful little box, he was given an order by telephone to invest £50 in Imperial Chemicals. More uncaring than careless, he took it down as £50,000 and passed it to the jobber who bought the shares. The blunder was discovered before it caused serious havoc, luckily for the firm. When August suggested that they should hang on to the shares as the price was going up he was ignored; City ethics—or City orthodoxy—had to be observed. He wouldn't have lasted much longer anyway. In the spring, when he said he was leaving, nobody was surprised and nobody tried to stop him.

His first cruise with Frank Carr in *Cariad* started at Pin Mill in Suffolk at Easter 1929. Also on board was a professional bosun, a tough old naval pensioner who cooked and generally did what he was told. They sailed to Holland, spent ten days exploring the Dutch waterways and ran back across the North Sea at a brisk seven knots. Boat and partnership were proclaimed a success. At Whitsun they started for Scotland, by Dover and Falmouth and the Scilly Isles, then up the Irish Sea.

Mollie, staying with friends on the Devon coast, had made August promise not to sail past without stopping. They cruised close inshore looking for the village, anchored in the evening, rowed ashore in the dinghy and spent half the night trying to find the house, with no luck. In Falmouth next day August discovered that Mollie had been bathing on the beach as *Cariad* sailed by and had now gone home to Essex. He sent off a furious telegram and then a letter telling her they had wasted a good wind, blistered their hands with rowing, landed on frightful rocks, climbed a cliff and got lost in the dark. He accused her of disgusting incompetence, not to mention callousness; she had now taken his sister's place as the ultimate biscuit. He was half teasing, but only half. But by the Scilly Isles he had recovered his temper ('you have no idea what a lovely ship *Cariad* is to be in after a racing boat') and only wanted to make certain that Mollie would be waiting when they got to Scotland.

She was. For a fortnight, with the bosun and another girl as chaperone, they sailed among the western islands. The boat, the scenery, a young man in love and his girl on board—it could hardly fail. But August put Mollie through a gruelling trial. He had already warned her that *Cariad*'s bunks were hard, with no sheets, and told her to bring her own gramophone if she wanted one. Though a new patent lavatory had just been fitted, *Cariad* was no luxury yacht. The gear was old and heavy, the bosun's cooking was elementary and irregular. Fresh water ran short and August, who gave up washing, expected the girls to use each basinful twice. He sailed the boat hard, making few concessions for the crew's inexperience. Afterwards, too late, he saw what he had done wrong and felt bad about it. He had behaved thoughtlessly, too tied up with *Cariad* to spare time for Mollie. If he could have another chance and start again, he could make her happier. He was a brute, she was an angel: 'I wish you wouldn't be so sweet to me when I am so beastly to you.' She could have no idea what their cruise meant: 'It will remain the most precious memory of a doing I have ever done.' More important, Mollie had passed the test. When he saw her off on the train at Oban he asked her to marry him. She refused.

A week later at Aberdeen it was Mollie who was seeing him off. Wordie's expedition embarked in the *Heimland* again and August showed Mollie round the ship. After she had gone and the *Heimland* had cast off, he wrote her a letter for the pilot to take ashore. Usually at the start of a voyage the faster the land disappeared and the further the ship sailed out to deep water the happier August became. Not this time. He was homesick as he had never been before. Why was he leaving her? Yet would she have it otherwise? There was nothing he could do, it seemed, that might be any possible use to her. But henceforth everything he ever did would be done for her. If they reached their mountain it would be Mollie who kept him going. If they got to the top it would be her inspiration that took him there.

Then he touched on something momentous: 'If only I had the chance of doing something really big, I feel I could do it—for you.' It was the Test described by Christopher Isherwood, the need for an ordeal, for a challenge to one's courage and maturity and manhood, felt by every generation but never so badly as by theirs. It was also a clue to the future. But if August had anything definite in mind he didn't say so. Probably he imagined something vaster than he could clearly see, something too elusive to determine until it became too obvious to avoid. It would be intensely private and totally infinite. Nothing so far had taken him to the limit: 'Fate always dodges me and does me down.' When it came he would do it in answer to an inner need, a secret voice which for convenience, if nothing else, he could call Mollie.

She had seen him off. Her last words, last looks—anything to give him hope—August took with him as the *Heimland* sailed out of Aberdeen harbour and set course for the Arctic. He felt the unhappiest—or the happiest—man on board and scribbled a poem, but not a very good one, on the last sheet of the letter before giving it to the pilot.

Though it was the same ship and the same leader, August was the only one of the other eight who had been to Greenland with Wordie before; the only one, as last time, who wasn't seasick. Among them was Vivian Fuchs, an explorer later to become famous for a journey at the opposite end of the world.

The object, as well as continuing the survey, was to climb Petermann Peak. But it was a bad year for pack ice, not much better than 1923 when Wordie had failed to get through to Greenland and two ships had been lost. In 1926 it had taken the *Heimland* three days to push through the ice before reaching open water off the coast. Now, in 1929, it was to take nearly a month.

They sailed into the pack on 8 July. With the captain or the mate up in the crow's nest, August took a turn at the wheel and found it hot work, putting the helm hard over one way, then the other, and working the engine-room telegraph. But the floes were scattered, the weather clear, and at first they made fair progress. They shot some seals and had fresh meat for the first time since leaving Aberdeen. Otherwise the deathly stillness, the silence of the frozen sea, was broken only by the throb of the steam engine and the twittering of thousands of little auks. The birds flocked ceaselessly from pool to pool or lay resting on the floes, reminding Wordie of penguins in the Antarctic.

Slowly the ice closed in. A gale to the north of Jan Mayen Island pressed the floes south-westward, compacting them too densely for a ship to penetrate. After five days the *Heimland*, within sight of land ahead, was lucky to get out of the ice the way she had gone in. They sailed 200 miles north and entered the pack for the second time.

For a week the ship was immobile, drifting in a trap. Neither crowbars nor dynamite could release her. When they could move at all it was often in the wrong direction. The mountains of Greenland looked tantalizingly close, heightened and distorted by mirage. Inactivity tested the men's patience, but Wordie, ever in pursuit of scientific study, sent them over the floes to bring back shells, seaweed and samples of fine mud from the surface of the ice. They skied or played hockey or went off to shoot bears. Some of them even bathed. On board, August suggested a relay race—start aft, sprint for'ard, touch the anchor, up the rigging, touch the crow's nest, on to the wheelhouse, up the mizzen shrouds, on to the deckhouse, touch the stern, finish at the bow—and gave a demonstration. But the rigging was iced up and a window was broken, so the course was abandoned for a medicine ball made from an old wrapped-up piece of sail. In the deckhouse the gramophone played *Tipperary* and *The Policeman's Holiday* till the records wore thin.

When the pack ice began to stir, shifting with a monstrous wind-blown force, the danger became acute. The first nip lifted high the *Heimland*'s stern and held it for several hours, but without damage. Next day the bows were pushed up, forcing her astern and bending the big iron rudder through thirty degrees. Then the entire ship was raised on flanges of ice that slid underneath and cradled her for a day and night before dropping her back into the water. A fourth nip, the most serious, lifted the stern again and tilted the ship alarmingly while jagged chunks of underwater ice, released by the motion of the pack, struck her violently from below. Probably Wordie had suitable tales of the fate of Shackleton's ship to tell his companions. But with luck and skill and occasional recklessness—just the kind of seamanship to appeal to August—the Norwegian captain drove his ship through into clear water. On 4 August, having taken more than a month from Aberdeen and twenty days to get through a hundred miles of ice, they anchored off the Greenland coast.

It was nearly too late; the short summer was almost over. Though the sun still shone at midnight it had lost its strength, the nights were very cold and such small plants as had flowered at all were already withering. They must press on if they were to achieve anything, or else settle down for the Arctic winter. Once more they sailed up the lovely twisting Franz Josef Fjord and two days later reached the head. Three men were left on board to do geological work around the fjord. Wordie and the other five went ashore with tents, sleeping-bags, climbing ropes, crampons, primus stoves, paraffin, heavy surveying equipment and food for twelve days—pemmican, biscuits, oatmeal, sugar and chocolate. After weeks of idleness on board ship, the first few days' haul, carrying fifty-pound loads above 7,000 feet, was painful business.

They were often in the clouds, but worked on the map of the Cambridge Peaks which had been started in 1926, and carried their camp westward until, after five days, they got their first clear view of Petermann Peak, still far away beyond a huge glacier. It took another two days, descending icefalls among seracs and crevasses, to reach the glacier and pitch camp beside a lake where sunshine danced on the snow and lit the multi-coloured rocks. Next day they crossed the glacier, four miles wide, and camped on the slopes below their mountain. August was full of admiration for Wordie's route-finding: 'It's all very well to toddle along in the rear and carry weights, but a very different thing to find the way.'

Toddling along in the rear was a humble description for such a strenuous way of travelling. In one place, without proper crampons, August slipped on a steep ice slope and fell the length of the rope. He expected the jerk to pull the others off too, but the next man dug in his ice axe in time. August dangled like a spider, unable to cut steps up the brittle ice, but with help from

Sledges were used to ferry equipment from the coast to the ice-cap weather station

Buggery Bank – a steep slope of sheer ice – barred the way to the ice-cap

above managed to pull himself up the rope hand over hand. 'He was basically an explorer, not a mountaineer,' one of the others wrote fifty years later, remembering the pleasure of August's unflustered company: 'He was a delightful tent companion. What matter if he left a boot outside by mistake one night, which took ages to thaw out in the morning?'

Wordie, knowing August's habit of losing things, carried a spare pair of gloves. But it was another man's boots that fell to bits; he could do no more climbing if he was to have anything on his feet for the return, and had to be left alone in a tent. The other five started for Petermann, crossing a col and climbing all day till they stood at the foot of the final slope. But now the weather, after four days of bright sun and opalescent clouds, turned against them. There was no time to wait for improvement, they were already short of food and would soon be overdue at the ship. Their only hope of climbing the mountain was to do it now.

Moving fast up hard snow they reached the crest of the south-west ridge at five o'clock in the afternoon and stopped for tea and a tot of whisky. The ridge itself, of alternate rock and ice, was difficult and needed great care, but at least they were sheltered from the freezing north-west wind that had grown from the morning's breeze, blowing straight off the ice cap. By seven-thirty in the evening they were on a ledge fifty feet below the summit with only a steep cone of ice above them.

The moment they stopped they realized that the wind was now a gale, too cold to bear unless they kept moving. To cut steps up the last ice would take a man an hour or more while the rest waited. August and Fuchs were left on the ledge. Wordie led the other two along the foot of the ice and then up dangerously glazed rocks, exposed to the full Arctic blast, to the summit. The temperature on top was ten degrees below zero, the wind was too strong for them to set up the plane table which they had carried for the last nine days; too strong even for them to stand upright. They waved and shouted something to the two on the ledge below, but it was lost on the wind. August and Fuchs, their feet frozen and the storm threatening to get worse, gave up hope

4

of reaching the summit and began the descent while it was still possible.

A year later, on his next expedition to Greenland, August started an argument about the motives of climbing and shocked his companions by saying that he had been quite content to stop short of the summit of Petermann. It didn't matter that he never reached the top, he had done the job he set out to do and got all the fun he wanted. Such mild ambition was heresy to climbers who took their mountains seriously.

But he insisted on measuring the altitude before going down. Somehow with numbed fingers he got the primus going, melted ice and boiled water for the hypsometer while Fuchs shielded him from a force eight gale. The height was 9,650 feet—not as much as they hoped but still, they believed, the highest peak in the Arctic.

A midnight storm in such a place was no time for lingering; cold and fatigue were enough without frostbite. But before hurrying down the three on the summit had just enough light to take photographs and bearings. The edge of the great Greenland ice cap was still another fifteen miles farther west. The big glacier they had crossed yesterday might lead up to it, but there would be some hard country to cross before sledges could be used.

Above that big glacier, perched on a cliff 3,000 feet high, August and Fuchs found a dramatic camping place and by two o'clock in the morning all five men were in their tents. The gale still blew next day, but after a few hours' rest the surveyors got to work again. That evening, descending steep screes which Wordie and August agreed was the nearest thing to their idea of hell, they rejoined the man who had been left behind with tattered boots.

Now that the sun had begun to set and the nights were very cold—now that they had climbed their mountain—they wanted only to get back to the fjord and the *Heimland*. They gave themselves two days to cover the ground that had taken seven on the way up, Wordie leading one rope and August the other.

It was a gruelling march over snow so soft that they sank to their thighs, or black ice swept of snow by the wind and so slippery that they could only creep across it. Besides his own gear August carried a tent, a primus, the plane table, the theodolite legs and the hypsometer, and under the extra weight his rucksack broke. He could hardly keep his balance. His ankles, twisted and bruised, swelled up with pain. Leading his party up a long steep slope, tired and ever slower with Wordie far ahead, he nearly stopped. Fifty years later, one of the others remembered August not only for his perseverance and philosophical view of his own limitations, but for his rather frail body: 'I didn't think he was going to last out . . . Anyone less courageous and determined wouldn't have done so.' Endurance wasn't a matter of physical strength. August too thought he could never reach the top. He thought he would have to give up. Why go on? What was he here for? Who cared anyway? Nothing had any point or purpose, everything was vile, he hated everybody. But not quite everybody; it wasn't the last time in the Arctic that he called to Mollie and she answered. He could almost feel her helping. Inspiration revived him and he got to the top before Wordie.

There was still an agonizing descent, slithering but mostly falling, down a glacier and more scree, but at last they reached the fjord, twelve days after setting out. 'Courtauld took some bad falls,' a companion wrote in his diary that night, 'and I still wonder how he got down.' August himself wrote, 'If getting to heaven is half as good as getting on board the *Heimland*, it will be worth trying for.' But he couldn't do justice to the cook's musk-ox stew; all he wanted was to get his boots off.

With pack ice already choking the bays and fjords along the coast, there was no sense in staying longer. On 25 August they sailed from Greenland, but the land remained in sight astern until the evening of the second day. The outward passage through the pack proved almost as troublesome as the inward had been. It was a matter of making quick thrusts down any channel that opened, before getting pinched again between the floes and stopped. The little ship would wait for hours at a narrow neck, sometimes steaming ahead against the ice until a gap appeared.

Once the propeller struck an underwater tongue which twisted one of the blades and bent the shaft. Often, as the frozen sea heaved on a gentle swell, a general loosening seemed likely but it never came, and though the captain called for extra steam they couldn't push the floes apart. Then a fog came down. After five days, with a spell of better visibility, full steam was raised and the *Heimland*, as if in a fit of impatience and heedless of knocks and bruises, forced her way out into the open sea. Remembering the bad summer of 1923, Wordie considered they were lucky to get away.

Once in the open sea most of the expedition collapsed on their bunks wishing they were back in the calm of the pack ice, but August's only complaint concerned the gramophone. On Jan Mayen Island they inspected the ruined blubber kitchens of a seventeenth-century whale factory, and in the Faeroe Islands they went to a cinema. August had a bet with Wordie, for a bottle of burgundy, over the time they would reach Aberdeen, and lost. On 9 September they docked and went ashore. The first pint of beer, according to August's diary, was a poem in itself. After dinner in a hotel, he took the night train south.

The day he got home Mollie went off to stay with an uncle who was British consul in Venice. They had time for just the briefest meeting, which only made it worse. August was miserable: 'How could you be so cruel as to go that very day?'

For the next month he bombarded her with lovesick letters ('I suppose you are having a simply wonderful time among the Venetians. Do they serenade under your window *every* night?') but he didn't often get an answer. Mollie still couldn't take his attentions as seriously as they were meant. Perhaps she had taunted him with her doubts, or perhaps he only imagined she had: 'You say I am polite and insincere. I, who have no manners and no finesse. You accuse my mind of not flowing. How can it flow, with no inspiration nearer than the other end of Europe?' Self-pity turned to self-mockery. He chided himself for being intolerant, selfish, sullen, bad-tempered, lazy. Only a letter from Venice could save him, but they seldom came. Among the comforts of his home and family he felt peculiarly deserted.

As before, he found relief with Frank Carr on board *Cariad*: 'The sea seems the only place whose sound and feel and sight and touch give me any kick now.' But it was tame sailing this time, just messing about in the Solent. Pottering round harbours was never August's idea of the proper use for a boat and after a week he went back home. At the end of September Gino Watkins came to stay, which should have been fun. They had met at last, but later August couldn't remember where or when—only that Gino 'seemed a virile and forceful fellow'.

They had already shared several experiences. Both of them had spent their childhood in a comfortable country house, both had tried to enter the navy at thirteen but failed, both had followed an uneasy career of nonconformity at school, both had conceived a love of travel and mountains and a horror of pomposity and authority. At Cambridge both of them had been befriended and encouraged by James Wordie, and both had got into trouble with the police for climbing lamp-posts on Guy Fawkes night. Both had taken flying lessons, August as a London stockbroker and Watkins as a Cambridge undergraduate, the first recruit of the university air squadron. When they met they found that their lives were ruled by the same compulsion, a passion for exploring. But differences as well as similarities marked the brief years of their friendship.

In his outward personality Gino Watkins had few points in common with August Courtauld and he was very different from August's other friends. Goose Gosling never understood what August saw in a man who, though clever and dashing and heroic, looked like a pansy. But it was Watkins's seriousness, not his frivolity, that was difficult to accept. To be a spartan as well as a hedonist, to enjoy rock-climbing and jazz equally, to spend one's days calculating the food needed by a sledge team on a winter journey in the Arctic and one's nights dancing at the Savoy till the early hours, was slightly indecent. The mixture wasn't quite right, nobody normal could keep it up—or nobody August had ever known. Till then, most of his friends had been total amateurs in life. Even among the men with orthodox jobs there was a suspicion that to be too much a professional was to be not quite a gentleman. Qualifications, which might be all very well for people who had nothing else, were considered rather vulgar and showed an earnestness that it was better not to advertise. To be keen was to be guilty of an almost deplorable virtue. Nothing mattered so intensely that it was worth working to the end of endurance for, as Watkins did. If he wished, he could be as gay or idle as anyone—after his first brilliant piece of exploration he ended up at a party north of the Arctic Circle, dancing the Charleston in his pyjamas—and he could loaf around all day doing nothing more energetic than turning over the gramophone record. But few men could also be so serious.

Since failing to get on Wordie's expedition to Greenland in 1926 he had done some spectacular travels of his own. In 1927, aged twenty and still an undergraduate at Cambridge, he led a party of eight men to Edge Island off Spitzbergen. The following year, leaving Cambridge without a degree, he took an expedition for nine months' exploring in Labrador. Now, for 1930, he was planning something much more ambitious in Greenland. The idea, dreamed up one day in Labrador, was to explore a possible air route across the Arctic from Europe to America.

As soon as he heard about it August wanted to join the expedition. He thought his father might help with the finance and invited Watkins to stay. A shooting-party was going on, but Watkins came prepared; when he was offered a gun he held up a bandaged hand and said he had sprained his thumb. The truth was that he couldn't afford to tip the gamekeeper. He needn't have troubled; the visit was fruitless. Samuel Augustine Courtauld wouldn't give a penny. Suspecting that his mother had been at work, August was disgusted: 'He wants me safe and stuck rather than run the risk that his family might ever get out of the rut of complacent money-making to bring a small spot of credit on this womanly old country of ours. I am so sick with my family

I can't even sit with it. Let it fug in its own noxious library. If only I could rake up some of its slimy past and do some subtle blackmail on it I could go to the grave grinning.'

If only, for that matter, Mollie would come home from Venice and cheer him up. He would drive down to Dover, Folkestone, anywhere, in his Alvis to meet her off the boat and bring her back. But she didn't even write, or not often enough: 'Just a line from you makes all the birds sing and the world grow green with envy . . . The days pass, people come and go, talk and scream, fuss and chatter while I wait, post by post, for the letter that never comes.' At last a letter did turn up at breakfast: 'Everybody wanted to chatter and pour things at me and feed me, but I didn't hear them.' He stuffed it in his pocket and took it out shooting with him, and read it over and over again during the drives, oblivious of the pheasants and partridges and the guns going off all round.

Mollie was having a marvellous time and told him so. The British fleet was in Venice on a visit, showing the flag with full naval pomp and gaiety, though for the happiness of so many young officers the consul might have wished he had a dozen nieces. Mollie's letter must have woken other, older pangs in August who wrote back rather coolly: 'So glad you like the navy. I think it has much to be said for it.' But there was much to disapprove of too: 'I'm not sure that all the high living is very good for you . . . It's absurd. How anyone can go through a month of such a life I don't see. Come back at once. I don't like it at all.'

She returned at last, but things didn't come right at once. Probably after the long separation August moved too fast. In his mind he had reached a stage beyond anything that the facts justified. There were bound to be disappointments, if not disasters. Within a week of Mollie's return he was feeling a hopeless oaf, consumed with remorse over his behaviour.

I seem to have absolutely put my foot in it. I was only trying to do the right thing. You see, I happen to be desperately fond of you. I love you more than my life, more than the whole world. And I thought that if you didn't want me to be like that, then I ought to go away and not worry you any more . . . You do know now, don't you, that if it's any good to you, here I am, the whole of me, for you when you want? I wish you would want me a little. Can't I be useful somehow? Can't I do something, give up something, for you? . . . How I hate being where I'm not wanted.

It was his turn next to go away. Three weeks after Mollie came back from Venice, he went up to Scotland to shoot. By November there was snow already on the mountains and he spent much of the time crawling over the landscape, stalking deer. A few years earlier, out on the Essex marshes, he had discovered that it didn't matter if the weather was too fine for shooting. It was the same now in Perthshire. Though there were plenty of deer to be seen through a telescope—stags roaring and fighting, hinds nibbling nervously—he couldn't get a shot all day. But the country was bright and still and cold, and he was happy enough; happier still if he had a letter from Mollie to take out and read at odd moments, or just to touch when he put a hand in his pocket for a pipe and tobacco. Mollie! He could shout her name to the mountains and brood on it in the evenings by a log fire, exhausted with the day's exercise: 'I wonder why everybody doesn't call themselves Mollie.'

For her there were times of surprise and puzzlement. A burst of fury, an act of kindness, a sudden departure, a moment of sentimentality, a spell of self-confidence, a fit of helplessness, a mixture of intense devotion and ferocious independence—all this in a man who had acute difficulty in declaring his heart. And though he may have often worn a carefree and vaguely haphazard boyishness, he also showed uncommon maturity. His vision, his ideals were consistent; his changes of mood were merely running adjustments, the sailor's constant trimming of the helm.

Mollie was a little frightened of him. She wasn't alone in this—

other people felt the same, though it would have astonished and perhaps upset him to know it—and in all their years she never quite lost the feeling. In a girl of twenty-two, three years younger than himself, he could inspire both admiration and intimidation. For her, still at the beginning, it was a comfort to be encouraged by someone who had got a little further. But if his first attentions were only what she might expect from a rich young man—and anything less would have been beyond even August's disdain for convention—his later adoration was more than she could grasp, let alone return. Though she liked him, and had done so since that children's party many years ago, the effect he had on her was not yet the influence it soon became.

Again August asked her to marry him and at the end of November 1929 they became secretly engaged; secretly, because Mollie was enjoying her carefree unmarried state and still felt unsure about a husband whose other love was so difficult to share. Her present life was heady, full of fun, expectant like spring and she was enjoying it as it was, without having it stirred too deeply by anyone. She wouldn't let herself be too impressed, she wouldn't be commanded. Obviously August could be depended on, not least in love, but Mollie wasn't ready to be tied for ever to a man who cherished a passion for polar exploration as well as for herself.

That other passion, stimulated by his new friendship with Gino Watkins, had been fired by Watkins's plan to explore an Arctic air route. Without a job and unoccupied except by his pursuit of Mollie, August threw himself into the scheme.

When in 1913 the *Daily Mail* had offered £10,000 for the first flight across the Atlantic, it was laughed off as a stunt. Neither machines nor aviators were taken very seriously.

The First World War changed everything. Flying was suddenly turned into something useful and deadly. In a few years, with the extravagance and urgency of modern war, aeroplanes were so developed that before peace returned Britain had planes capable of flying to Berlin and back with a load of bombs. In 1919 it was a converted bomber that flew the Atlantic in sixteen hours and earned the *Daily Mail*'s prize. Three weeks later a British airship made the first two-way flight to America and back, and in the same year a regular air service from London to Paris was opened.

Britain was poised at the beginning of an age, though few men noticed it. 'Our future is in the air,' one of the rare visionaries said. 'In the last four years we have made the most astonishing developments in aviation. We have greater advantages than any other nation in the world, and with an empire that spreads all over the world we have a wonderful incentive to throw ourselves into the work . . . Aviation will be the greatest factor in linking up our world-wide empire.' The empire, more than anything else, got Britain off to a good start, and because most of it lay in either the direction of India and Australia or of South Africa those were held to be the proper routes for pioneering. In particular the stage from Cairo to Karachi, which had good flying weather all the year round and no long sea crossing, was considered important. Churchill, the Secretary of State for War and Air, said that it 'buckled' the empire together. But though air transport was recognized as vital in imperial communications, the idea that it should be owned or even aided by the state was ridiculous. Churchill also said that civil aviation must fly by itself.

The flying men battered away at the government and cursed it for lack of foresight. They believed they had a chance to make Britain as strong in the air as it was at sea. Mostly they were ignored. Civil aviation was insignificant in the national economy and a general nuisance to politicians—'the Old Men'—who had no patience with anything so unnecessary and unprofitable. In the early 1920s, while air routes were being opened across Europe and Asia and Africa, British airlines found themselves constantly beaten by foreigners. When Imperial Airways was founded in 1924 to give government protection, it was too late to save Britain's lead.

An airline to America was still a dream. When a British businessman who wanted to survey a southern route by the Azores and Bermuda asked the treasury for £5,000, it was refused. Money was tight, and for many years British officials were too taken up with their empire lines to Australia and Africa to have time for the Atlantic too. Anyway aeroplanes couldn't be trusted to fly long distances over the sea. They caught fire or iced up or ran out of petrol. Navigation was rudimentary, instruments were unsophisticated, airmanship was primitive. Besides, there were several fast transatlantic liners sailing every week and crossing in five days, which was good enough for most people.

Other countries were testing new ideas. Two liners, one French and one German, were fitted with catapults that could launch an aeroplane 500 miles before the ship reached land, saving twenty-four hours for airmail. The Americans were getting ahead in long-range flying. As the southern route by the Azores meant a 2,000-mile ocean hop, which was too far for regular traffic, Pan-American Airways sent Colonel Lindbergh, fresh from his famous solo flight across the Atlantic, to investigate a northern route. There were problems—it would need bases and planes that could operate through the Arctic winter, so flying-boats were ruled out—but at least it would follow a great circle, the shortest line across the earth's surface.

Meanwhile British aviation, apart from the empire-buckling in pleasanter climates, seemed to be typified by the race run from London to Edinburgh between an aeroplane and the Flying Scotsman. The plane had to come down twice for fuel and made the mistake of circling the wrong train at Berwick, but it did just manage to win.

In Labrador during the previous winter Gino Watkins had pondered these things.

It is certain [he wrote in his diary] that nearly all the great air routes of the future will lie across the Arctic. The safest and quickest air route from England to the American continent is by Iceland, Greenland and Labrador. The quickest route to Japan and the Pacific is by Spitzbergen and Franz Josef Land. But before anything can be done these places must be scientifically explored . . . It will of course be denounced and hampered in England as every new idea is. People will say how dangerous, and every possible restriction will be put on it. England is behind other countries in commercial flying—why? Always the same reason. No one may do anything dangerous and everything new is bad.

When he got home Watkins typed out a memorandum and sent it to anybody who ought to be interested in an Arctic air route to Canada:

The amount of time saved by using this route would be very great indeed, and it has the great recommendation of relative safety since there are few long sea crossings . . . The whole journey would take about five days . . . The part of this route least known at present is the east coast and central ice plateau of Greenland . . . My aim is to take an expedition to Greenland for one year to thoroughly investigate the possibility of an air route over that country. This expedition would be equipped with two suitable aeroplanes, a large number of dog teams and two motor-boats.

Maps would be drawn, air photographs taken, test flights made over the ice cap, and a survey made—by motor-boat and aeroplane in the summer, by sledge in the winter—of the route which future airlines would fly over. Most important, a weather station would be set up far inland on the ice cap where daily recordings could be made at all seasons. And between the ice cap and the coast there were unknown mountain ranges, often covered by mist, to be explored—even to be discovered—before commercial pilots could be tempted anywhere near. At the end of a year the two aeroplanes would make a trial flight from Greenland to Canada and back along the entire Arctic route to England. The cost of the expedition would be about £12,000.

The winter of 1929–1930 wasn't the best moment for a young man to raise money, but Watkins was an extraordinary person. With his record of two successful Arctic expeditions, with his persistence and idealism and charm, he enrolled one very important ally, Admiral Goodenough, president of the Royal Geographical Society. The Admiral offered a room in the society's house overlooking Kensington Gardens, which promptly became headquarters of the British Arctic Air Route Expedition.

J. M. Scott, a member of the expedition, wrote,

It would have been hard for a stranger to guess the purpose of this room. From the pile of letters on the table, the upright wooden chairs, the shelves of imposing books and the metal file in the corner by the door, one might have taken it for an office. But the men who used it did not look like office workers. They were all young, not long down from university, one might guess, and chiefly interested in passing a pleasant morning. They had a gramophone in one corner, and if the file were opened one would see not only letters but a heap of dance records and a box of tea cakes. It was a noisy room.

So noisy that the elderly surveyor instructing a class next door, who had taught mapping to generations of explorers since the time of Scott and Shackleton, sometimes had to complain.

But the gaiety concealed a very real seriousness. Support was gradually mustered. Watkins drummed up both private and official interest while August, as treasurer, had another shot at getting money out of his family: 'I tackled the cousins and aunts . . . They stumped up nobly.' The most generous of all was his father's cousin, Stephen Courtauld, who became chairman of the expedition committee. James Wordie also joined it and the Prince of Wales was honorary president.

Though professionalism was something Watkins might never

have claimed, it was his own and that of the men he collected—companions in the field or supporters at home, in science and commerce and government—that launched the expedition. His energy and stamina, astonishing in someone who didn't look robust, who looked hardly more than a boy, became a legend. Between the autumn of 1929 and the spring of 1930 he filled the months with enough activity to occupy most men for as many years. He joined the air force reserve, completed his flying training and got his pilot's licence, went back to Cambridge in the hope of finishing the degree he had broken off in 1928, attended lectures on geography and gave one himself to the Royal Geographical Society on Labrador, studied dietetics, calculated rations, tested different types of margarine, swam and went for long country runs, wrote letters, read books, ordered stores, designed tents, questioned other explorers and interviewed prospective ones, got commercial firms to supply their goods free, tried out aeroplanes for the Arctic, arranged to write articles for *The Times*, went to Denmark to charter a ship and to Switzerland to ski, went to several parties a week and frequently danced all night, had his twenty-third birthday, and fell in and out of love quite often.

Watkins said that a man should have done everything by the age of twenty-five, as if he knew that he was to get no further. He crammed his time with the pursuit of some of the ideas that streamed from his mind, letting nothing divert him. Charisma, an overloaded quality, fitted the essence of his character, the force that impelled and pervaded the young men preparing to explore with him in Greenland. J. M. Scott wrote, 'He went straight and ruthlessly for what he wanted . . . He was essentially interesting, often inspiring and sometimes annoying. But you could never get tired of him.' He put his life into what he cared for, and his achievement was famous. Once a telegram, addressed merely to 'Watkins Explorer England', was delivered straight to him.

The choice of expedition members was entirely up to Watkins, who never went on an expedition except as leader. He picked his men not for their specialist knowledge but because he liked them and thought they would fit in with his ideas of travel. He didn't want hardened old experts who might have fixed opinions, he preferred beginners who could adapt while he watched and came to understand them. Technical experience would soon follow. Of the fourteen only three—himself and J. M. Scott and August Courtauld—had been in the Arctic before. Only August, veteran of two expeditions with Wordie, had ever been to Greenland.

All of them were given special functions and together had many skills, though their average age was only twenty-five. The navy lent a doctor, Surgeon-Lieutenant Ted Bingham, and the army a signals officer, Captain Percy Lemon, as wireless operator. The air force sent two pilots, Flight-Lieutenants Jimmy D'Aeth and Iliffe Cozens, to fly the expedition planes. Wilfred Hampton went as aircraft engineer, Lawrence Wager as geologist, Quintin Riley as meteorologist, J. M. Scott as dog-master and Freddy Chapman as ornithologist and surveyor. Martin Lindsay and John Rymill and August were also surveyors—after a crash-course of mapping at the Royal Geographical Society—under Alfred Stephenson, who like Watkins was still finishing his degree at Cambridge. Long afterwards the poet-climber Wilfrid Noyce, noting that August was in many ways typical of a remarkable expedition under a remarkable leader, wrote, 'They were all still undergraduate in humour, yet deadly earnest in expedition matters; flippant in tone but serious in judgement and as ready to pass judgement on the world, the flesh and literature as in the twenties one normally is.'

Working closely with Watkins during those months August found him fascinating—a 'truly remarkable man'. Perhaps he recognized a less introvert, more demonstrative version of himself. Perhaps he dimly saw that somehow with Watkins he would get his chance to do 'something really big'—the ambition that he had written to Mollie about.

Mollie had reason to be a little jealous. Her own enthusiasm for Arctic exploration was negligible, though under August's influence it was to grow. At the moment Gino Watkins only got in the way. He was so dedicated, he infected August with his own ambition, he seemed a real challenge to herself. She felt that August was too much in awe of him, too involved in the plots and plans of this gifted, compulsive man. When she first met Watkins she wasn't reassured. She may have been right to worry, but she underestimated August's feelings: 'You know I love you now as I have learnt to love you during the last few months. It gets worse and worse when you are away. You will always be *the* person to me.'

That winter they found a new and surprising common pleasure. Almost by chance they started going to concerts and operas, and discovered something they had hardly been aware of before—a love of music. Mollie, who already sang in the London Philharmonic Choir and saw August's delight in going to rehearsals with her, persuaded him to take up singing too. He went to Mollie's teacher, who turned him into a baritone and made him learn old English songs and ballads, and later, when he got better, the second part of a duet from *The Beggar's Opera*. August wrote to Mollie, 'I think I'm going to be rather good at it,' and they sang it together. Flying lessons had given way to singing lessons— an odd departure for a Courtauld and a measure of Mollie's influence.

They announced their engagement in May 1930, two months before the British Arctic Air Route Expedition was to leave for Greenland. A notice was put in *The Times*, a photograph appeared in the *Evening Standard* and letters poured in, congratulating them both and commiserating with Mollie on the year's separation she would have to endure before her wedding. It was no more than she expected. August had always made it clear that having got engaged he would be in no rush to get married.

The last weeks—the first weeks of August's and Mollie's engagement—were a hectic time for everyone. Final stores were bought, equipment was packed, the two Gypsy Moth aeroplanes were crated, and Scott was sent on ahead of the rest of the expedition to buy fifty sledge dogs in West Greenland where there was a better breed than in the East. As it happened to be the

height of the London season, there were countless parties to be
fitted in too. Watkins would go to two or three dances in one
night and run home in the early morning for exercise. A little
later, spruce and dapper in his double-breasted suit with smooth
hair and rolled umbrella, he would be driving his old two-seater
Morris to the Royal Geographical Society or down to the London
docks. A few days before the expedition sailed, a wild and glorious
treasure-hunt was run round the West End in ancient sports cars,
with August and Mollie laying the clues.

On 4 July the expedition ship, the *Quest*, sailed up the Thames
to load at St Katherine's dock. She was 125 tons, a wooden coal-
burning sealer like the *Heimland* but twice as big. Once she had
belonged to Shackleton who had sailed in her on his last
expedition to the Antarctic and had died on board.

On the evening of the 5th the ship was dressed with flags and
coloured lights for a cocktail party and a dance. The blessing of
authority was bestowed by the Secretary of State for Air and the
Director of Civil Aviation—both soon to die in the crash of the
airship R101; on his return next year Watkins found that he
had lost two of his most useful friends, but tonight all was
jollity in the docks. A band played, George Robey entertained
the guests, the East End Londoners came out to cheer, and everyone—Norwegian sailors, English explorers, friends, families,
fiancées—sang and danced and drank and climbed the mast.
Not far away another polar ship was getting ready to leave on a
long voyage to the Antarctic, but her own restrained farewells
were quite unlike the high spirits aboard the *Quest*. As in most
things, Gino Watkins and his men had a special style of departure.

Early next morning they hoisted the expedition flag—a polar
bear with wings—and slipped down river to Gravesend where
Stephen Courtauld, patron and committee chairman and untiring
friend, gave one last party on board his private yacht. After lunch
the good-byes were said and the *Quest* sailed out into the North
Sea.

Chapter 6

The Quest

OFF THE NORTH of Scotland they passed the Graf Zeppelin heading for Germany, and in the Faeroe Islands they picked up Scott and his fifty dogs. After six weeks on a lighter anchored in a fjord, the dogs were in a wild state; one had swam ashore and killed nine sheep before being shot. Feeding them with slabs of whale meat was a noisy and alarming business and even Scott, who had driven dogs with Watkins in Labrador and could handle them like pets instead of the dangerous wolves they seemed, got so badly bitten on the wrist that he temporarily lost the use of his hand.

Watkins and August, who occupied Shackleton's old cabin on the *Quest*, now had to make room for Scott too. August hadn't met him before and found him 'quite the most charming person in the ship, but unavoidably large. We both smoke pipes when we turn in, much to Gino's annoyance'.

They also took on board a ton of whale meat, for both dogs and men. Some of it was already dried and could be stowed in the hold, but the rest was tied up in the rigging where it gave further distress to anyone inclined to seasickness. Before they reached Iceland the weather became very rough, the ship rolled forty degrees each way and the deck was soon awash with seawater and dogs and baggage and lumps of putrid meat that fell from above. Among the cargo were some barrels of a mysterious and particularly nasty blubbery stuff dug from the boilers of a whale factory, which was said to be useful winter dog-food. Two of the barrels burst, adding to the mess that was hurled from side to side across the ship and making even August uncomfortable.

At Reykjavik they took on coal, which meant shifting the dogs and much of the cargo to reach the hatches and brought more filth on board. Some of the crew got at the captain's brandy and some of the explorers got drunk ashore. The rest had dinners and hot baths at a hotel, the first for twelve days and the last for twelve months. Chapman ('a charming chap but horribly hearty' in August's view) was impatient to begin exploring and led a party with rucksacks into the interior for a night's camping. August didn't join them; there would be enough of that sort of thing once they were in Greenland.

The last stage of the voyage—sighting their first whales, entering the pack ice, hunting seals, tasting seal steak, observing Arctic birds, walking across the floes and cracking walrus-hide dog whips—was exciting even for August, who was now making his third Greenland landfall. The passage through the pack ice took only three days, as it had in 1926; and three weeks after leaving St Katherine's dock they started to unload their cargo on the East Greenland coast.

For his base Watkins chose a stony little promontory near the head of a small fjord, thirty miles from the settlement of Angmagssalik, 500 miles south of the region explored by Wordie's expeditions; a lonely place disturbed only by the roar of glacier streams and the buzz of summer mosquitoes. Sometimes an almighty lump of ice broke off a glacier and splashed into the fjord or an iceberg rolled over in the water sending waves rippling to the shore. But there was no ring of mountains to hinder wireless transmission, there was deep water for the *Quest* to anchor close inshore and a sheltered landing-place for the seaplane, and the hunting looked good; with luck, men and dogs would get fresh meat and fish for the year they stayed there. Most important, at the head of the fjord a glacier tongue came licking down from the interior, promising a route up on to the ice cap.

The next fortnight was spent ferrying stores from the *Quest* and building a base. Immediately they were visited by Eskimos— family parties paddling their big *umiaks* into the fjord to watch the strange young men, and hunters in small *kayaks* bringing presents of duck and seal and fish. The explorers worked day and night in twelve-hour shifts, humping timber, scientific equipment, sacks of coal, a stove, a kitchen range, drums of petrol and paraffin and the first of the two aeroplanes; the second was coming in another ship. With the help of the *Quest*'s carpenter they built a wooden hut on the promontory. Its walls were of double layers of matchboard insulated with windproof felt, with a double roof and double floor. Inside was a living-room lined with bunks, a kitchen, a tiny darkroom, wireless room and workshop. August wrote to Mollie that it was guaranteed to keep in any fug they could generate: 'It seems an awful waste to be here only a year.' They ran electric light off the wireless engine, installed a central heating system, fixed up bookshelves and curtains, and hung over the door an oak panel with a gilded quotation from Masefield given them by Admiral Goodenough. With free shooting and fishing at hand, August said it was like living in a cross between a Scottish shooting-box and a Clacton seaside villa.

Lemon erected a pair of masts for his aerials and tested the portable wireless that was to be taken up to the ice-cap station. Wager went off with a rucksack and presently the fjord echoed with the ring of his geological hammer. Scott saw to the dogs, marooning them on an island and building a store for their food. Rymill, an immensely strong Australian, impressed August with a 'frightful habit of taking all his clothes off and sluicing himself with cold water, or running about on the ice stark naked, cracking a whip'. Lindsay, who claimed to have seldom carried anything heavier than a message, now found himself a common labourer and to August was 'an unfailing source of mirth; he does everything and says everything wrong with the completest good humour and cheerfulness—one doesn't know whether he ought to be in a lunatic asylum or a stained glass window'. Riley ('pleasant, good-mannered, good-tempered, intelligent') assembled his meteorological instruments. Stephenson ('a nice chap, very keen on his job') prepared his survey equipment.

Bingham, the doctor ('a comic Irishman with a fund of the lowest and funniest yarns ever'), was summoned by wireless to attend an injured man at Angmagssalik; August went with him in a motor-boat, travelling thirty miles overnight and learning practical anaesthetics on the way, but to his relief an operation wasn't necessary.

D'Aeth and Hampton unpacked and rigged the aeroplane, only to find that the ski undercarriage for winter flying had been left in England. But this was still summer, they stretched ropes across a bay to stop ice floes drifting on to the runway and the engine started first time. The plane took to the air, to the wonder of the Eskimos, and was soon making survey flights of the coast and the route up to the ice cap.

The first ascent of the glacier at the head of the fjord was made by Watkins with Scott and Chapman and two dog teams. The lower part was too scored with crevasses and icefalls to be climbed with heavy loads, so everything had to be taken round the side. August and Lindsay went to help. Carrying two sledges, as well as supplies for future ice-cap parties, over ground littered with huge boulders, then up a cliff of bare rock and finally down a steep slope of loose scree on to the glacier, was tough work. At last a tent was put up and the two helpers went back to the base. Next day, through binoculars, they watched Watkins and his men and dogs crawling over the vast sheet of ice—like microbes, August said; in fact they were the only living things in that frozen world.

One of those three, J. M. Scott, has likened the Greenland ice cap to an enormous plate surrounded by a rim of coastal mountains, on to which sugar is constantly being poured. After millions of years the falling snow has been pressed by its own weight into solid ice as much as 10,000 feet deep—solid, but very gradually slipping outwards as it is piled up in the middle, sloping down towards the edges and overflowing in glaciers between the mountains; spewing its surplus body into the sea. Except for a narrow fringe round the coast, the biggest island in the world is a lifeless desert where the Ice Age still exists, racked

by terrible winds and inhabited, according to the few Eskimos
who live along its shores but never venture inland, only by evil
spirits and monstrous superhuman beings.

The Norwegian explorer Nansen made the first crossing from
coast to coast in 1888, and was followed by other bold men
journeying on to the ice cap. They went in summer when the
weather was favourable; nobody had been there in winter.

Watkins and his two companions, on that first reconnaissance,
found the country more difficult than they had believed. The
glacier was a mass of small hummocks and the ice so slippery
and glasslike that it cut the dogs' paws. They had brought
special dog boots, but by an oversight only fourteen boots for
fourteen dogs. After a long uneven rise they reached a high, very
smooth slope of sheer ice which could never have been climbed
without ice axes and crampons. Promptly it was named Buggery
Bank and was to be the agonizing prelude to all ice-cap journeys.
Above it the ground was less steep but no less difficult: crevasses,
hollows of soft slush, ridges of ice divided by knee-deep streams.
One of the dogs fell through into a crevasse, but luckily was
rescued. They slogged on a short way, marking the route with
flags, before turning back. The descent, with the men riding the
sledges and the dogs at full gallop, was short and thrilling.

In the second week of August a Danish four-masted sailing-
ship entered the fjord with further stores and the second aeroplane. But the season was advancing, and after unloading his
cargo the captain was in a hurry to get away before the ice,
which was already gathering in the fjord, closed in. Next day
the whole expedition, with half-hearted help from the Eskimos,
carried two tons of stores from the head of the fjord up over the
rocks on to the glacier for the ice-cap station. Some of the ration
boxes and paraffin cases weighed eighty pounds and some of the
rock slopes had to be climbed on all fours.

That night, 10 August, they were all together for the last time
for many months and celebrated with a party on board the *Quest*.
The work of real exploring was to begin.

Five men—Riley, Lindsay, Bingham and Rymill with Scott in charge—climbed the glacier and set off north-westward to establish the ice-cap station about 130 miles inland. Riley and Lindsay were to be the first pair to stay at the station for a month, perhaps longer, and make weather recordings.

Lemon remained alone at the base to keep a regular wireless watch. The other eight sailed away in the *Quest*, with an aeroplane and a motor-boat, and headed for Kangerdlugsuak, a long and intricate fjord which no explorer had ever penetrated, 300 miles further north. With fewer men on board, and without the dogs and paraphernalia that had cluttered the ship before, conditions were pleasanter; August had a cabin to himself. But when it was known that a ship was sailing up the coast a number of Eskimos turned up, hoping for a free passage, and soon the deck was crowded with families, dogs, boats and sealskin tents. The three-day voyage became a cruise. The weather was warm, there was no work to do and plenty of time to admire the passing scenery—an archipelago of rocky islands and straits with drifting icebergs and spouting whales. For August, no longer a stevedore or a coolie but not yet an active explorer, all was pleasure, apart from a brief touch of nostalgia on the Twelfth at the thought of everyone at home shooting grouse.

The mood was set for the next month, when the comforts of hut and ship were exchanged for the rigours of hard travel and difficult survey work. That journey up the coast during the last weeks of the Arctic summer was remembered by many of the members as one of the best parts of the whole expedition. The weather was usually warm and bright, there were patches of wild flowers and crowberries on the hills, there was often sea trout or salmon for breakfast and ptarmigan or seal steak for supper, and though the day's business of surveying took sixteen hours or more it was enjoyable as well as arduous. Chapman wrote that he had never been happier:

Life in Greenland was remarkably satisfactory . . . We were a group of young men with more or less kindred interests and all intent on the same object. The work of mapping and flying over unknown country was inspiring, and the mere struggle to keep alive in the Arctic absorbed all one's spare energy, enthusiasm and inventive powers. Instincts inherent in man but dormant through long years of 'civilization' were called into play.

Chapman, Wager, Stephenson and August went off one evening in the motor-boat with a week's food while Watkins and the flying men stayed on the *Quest* with the aeroplane to do aerial photography. The boat party soon found themselves in a maze of ice at the mouth of a fjord and were in danger of being benighted or even crushed. The channels and pools between the floes opened and closed in an ever-transforming pattern. August, handling the outboard motor, was ready to throw it into reverse and the other three stood by with oars in case of collision, while floating towers of ice loomed over them in the dusk. One of those monsters, overturning as they often did, could have toppled on to the boat or swamped it with a wave. Somehow they got through, but landing on the steep rocky shore and finding a camping place was no easier. They pitched their tents on a ledge of mossy turf and heather, the only level spot for miles, and watched the moon rise over the mountains while they cooked supper. Nothing but the muffled, restless noises of the ice in the fjord disturbed the night.

It was in that same fjord, two summers later, that Gino Watkins's kayak was seen drifting, waterlogged but empty. He had gone hunting alone in a bay near the tongue of a glacier, a hundred-foot wall that frequently shed immense pieces of ice— 'calving' as explorers call it. Once before, while he was inflating a seal he had shot before towing it back to camp, the glacier had calved with special violence, sending a wave that upset his kayak and threw him against the cliffs. Some such accident must have happened again, but his luck had run out. His drenched trousers lay on an ice floe not far away, adding to the riddle; his body was never found.

Stephenson was in charge of the plane table, August of the theodolite observations. Wager broke rocks with his hammer and Chapman did most of the hunting. The days passed in activity and harmony. Every inlet they entered, every island they landed on, every hill they climbed, was unexplored; no man, save perhaps an adventurous Eskimo on a rare hunting trip, had been there before. Not that they didn't have mishaps. Having lost an oar, they struck a submerged rock and broke the propeller shaft. Paddling with an ice axe, a thwart and the other oar they crossed two miles of ice-strewn water before reaching land. August in particular, far from being perturbed, could call up his finest resources at such misfortune. When things went wrong he seemed to like it all the more.

Two days after being picked up by the *Quest* they entered the unknown Kangerdlugsuak fjord, sailing forty miles inland to the head. All around rose enormous snow-covered mountains with glaciers sweeping down from the distant ice cap. They left a dump of stores for a possible sledge journey next spring and covered it with stones to save it from polar bears, then set about mapping. August, with the boat party, went off again with tents and hunting gear.

The first day they shot two bears. The second day, 26 August, was August's twenty-sixth birthday, and in an uncomfortably stony camp they celebrated with bear's tongue soup, sea trout, seal's kidneys, stewed crowberries and Horlicks. The third day was the beginning of a run of disasters. First, Chapman dropped August's ice axe overboard and they couldn't recover it. Next, while they were working ashore at the plane table, a glacier discharged a thunderous salvo of icebergs into the water. They stood watching (August would have been transfixed by such a display of nature, like the earthquake in his school essay) without realizing the size of the wave that was rolling towards them. It lifted their boat, bounced it on the rocks, half turned it over, filled it with water and sucked it out to sea. Chapman jumped in to catch it, but their cameras, guns, binoculars, wireless, primus stove, sleeping-bags, tents and food were soaked.

Three mornings later, in camp ashore, they woke to find the boat had been tipped up by the falling tide and everything in it thrown into the water. Worst of all was the loss of a precious instrument box, the property of Francis Rodd, containing his theodolite. They recovered what was still afloat and spent the day searching the rocks along the shore for the rest, but found only a tin of petrol, a boat hook and some wet tobacco. At low tide that evening August saw a glint of the box in twelve feet of icy water. Chapman, indefatigable as ever, dived down and prised open one of the handles, then they fished it up with the boat-hook lashed to two oars. Rodd's instruments were not quite ruined; August carried them up to a freshwater lake and carefully rinsed out the salt. When he got a chance, he dismantled them and cleaned the parts with petrol: 'Francis will be interested to know that in two days I took the theodolite completely to pieces and got it going again.'

After that it was only mildly annoying, in the middle of a windy night, to have his tent blown down on top of him and then, when he had put it up again and got back into his sleeping-bag, to be disturbed by the grunts of a polar bear. In summer, finding it hard to catch seals and living off grass and berries, bears could become dangerously hungry. But August went back to sleep.

The summer was nearly over. Each morning a layer of new ice had formed on the water; they had to wait for it to melt before starting work. Any hope of continuing in the motor-boat all the way back to Angmagssalik, surveying as they went, was given up, and they decided to return in the *Quest*, though the boat party could congratulate themselves that they had lived rougher, travelled harder, seen more—explored more—than the men who had stayed on board the ship. But Watkins on his aerial survey had made one great discovery. On 1 September, while he and D'Aeth were flying at 10,000 feet, they saw a big frozen lake inland and beyond it a range of mountains sixty miles away, higher than themselves—higher than Petermann Peak—invisible from the coast and till then unsuspected. Later they were found to be the highest in Greenland and named the Watkins Mountains.

For the captain of the *Quest* to linger on the coast was to risk getting caught by winter. The salmon and the Arctic terns had already gone. But the surveyors couldn't desert their map, and all down the coast they tried to fill the blanks. Though the days might be colder the nights were now dark enough for star sights. While the captain fretted, Stephenson was busy with his plane table and August made interminable astronomical calculations.

On 14 September they got back to the base and found that Lemon, the wireless operator, had set himself up in fine style. Fittingly, as headquarters of the biggest British polar expedition since the days of Captain Scott and Shackleton, their hut was going to make a comfortable winter home. The final domestic touch—not one to interest an earlier generation of explorers—had been added by an Eskimo boy and three girls who turned up one day and enrolled themselves on the staff, cheerful and willing and ready for anything. The boy's job stretched from butler to bootboy, though mainly he carried coal for the stove and ice for drinking water. The girls were trained to cook and wash up and mend clothes. They were supposed to live in the loft, and worked for their food and lodging and a few cigarettes. Sometimes they were allowed to play the gramophone.

Before the end of the winter the girls were to become something of a controversy. Lemon was the first to adopt an Eskimo mistress. Watkins soon followed. And Chapman, returning to Greenland on another expedition, was astonished and delighted to be introduced to his own half-Eskimo son. Other members of the expedition were less happy with these arrangements. Sleeping with the natives was quite improper for most true Englishmen; it was demoralizing and demeaning. Lindsay for one found it intolerable. He believed that what a man got up to in London or Paris was all very well, but in a crowded hut on an Arctic expedition he didn't fancy it for himself and objected to it in others. All winter he had an Eskimo woman climbing over him to reach Watkins in the bunk above and by next summer he had had enough. In Greenland there was always the danger of the relief ship not getting through the pack ice. If that happened, and they faced a second winter in the hut, Lindsay meant to protest to Watkins about his public love-life, and tell him to pitch a tent elsewhere and take his women with him. Among the others whom he could count on to back him up, Lindsay was sure of August.

August's own complaints were not so moralistic. The days of the summer journey—working hard, hunting, climbing, exploring in a small boat, camping in wild places, arguing in a tent with friends—were finished and he was back in the feckless atmosphere of the base. In a mood of discontent he wrote to Mollie: 'How terrific it will be to get home and see you after all these boring people and to find gentle green England after this jagged, zig-zag, see-saw jumble of rock and ice that calls itself a country.'

The ice-cap station had now been manned by the first pair, Lindsay and Riley, for nearly a month. Soon after the *Quest* got back to the base, Watkins and Scott set off to relieve them, with Bingham and D'Aeth who were to be the second pair at the station. A few days later Chapman and Rymill followed them.

August, who might have wished he was himself going up to the ice cap, found that his first job after the coast journey was to help the two parties over the rocks to the glacier and then up the ice slope of Buggery Bank. Sledges capsized and broke, loads burst open, dogs fell into crevasses, food ran out. At night it rained and August's tent leaked, adding a wet sleeping-bag to the other pleasures. In the end they drove iron pegs into the ice at the top of Buggery Bank and slowly got everything up, load by load, with block and tackle.

Anchoring the base hut to the ground with wire cables against the winter gales and building a hangar for the two aeroplanes were the next jobs—not the sort of work that August would enjoy but he managed to fit in some shooting and fishing too; and one sunny morning he spent sitting on the rocks writing to Mollie: 'This expedition is pretty unpleasant sometimes and I think I could hardly bear it if I hadn't got you to think about.'

At the end of September he and Stephenson and Wager set off in an *umiak*, a large open boat made of driftwood and sealskins, on what was meant to be a three-week survey trip to the south before the coast was locked in ice. They piled into the boat with all their baggage and a crew of Eskimos—an old man as pilot and two women to row—but they hadn't gone far down the fjord before being beset by fog and a heavy swell. Though the old man put on a big pair of spectacles, he admitted he was lost. Rocky islands with surf bursting on the shore appeared ahead, but didn't tell them where they were. August told the pilot to steer on the sun, faintly showing, till they hit land. In time they reached the far shore of the fjord and after much rowing camped only two miles from the base hut. The Eskimos had never put up a tent or worked a primus, but they quickly learnt; and they had no bedding, so slept in borrowed reindeer sleeping-bags.

For the next two days it rained or snowed almost without cease. They did some desultory fishing and shooting, or lay in their tents reading and being leaked on. On the third day the old man announced that it was fine enough to start again, but at the mouth of the fjord the swell still rolled and he changed his mind. They gave up all hope of a boat journey and went back to make a map of the base fjord instead.

On 1 October the *Quest*, which had made a trip to Iceland, returned with the ski undercarriages for the aeroplanes, more stores, and mail. August had sent a wireless message home asking for suet, which he badly missed. Instead he was sent a suit, including tweed trousers and a pair of plus-fours. Now he would have to wait a year for treacle pudding (it was with a treacle pudding that he had broken his three-day fast at Cambridge) but when he got back—whenever that might be—he would have it for breakfast, lunch, tea and dinner every day for a month. Meanwhile not even a letter from Mollie, who was enjoying herself in Salzburg, could cheer him up: 'The Mozart must have been almost heaven. Why did I ever sign on for this trip? One misses all that is worth living for.'

That night they had a feast in the hut, with roast lamb to

brighten the diet of cod and gull, and a dance that went on till morning. Eskimos from neighbouring settlements turned up in strength and at the height of the party the captain of the *Quest* and one of the girls were found to have disappeared, until someone went outside and fired off a Very light which lit the entire countryside, including the missing lovers. Next morning, while the rest were sleeping it off, August wrote a letter to Mollie, the last he could send her before the Arctic winter clamped down.

Was he getting any fun out of Greenland? she had asked. 'The answer is no,' he replied, 'except watching people hurt themselves and tread on each other's toes and nerves.' More and more, since being at the base, he had been struck by the futility of the expedition: 'I have come to the conclusion that it is a poor show altogether.' He felt it was misconceived, or else he was too romantic, too individualistic, too old fashioned for it. The modern idea of exploring from a base was all wrong: 'One should travel on and always on, never coming back to the same point, never having a base, but always moving towards the next horizon.'

His dissatisfaction extended to his companions: 'Everyone seems to be out for their own interests or to accomplish some feat for themselves, except me. I don't want to do anything much and get more disagreed with and more unpopular every day.' He did, in fact, want to accomplish something of his own but he wasn't clear how it could be done. Everyone else, it seemed, had a purpose on the expedition, whereas he had nothing to contribute. The feeling of being a passenger, which was absurd, grew into a feeling of being generally disliked, which was more absurd. It was a passing mood, based on nothing at all—perhaps just an early morning attitude put on for Mollie's sake—but for the moment it obsessed him.

Things were not too bad, as he had to admit: 'I get on well enough with most of the chaps who are a damn good lot, but the few who really are the best fellows one could know I never seem to have the luck to be with.' Some of them were to be his close friends always. J. M. Scott wrote that no bond linking men together could be stronger than that forged on an Arctic expedition; the British Arctic Air Route Expedition in particular was free of dissension. Watkins's style of leadership—informal, trusting, discreet, sensitive—must have set the tone. Lindsay thought they all got on so well together because most of them were gentlemen and only three hadn't been to public schools: 'We had no member of the so-called working classes and no hard case.' There were disagreements—it would have been odd, given the temperament of fourteen young men who had chosen to spend a year in the Arctic, if there hadn't been—but nothing serious.

Gradually August was getting to know the others better, and for Mollie he wrote thumbnail sketches of them all, beginning with Watkins: 'Brilliant organizer and leader. Has more brains than most people would think. Foresees situations and plans details quite amazingly well. Tastes v. lowbrow, likewise conversation. Somewhat of a poseur and a great liar. Fond of Eskimesses, has broken one heart already. Inclined to do too much himself, but on the whole the best man one could want for the job. Everyone will follow him.' One by one he went through the whole list and ended with himself: 'Lazy, selfish, crabbed. Likes annoying other people and is most unpopular member of the expedition. Has managed to evade most responsibilities and is trying to evade that of general help as hard as possible. Dislikes expedition quite enormously, but is too tough to come to any harm and will come out much as he went in—acid, bitter and bad-tempered.'

He can't have believed it was a true self-portrait. It was written early in the morning after a party, while the others still snored in their bunks and he feasted on some photographs of Mollie that she had sent: 'I get a terrific thrill every time I look at them.' In a few hours the *Quest* would sail away, leaving the expedition to settle down for the winter with no hope of a ship reaching Greenland before next June. Anything might happen before then. Perhaps August could dimly see something important, something calamitous, in the future months; eight months without a letter but surely not without event. At present, before the last tie with England was cut, his mood passed through clouds of varied discontent—homesickness, lovesickness, inadequacy, hopelessness. Mollie was his one inspiration: 'If I get the chance to do anything worthwhile it will be for you ... It is because of you I am able to live my own life and not care a hoot for anybody ... I live all the days in a dream, so that our petty shoutings and tumults and endeavours seem unreal and vanities of no consequence.'

Then, looking round the hut that early morning, he had an idea. The old Norwegian carpenter off the *Quest* ('who might have come straight out of *Alice in Wonderland* and when sober is an awfully decent old sort') had built such a good house that August would invite him to England where he could build another for Mollie and himself: 'You have only to choose a place and we will buy a little bit of land and some timber, and build the house ourselves as we want it, instead of how some damned architect wants it. Also it would annoy the trade unions.' But perhaps she could never bear to share it with him: 'I can be very tiresome to live with. All I need really is a sort of dark corner somewhere which is never tidied, where the explosions of my earthquake can be confined.'

Once the *Quest* had left, taking his letter, there would be silence until next summer unless Mollie sent him messages by wireless: 'You have friends and family, and dos and comes and gos, but I have nothing except those little squeaks through the ether.'

The *Quest* sailed away, the fjord was frozen over, the boats were hauled ashore. Then one morning the men in the hut were woken by their bunks lurching under them and a strange roar that filled the air. The first winter gale—the first fornicator, they called it—had begun. They just had time to secure the boats and tie down the aeroplane hangar. At breakfast the hut swayed and creaked, the walls bulged, the cups and plates jumped on the table. In the fjord the new ice broke up and icebergs tossed like flotsam. When August went out to read the weather instruments he had to crawl. The wind gauge measured 129 miles an hour, then blew away. During the afternoon one of the wireless masts fell down and a seaplane float landed in the dog-meat store. Pieces of ice and stones flew everywhere. The noise was terrifying. The men sat in the hut waiting for the next gust, thankful to have put wires over the roof and wondering what it was like for anyone up on the ice cap. No tent could withstand such wind.

From the hut, on a bright morning soon afterwards, small dots at the top of Buggery Bank were seen. It was Chapman and Rymill coming back from the ice cap with Lindsay and Riley, the first pair to man the station. The journey had taken ten days; for three of them they had been stormbound in their tents and all four were frostbitten. Chapman had never felt so miserable. Bingham and D'Aeth were now manning the station. Watkins and Scott were on a two-man sledge journey over the ice cap, south of the station, and nobody knew when they might come back. But it was clear that a party must start now to relieve Bingham and D'Aeth and take supplies to the station to last for several months. Plans for winter travel on the ice cap had to be revised. Previous ideas of the weather had been absurdly optimistic; they had even thought that relief teams might be taken in by aeroplane, but now, if the fornicator gave any hint of things to come, there was a chance that nobody would get through before next spring. They could only hope that up in the middle of the ice cap, where the gales came from, their force was less than down here on the coast.

August was in charge of making a dump at the foot of the glacier. They tried to be quick, but it took ten days to prepare a big ice-cap expedition. Tents and sledges had to be repaired, dog harness spliced, rations sorted. To save weight all the pemmican was taken out of its tins and packed in cotton bags made by the Eskimo girls. The portable wireless, the most vital item after food and fuel, was loaded on to a sledge; its generator alone weighed 150 pounds, but with their own transmitter the men at the ice-cap station would be in touch with the base.

The two best dog teams were away with Watkins and Scott, somewhere on the ice cap, and a motley bunch had to be collected locally to make up teams for six sledges, one for each man on the

5

party. Chapman was leader, with Stephenson, Hampton, Lemon, Wager and August. Stephenson and Hampton were to be the new pair at the ice-cap station in place of Bingham and D'Aeth. On 26 October, after being held up one more day by a blizzard, they started from the base.

Scott wrote, 'Nobody could have led this difficult journey better than Chapman did. He had faith and vision. He was a tremendous driver, chiefly of himself. He had reserves of imaginative re-creation, and he was an unconquerable optimist.' It was as well. Chapman himself wrote, 'I think this journey is going to be one of the bloodiest ever made—if we make the ice-cap station, that is.' Of the six men he alone had any experience of driving dogs. Three of the dog teams had never been driven before, and one sledge carried only the wireless, making the others extra heavy.

When they reached the dump at the foot of the glacier they found that two tents had been blown down by the previous day's blizzard and another had vanished. Next day, in a rising gale, they started up the glacier. The ice had been swept bare of snow which, with the fierce wind, made travel difficult. Men wore crampons, dogs wore canvas boots. In a storm on the second night one tent collapsed and its outer sheet sailed away, though it was pegged to the ice with a metal spike and its walls weighted with ration boxes. The occupants had to cram in with the others. August, with Chapman and Hampton, lay listening to the fury and wondering how long their own tent could hold out. When one man turned over in his sleeping-bag the others had to follow; when a gust came all three were lifted off the ground. With daybreak the wind eased and they could get some sleep. Chapman wrote, 'It was as if the earth had suddenly stopped spinning and we realized how tremendous the nervous strain had been.'

It took three days to haul the loads up Buggery Bank, using block and tackle. Woollen balaclavas became clogged with lumps of ice, pockets and shirts filled with powder snow, beards and eyelashes grew icicles. In camp, inside the tents a lining of hoar frost formed on the walls; outside, the dogs lay buried in the snow. Sometimes when the weather cleared—such were the extremes of this Arctic land—they were treated to a marvellous aurora in the sky.

While riding his sledge empty on the way back for another load, August was thrown off; the dogs careered off alone in the direction of open crevasses and were only stopped at the brink. The wireless sledge also broke loose, ran downhill and overturned; August thought they would be lucky if it still worked when they reached the ice-cap station. One team of dogs broke into a bag of pemmican (the tins would at least have been dogproof) and ate several days' ration. Others fought among themselves or chewed through their harness and escaped. A particularly wild one in August's team bit his hand and then his arm, through all the clothes; after a beating, August chained him up but he broke the chain and took no further part in the expedition, happy to watch the others from behind a ridge of ice.

A region of crevasses had to be crossed before they were up on the ice cap proper. One man went ahead on a rope, probing the ice bridges; once a sledge fell through. By now they had discarded their climbing boots, which had to be unfrozen every morning, and wore deerskin moccasins, but nothing could protect them from the sting of driving snow. On 2 November they were hit by another storm, and though all six men struggled with each tent they could only put up two before collapsing inside, encrusted with ice. There they lay for two nights while the snow piled against the walls and reduced the space inside still more. But they were glad of the rest and read books, wrote diaries, and sang sea-shanties.

Dogs, as well as sledges and baggage, had to be dug out of the snow; their harness, in tangles, was frozen into the ice beneath them. The wireless sledge was broken and needed repairs. But a day of calm saw them through the last of the crevasses before the storm returned with a vengeance. In his diary August wrote,

The fornicator blew all night and all day. Snow drifted right up over the tent entrance, causing the walls to come together and make it very cold. Got out about three p.m. to feed the dogs. Wind furious. Could only walk against it with face turned away. Most of the dogs were buried in the snow with only their noses out. Some of them didn't seem to want their pemmican. Inside of tent covered with hoar frost which drops on to us. We are now on half rations.

They had covered only ten miles in ten days—the time taken by Chapman on his return from the ice-cap station the previous month—and had to stay in their tents three more days while the storm raged. August wrote,

Still blowing. A lull in the night proved a false hope. Tent shaking and beating all day. Finished *Tess of the D'Urbs*. Only have Conrad's *Victory* left now. Towards evening the wind increased in violence and as darkness fell the tent was thundering and shaking as if it would be torn in pieces at any moment. Had to shout to make Hampton hear, although he was only a foot away. Everything covered with rime and snow. Sleeping-bags wet. We slept in our clothes and prayed that the tent would stay up. One dreads to think what it would be like if it blew away.

The wind was over a hundred miles an hour, according to Chapman who thought it must be like being under shellfire in the war: 'If the tent goes we are corpses.' His anxiety for the rest of the journey grew. The weather might get worse, the days would certainly get shorter, the tents couldn't possibly stand much more. The dogs, who were on short rations after getting at their food again, were already weakening; soon it would be the men. When they opened a fresh ration box they found that all the chocolate had been stolen from it on the voyage from England. It was a terrible discovery.

After three days in tents they could move again. August's dogs had bitten through their traces and everything was buried under a mess of snow and frozen urine. (At least the dogs were good scavengers and disposed of all excrement, human and their own.) One of Chapman's dogs was frozen into the ice by its tail; by mistake, trying to cut it out, he cut it off. That day they passed the Big Flag, put up by the first party to mark the end of the climb up on to the ice cap, and celebrated by opening their only tin of beef. Frozen solid, it had to be cut with an ice axe.

Now they were on the regular ice-cap track and the going should be easier. The first party had planted a line of numbered flags on bamboo poles at half-mile intervals, a dotted trail across the waste. Beyond the Big Flag they had only to steer north-west along the line, with 112 miles to go. The plateau stretched ahead, rising gently to the horizon, though usually even the next flag was obscured. To lose the trail might be fatal; in such weather, with the sun seldom showing and then only barely clearing the horizon, there was no hope of getting a fix. But the bearing and distance between each flag had been recorded in a logbook, and with compass and sledge wheel (a bicycle wheel attached to one of the sledges to measure the distance run) the route to the ice-cap station should now be straightforward. They were overdue; Bingham and D'Aeth would be already expecting them.

Then on 10 November, fifteen days but only fifteen miles from the base, an extraordinary encounter occurred. Chapman was out in front when he suddenly saw, far ahead in the blankness, something moving.

It was Watkins and Scott who had been travelling for two months on the ice cap and were now worn out but nearing home. During their journey the season had changed from autumn to winter, the weather from benign to murderous. They had never imagined the viciousness of an Arctic gale. One day they had progressed only 200 yards. They lay in their sleeping-bags while the wind blasted the tent with snow, the poles bent and the canvas cracked like a sail. 'It was rather frightening at night,' Scott admitted. If anything broke they would be flung out into the mad world outside, to struggle blindly and probably to die. During the storm Watkins read aloud to Scott—*A Christmas Carol*, 'which was in a way seasonable'.

Joy at meeting vanished when Watkins found that Chapman's party, which by now should have been coming out from the ice-cap station, was still on its way in. 'Good Lord,' he said, 'you'll never get there.' Chapman said, 'I know,' and they all laughed. But Watkins was very worried. He didn't give orders, he left the decisions to Chapman. The most important job was to get Bingham and D'Aeth out. The wireless could be dumped. The ice-cap station itself could be abandoned once the men were relieved. If food ran out, the dogs could be fed on each other, or men could eat dogs. They didn't stand talking long. Soon they parted, Watkins and Scott for the coast, Chapman and his five men on across the ice cap.

Chapman announced his plan. Rymill, Lemon and Stephenson would now return to the base. Wager and August would be the next pair to man the station, possibly for the whole winter. Chapman would push on with them, taking only three sledges, and bring back Bingham and D'Aeth. Next morning, 11 November, the wireless was left near a flag, never to be seen again. The three men for the base gave up their books and spare clothes to the three for the ice cap, who took the best dogs and all the food they could carry. They arranged a code of signals in the snow in case the aeroplane was able to fly in and drop food. Too late, in the business of sorting and re-packing, they remembered it was Armistice Day and they should have observed two minutes' silence at eleven o'clock, but they promised to have a dinner together in London next year. At noon they separated and went their opposite ways.

Chapman, Wager and August trudged on. The wind had blown the surface into a sea of frozen waves which constantly over-turned the sledges. Often the loads had to be unlashed and taken off before the sledges could be righted. Fingers and faces got frostbitten. Chapman's toenails came off and his raw toes stuck to his socks. The bunting on most of the flags had been torn to

shreds which made them hard to see; some had already sunk out
of sight in drifts. Steering by compass was almost impossible: the
dogs lost direction and the needle moved sluggishly in the frozen
liquid. At night the temperature dropped to thirty-five degrees
below zero. The hoar frost inside the tents hung over the men;
there was no escape from the ice.

Meanwhile they were eating the food intended for the ice-cap
station.

> Courtauld came into our tent this morning [Chapman wrote
> in his diary], and suggested he should stay alone at the ice-cap
> station. He stresses what has been worrying me, namely that
> we shall take so long to reach the station that we shan't have
> enough supplies to leave for two people. The bad weather,
> having started so early, may continue till February and even
> over March, so that no sledge party could come up and the
> aeroplane could not land. Courtauld says he is used to being
> alone and is very keen to try the experiment in such conditions.
> With so many books, a good supply of tobacco and ample food
> for one man he says he will be perfectly happy and is most
> anxious to do this . . . We can't decide anything yet. We've got
> to find the station first.

August's idea may have come suddenly or he may have ruminated
on it for several days. Probably it grew unconsciously until he
saw that it was the only answer. Everything fitted. The sledges
were beginning to break up after so many spills; they could be
lightened by taking on food for only one man at the ice-cap
station. August's partner at the station was to be Wager whom
he had come to dislike. Wager was tough, an expert climber as
well as geologist, but August thought he was too fond of doing
other people's work or telling them how to do it: 'Fussy, quick-
tempered and rude' was his judgement, a harsh one and later to
be amended (in 1935 they returned to Greenland on their own
expedition together) but present conditions were not the best for
frayed relations and August believed that Wager returned the

dislike; he dreaded being confined with him for the whole winter.
They could abandon the station and all go back to the base, but
August was tired of the company and would rather be manning
the station alone than face idle, aimless months in the crowded
hut. He could contribute to the expedition in his own way. It
might be a chance to do 'something really big', to test himself
to the limit as he had always hoped. Everything fitted; something
formed. He saw what would happen as nobody else did. His
mind was cleared. That done, he persisted. Quite simply, 'I
decided to stay on my own and keep the station going.'

But they hadn't got there yet; they were less than halfway in
from the Big Flag. The coastal fringe of mountains had long ago
disappeared behind them, but sometimes in fine weather the
white dome of Mount Forel rose to the north-east, refracted
strangely above the horizon and fantastically enlarged. More
often there was nothing to see at all.

Every night in a thin pencil-scrawl August wrote his diary:

November 16th: Another gale got up in the night so again we
lay up all day indulging in alternations of cooking and reading
aloud. The results were oatcakes of a sort, toffee, peas, the
whole of *King John*, sundry sonnets and the whole of *Alice in
Wonderland* . . . *November 17th:* Lay up again all day although
late in the morning (when it was too late) it dropped and we
might have travelled. Culinary efforts included a rice and
prune pudding, rather stodgy and tasteless . . . *November 18th:*
Wind increased in night to gale force and blew all day . . .
November 19th: A fine day at last. Got packed up very late
after lying up so long and found not a single trace on any dog.
They had all chewed them off . . . Found some old bits of
string and knotted up seven traces. Then we started. We
hadn't been a quarter of a mile before all the sledges were over.
The surface was alternately knife-edge drifts as hard as concrete and soft snow. The drifts lay in islands and always the
dogs seemed to make straight for them and plough through
the middle while we ran cursing beside our sledges, now pull-

ing, now pushing to prevent them upsetting. Every ten minutes
the sledge would capsize and the dogs sit down with a satisfied
look while we turned it right side up. Every time this happened
it made the sledges weaker and nearer breaking point. The sun
set and all the western sky glowed, but still we tried to get on.
The stars came out and found us at it as hard and futilely as
ever . . . We were forced to camp, having made a bare five
miles . . . *November 20th:* Another awful day travelling over
the drifts . . . Just when we were ready to start all my dogs ran
away. Had to go after them for a quarter of a mile and drag
them back. Traces were breaking all the time. Sledge over-
turned about every hundred yards. In spite of all we made
seven miles . . . *November 21st:* Another day even worse than
yesterday . . . Got away about ten. Traces still in hopeless state,
constantly breaking. Drifts awful, hard concrete ridges with
soft deep snow between. Sledge overturning all the while . . .
My dogs got worse and worse . . . Sledge beginning to pass
out. Camped at last, thoroughly worn out after doing six miles.
Now we are halfway from Big Flag. The continued effort at
this altitude (six or seven thousand feet) of struggling through
the snow without snow shoes (which the dogs have eaten),
keeping one's sledge upright, cursing one's dogs and continuously restarting, tires one out almost beyond endurance.

That day they killed the first of the dogs, a little bitch in Chapman's team, too weak to pull and not worth her pemmican. She
was knocked on the head with an ice axe and fed to the others.
Yet the men, whipping and cursing and putting them through a
cruel ordeal, marvelled how their dogs still pulled.

The days of compulsory rest, though irksome, had their
consolations. In agony with frostbite and crutch sores, Chapman
enjoyed the inevitability of a storm and the enforced surrender.
Wager happily worried away at geological problems. August
read and cooked. All of them found pleasure in companionship
and the comparative warmth of a tent after the struggle of trying
to move on.

In August's diary the fatigue began to show:

My moccasins have split and I got very cold feet . . . Sledges overturned all the time. All feeling the effect of the height combined with cold. Everything seems an effort to do. It takes us five hours to get away in the morning. Did six miles and camped, tired and feeling we had done sixty . . . Expected to make a good distance as it was a clear and sunny day (though the sun was only a few degrees above the horizon) with little wind. But the going was worse than ever. Sledges upset and broke and then a head wind got up. Only did two miles by lunch time.

When they started again after ten minutes' halt for lunch August found that a bitch in his team had produced a puppy. There was no hope of keeping it warm, so after the mother had bitten the cord and the father had licked the snow off it, August let Wager's dogs eat it. The bitch pulled for another hour, then scraped a hole to have a second puppy which went the same way. That evening, when they camped, she produced a third: 'So I made her as comfortable as possible with ration boxes and left her to do her best.' If any more puppies were born that night, by next morning they had gone.

Now they had been on the ice cap for a month, with forty miles to go. For two days they lay in their tents imprisoned by a gale. Chapman, who had a touring atlas, planned a yachting holiday and remembered places he knew in England: 'It's odd to think of life going on just the same there. And us, poor shits, slaving our silly souls out here—and why? God knows, but it's bloody good fun really.' The dogs prowled round the tents, chewed holes in the canvas and broke into a kitbag. When they could travel again the temperature rose above zero and August had to take off clothes to keep cool, but the warmth brought a mist which hid the drifts and flags; they only did four and a half miles. Next night the dogs ate a leather binocular case.

On the last day of November they broke all records—twelve

and a half miles. It started badly with driving snow and they
wasted time looking for the first flag. But the weather cleared
and the sun even lifted above the horizon for an hour or so: 'Too
low to give any heat. It looks quite nice however.' One of Chapman's dogs, too ill to work, was let loose and soon got left behind
to a lonely death. But for the first time since leaving the base the
men could sit on their sledges and be towed. Later, when the
moon appeared, they travelled on into the evening and celebrated the day's run with full rations for supper.

For the first two days of December the good weather held, the
moon shone and they covered twenty-two miles. Late the second
night they reached a flag and struck a match to read the number:
only half a mile more. They could hardly get the dogs to go on
again, to pull the last stretch. But there was no sign of the
station, to August's despair:

> We searched in all directions expecting every minute to see it,
> and then warmth and dryness and *food*. It was freezing thirty-
> five degrees below zero and the wind bit through our clothes
> as if we were naked. We went on a short distance and searched
> again. At last we had to give it up and wearily pitched our
> tents and got into our stiff frozen sleeping-bags. It was a bitter
> disappointment after what we had hoped. We slept little that
> night, shivering with the cold of our frozen bags.

In the morning Chapman went out alone, without a balaclava,
to look for the station. Half an hour later he was back, having
seen nothing but with both ears frostbitten. He warmed them too
quickly in the tent and a minute later was writhing and nearly
weeping with the worst pain he had ever known. Wager then
went out to search and reported that the line of flags seemed to
extend ahead. Somebody must have made a mistake. They looked
up in the logbook where the flags had been recorded last summer
by the first party, and on the back page found a continuation.
They still had twelve miles to go.

Already it was past noon. They struck camp, loaded up the

sledges and got going, desperate not to spend another night like
the last. The sun set, the light failed, Chapman steered on the
stars. At six in the evening, beside a flag, they found a tin of
Horlicks and a cheerful note of welcome from D'Aeth written
many weeks before.

It was the thirty-ninth day since leaving the base and August,
for one, had had enough:

> We plodded on and eventually the sledge wheel showed we
> had done the distance. It was then freezing forty-five degrees.
> Another night in our frozen bags was unthinkable. We all
> separated to do another moonlight hunt. I walked out across
> the snow until I lost sight of the sledges. Nothing. Would this
> be another trick of fate after another never-ending day? Must
> we again shiver in those frozen tents? I wandered back to the
> sledges, feeling hopeless.

Suddenly Chapman shouted.

'He had seen the flag, the Union Jack! I have never felt so
suddenly overcome with joy.' In a moment August saw the
tattered flag in the moonlight, marking a mound of snow that
shortly was to become his home.

The party which established the station in the summer had had
plenty of choice for the site. It merely had to be far enough from
the coast and near the probable air route across the ice cap. The
view was the same in all directions; this was as good as anywhere.
Its position was fixed by sun and stars with theodolite and wireless time-signal, and the altitude was estimated at nearly 9,000
feet. Then the special tent was put up.

The inner tent, a canvas dome ten feet across and six feet high,
was hung by tapes from a frame of curved bamboo ribs, with the
ventilator pipe at the top. The outer tent was put over it, leaving
a space between the layers. A skirt round the foot of the walls was
piled with snow to hold it down and an entrance tunnel dug,

starting several yards away and coming up through a hole in the floor. With reindeer skins spread inside and ration boxes for furniture the place was made as comfortable as possible. Lindsay, who lived in it with Riley for the first five weeks, wrote, 'This funny little dwelling was a very happy home.'

Weather observations had began at once. Instruments were set up for measuring temperature, pressure, force of wind, speed of clouds and depth of snow. To protect the station a high snow wall was built, making a small yard round the tent. An 'ice closet' was dug outside the wall, with a snow shelter over it and a sledge for a seat. Soon it was found that the yard acted as a trap for snowdrifts and often needed digging out; the closet also filled up. Two small igloos were built of snow blocks, connected to the entrance tunnel, for stores and the wireless that would be brought up from the coast one day. Finally the Union Jack was hoisted on a pole.

The first pair of occupants read, played chess and developed a code of private jokes. Lindsay began writing a book, Riley hung up a crucifix. The question of relief was a constant topic and they discussed the possibility of walking out if nobody ever came; they were not going to be martyrs to meteorology. Lindsay wrote afterwards that although they had little in common in the way of tastes or temperament, they never got tired of each other's company. In the end they were sorry to leave.

The second pair, Bingham of the navy and D'Aeth of the air force, had extended the entrance tunnel and built a dome right over the tent, to encase it in a shell of snow. Digging snowdrifts out of the yard took up much of the time. Being used to routine, they kept the place neat and tidy, their pots and pans clean and their beards clipped. They read, told stories and played cards. After a month, when they expected daily to be relieved by Chapman's party, they took to walking down the trail to clear the flags. On 3 December they had been nearly nine weeks at the station and were smoking their pipes after supper when they were startled by shouts of '*Evening Standard! Evening Standard!*'

at the end of the tunnel. Chapman, Wager and August burst in, their faces unrecognizable under layers of ice.

Bingham and D'Aeth, as hosts, cooked up a brew of pemmican and the five explorers sat up late exchanging news. For August the joy of having reached the station was marred by acute frostbite —both his big toes were swollen and his fingers so sore, with a huge blister on one, that he couldn't undo his buttons—but next morning, sleeping in one of the snow igloos, he could lie in his bag till ten o'clock without thinking of having to get going, and they had a 'really late gentlemanly breakfast'.

For two days a gale blew over the ice cap and nobody could move. Chapman was impatient to be away back down the trail— delay meant shorter daylight and worse weather—but a rest would be good for men and dogs, and they could mend the sledges, though with frostbitten fingers in the bitter wind it was painful work.

They discussed what was to be done. After sharing the station in worsening weather and with increasing uncertainty of relief, Bingham and D'Aeth disapproved of one man staying on alone. Both of them were now unfit, they had lost appetites and weight, they slept badly. Bingham would get breathless and lie awake sweating and panting. As doctor of the expedition he gave his opinion against August being left with nobody. He himself had had an unnerving experience which he thought would have been more serious if he hadn't had a companion; one day, standing by the tent, he had been startled by a sudden loud bang and bolted inside to safety, but it was only the Union Jack flapping in the wind. Another time D'Aeth caught sight of a strange man in the snow—one of the weather instruments—and also rushed into the tent.

August quietly repeated his argument. The ice-cap station was one of the objects of the expedition and it would be a pity to abandon it now after manning it since the summer. The winter, when nobody had ever lived on the ice cap, was the most important season for recording the weather. There wasn't enough food for more than one man and he would like to be that one. He enjoyed being alone, and now that his frostbite was giving such pain he was in no hurry for another journey like the last. His private reasons were harder to explain; nobody else could be expected to understand something which, however strong his conviction, he never quite defined.

He already had a reputation for being inflexible once he had made up his mind and in Chapman, leader of the party, he had an ally. There were not many members of the expedition—only Chapman himself and Watkins perhaps—who would have cared for the unknown ordeal of solitude all through an Arctic winter. Chapman (who ten years later, in the Malayan jungle, was to put his ideas to a triumphant test) believed that almost all difficulties could be overcome, that a man could exist for a long time on very little food, that the human body was capable of bearing immense privation, that it was a man's attitude of mind that determined whether he went under or survived. He saw that for August it wasn't just a matter of keeping the ice-cap station going, but recognized a compulsion beyond the daily routine of reading a few instruments, beyond the challenge of doing something nobody had ever done before. It wasn't a whim or a stunt or a gesture of bravado. There was a need, a light, a fire involved —an act of courage to reflect the truth of one man's imagination.

'Courage is a moral quality,' Lord Moran wrote. 'It is not a chance gift of nature like an aptitude for games. It is a cold choice between two alternatives, the fixed resolve not to quit; an act of renunciation which must be made not once but many times by the power of the will. Courage is will power.' August had made a decision, he was responsible for himself, and with food and fuel to last until the spring he would probably be all right. 'Courtauld is determined to stay,' Chapman wrote in his diary, 'and eventually we gave in . . . It's a marvellous effort and I hope to God he gets away with it.'

That evening they had a premature Christmas dinner with the last of the luxuries—game soup, fried sardines, roast ptarmigan, plum pudding with rum sauce, mincemeat, dates, raisins, tea and rum punch—and no pemmican. Dinner had never been so good. Nor were the dogs forgotten; one of them was killed for the rest to feast on.

Next morning, 6 December, the gale had blown out and the weather was fine. August got up early to make breakfast for the other three and by ten o'clock they were ready. They whipped up their dogs and soon were away down the trail, while he stood outside his tent and took a last photograph.

Possibly at the moment of his friends' departure he wondered about his decision not to go with them (more likely he felt an intense, powerful exhilaration at the experience ahead), but neither then nor later did he give anything away. A feeble sun, hardly rising above the horizon, shone on the pink snow for the occasion. 'It was bitterly cold and I didn't watch them long. Coming out an hour later I could just see them as a speck in the distance. Now I am quite alone. Not a dog or even a mosquito to look at.'

Chapter 7

Solitude

MANY MEN—or many more than care to admit it—have a desire to experience a spell of solitude; a time to keep silence, a time for peace. It might be a need for simplicity and purity; an atavism, a yearning for reversion, a wish to be alone on the surface of the earth once more; not just to be in Eden before the Fall, but to be Adam before the birth of Eve. It might be what the Everest mountaineer, John Hunt, writing of another lone explorer, called 'an urge which lies very deep in man's nature to find out more about himself, to discover where his limit lies'. But no man knows how he will survive the ordeal, any more than he knows how he will behave in battle. The obvious qualities are not necessarily the most useful; others, suppressed or never summoned, can save the unlikely survivor where the expected hero fails. In *They Survived* Wilfrid Noyce wrote, 'Nothing but the situation will show who has the life-urge, who the death-urge.' The instinct for self-preservation, common to all animals, isn't enough. Nor is discipline from outside—the discipline of orders or drill. Soldiers, left to themselves, don't always last longest; military control must be replaced by a higher and better one, from within.

For August solitude was a pleasure. Far from feeling lonely, he was glad to have nobody to bother him, nobody to interrupt his activities or moods or thoughts, nobody wanting to share the smallest part of their personality with him and expecting something of his in return. There was nobody to thank or blame; he was master of his fate. Now he could be himself, resolving the pattern of his life, conceding nothing to anyone else's. In his last letter to Mollie his claim to be selfish, coming from a man known by his friends for quite different qualities, was true so far as it was wishful. Perhaps he would have liked to be more ruthless than he could be. If so—if he hoped to practise a kind of harmless egoism—here was fulfilment. If it was really what he wanted, he could now be as unconcerned with other men as he cared, because the nearest were already far away and getting further.

'There is nothing to complain of,' he wrote in his diary that first evening alone, 'unless it be the curse of having to go out into the cold wind every three hours to observe the weather.' Though the routine of the observations saved him from his own haphazard ways, he felt they were someone else's invention, distinct from his more private line of study. He would perform them faithfully, for they were the public reason for his being there and he was loyal to the expedition; six times a day he dressed up in full Arctic clothing and battled out of the tent, down the tunnel and out into the snow to read the instruments. But soon it was the weather itself and its sudden changes, not its mere measurements, that excited him—days of half-lit stillness and nights of dead silence with auroras streaming magically across the northern sky, followed by blizzards that obliterated day and night in one terrible roar.

There was plenty to do: the ice to be thawed from his frozen sleeping-bag, his clothes to be dried, snowdrifts in the yard to be dug out, stores to be brought into the tent. With two layers of canvas and a thick casing of snow blocks, with no window and a long tunnel for a door, it would have been dark in the tent even if there were any sunshine outside. On 8 December, his second day alone, he wrote in his diary, 'Sun did not rise and I suppose will not until the middle of next month.' But the paraffin lamp gave him enough light and also raised the temperature above zero, and he kept the primus stove going for several hours even when he wasn't cooking. 'My house was warm and I lived an untroubled life of ease if not of luxury,' he wrote later, when the memory of discomforts may have faded. There were unexpected advantages in the climate and when, after mysteriously itching for a few days, he found bugs in his underclothes ('this is what comes of lending one's sleeping-bag to Eskimos') he simply put them out in the snow to be killed by the cold. Otherwise he was content enough and his pipe, a present from Mollie and a precious link with home, tasted as good as ever.

After a week, when he checked how much tobacco he was smoking, he worked out that he had enough for seventeen weeks. He also had six ration boxes, twenty-six gallons of paraffin, two bottles of lemon juice and a bottle of cod-liver oil. To decide how to manage his supplies of food and fuel he tried to estimate how long they had to last. For safety he could have picked the latest possible date for his relief and given himself the smallest allowance, but that was not August's way; it was mean, gloomy, pessimistic, cautious. 'I prefer,' he wrote, 'to eat my cake rather than have it. *Carpe diem* was a tag which served as an excuse whenever I felt hungry.' Also he wanted more fuel now, for drying his clothes and for reading, than he would need later. So he chose to assume that the relief would come by 15 March (if it didn't, at least the days would be warmer and lighter) and scaled his supplies to last till then, leaving a bare allowance after that.

Mental exercise concerned him from the beginning. On the fifth morning, though his fingers and toes were in pain from frostbite, he took a star sight with the theodolite to check the error of his watch (quite unnecessarily unless he thought he might ever have to navigate his way out) and laboriously worked out the calculation in his diary. Next day he played a game of chess against himself. Luckily as well as the books he had brought with him, he had others left by earlier occupants—a random library varying from Thackeray and Scott to Galsworthy and Whitaker's Almanack, but probably as good as anything he might have chosen. 'There were times,' he wrote, 'when the Bible made very good reading.'

The frostbite hurt badly. He bandaged his big toes which now seemed quite dead, though oozing, and when he took the bandages off after three days it was an unpleasant sight: 'Left toenail came off. Other will soon, I expect.' Five days later it did, and looked no better: 'V. nasty, soft, dead and gooey.' Every movement of his feet was painful but he couldn't nurse them properly. Too often when he went to take the weather readings he found a pile of windblown snow blocking the tunnel and he had to dig his way out. In stormy weather he would excavate himself six times a day, then wade knee-deep through the soft snow in the yard, flounder up a six-foot drift that marked the wall, trip over ridges and fall into holes before reaching the instruments. Sometimes they were hard to find in the dim, diffused light, even without a blizzard. One evening he lost his way, lost direction, lost sight of everything—briefly, but long enough to learn another of the weapons of an Arctic winter. For a man whose stoicism was quite unselfconscious, frostbite was just one of the trials he had solicited, to be recorded and endured. It was the only attitude if he was to survive.

Food—its monotony rather than its supply—was always a worry. Scientifically the rations might have been excellent, but there was no fun in opening another pack of peaflour or oatmeal, of spreading margarine on one more ship's biscuit, of again brewing up the eternal pemmican. His few luxuries didn't last long; nor was there much scope for variation, though within the first week he had made a kind of jam from cocoa which he decided was better than drinking it.

It was thoughts of good food, after reading a passage from Isaiah on the Sunday of his second week, that invoked the first suggestion of a future beyond the ice cap. One day he would give a tremendous dinner for his friends, and in his diary he drew a table plan for thirty-six (all men, all bachelors) and ordered the menu: oysters, soup, sole with mushrooms, *tournedos* of beef, woodcock or grouse, chestnut and orange pudding, strawberry or raspberry ice, caviar or pancakes *flambés*. He gave the wine for each course and the dates of the port and brandy to be served. After that, he could have had little appetite for his evening pemmican.

The first day without a diary entry was 18 December, and next day he explained: 'All today and yesterday north-west fornicator which completely snowed up the tunnel again.' He had to dig himself out every three hours, but because he was digging from inside he could only pile the snow up behind him. Soon there was just a small gap below the roof of the tunnel for him to crawl through. His digging couldn't keep pace with the drift; in half an hour the entrance was filled again. If the storms continued, he had no hope of keeping the tunnel open.

On the 20th the gale was still blowing, and although it calmed down in the evening the temperature dropped to forty degrees below zero. On the 21st peace returned and at midday, for the first time for a fortnight, he saw the half-sun above the horizon, through refraction. That night he was granted one of the moments of thrill which shone through the drudgery: 'Aurora wonderful tonight, like purple smoke wreaths twisting and writhing all over the sky. At ten o'clock it was completely still. The silence outside was almost terrible. Nothing to hear but one's heart beating and the blood ticking in one's veins.'

The silence of calm days dominated the ice cap, a rule of nature which he couldn't disobey. He was glad not to have even a wireless: 'For the first month or so I was very averse to the least noise. The complete silence all round seemed to urge one to keep in tune with it by being silent oneself. After a time I got over this, and used to get great satisfaction out of a sort of singing.'

The fine weather lasted several days, though on Christmas Eve he was still clearing up the mess left by the gale: 'Spent as much time outside as daylight and toes would allow, digging away the results of the fornicator. Thank God the shortest day is now past.' Then he made a discovery: two of the paraffin tins were damaged and four gallons had leaked away. He would have to economize drastically, using the primus only for cooking and relying on the lamp alone for heat. It was a bleak outlook, not improved by finding a second generation of bugs in his clothes. And the memory of more cheerful Christmas Eves brought the first faint pangs of loneliness: 'This time last year I had such a

marvellous Christmas . . . I really don't miss the good things of
Christmas very much, though I should rather like a bit of fresh
meat and a mince pie, and even more a bit of plum pudding.'
    On Christmas Day the pangs struck harder:

> How jolly to be at home or even at the base. I suppose they will
> be having a blind and finishing the last of the alcohol. How-
> ever I haven't done so badly. Excellent porridge for breakfast,
> a tin of shrimp paste and peas for lunch, and a dinner of rice,
> honey (made from sugar and margarine), toffee (home made)
> and chocolate. Mollie's pipe going v.g. Books good—Jane
> Austen and *Great Sea Stories*—and nothing to disturb the
> peace except the wind whistling up to an increasing gale and
> the house which is making rather frightening cracks and
> thumps. Hope it isn't going to fall in. If only I could put the
> clock on to next Christmas.

He consoled himself by making plans. He would buy a house in
Suffolk—not far from Ipswich for the trains to London, and near
the sea, perhaps at Pin Mill: 'No land except a garden. Fewest
possible servants and no waiting at table.' Then he changed his
ideas: he would spend his money on a boat and keep her at
Falmouth.
    For the next two days he dug snow out as fast as the wind
blew it in. The high wall round the yard was a mistake, he
decided; it acted as a snow trap. Without it the snow would have
blown straight past the tent and on for ever across the ice cap.
Without frostbite, for that matter, it wouldn't have been such
hard work; he couldn't bear it for more than a few minutes at a
time.
    Two days after Christmas, in the early morning when he had
just got back into his sleeping-bag after the seven o'clock
observation, he had a bad fright: 'There was a soft rumbling close
to my head which increased and ended in a dull crash. It flashed
across my mind as it began that the weight of snow was too much
and the whole house was going to come in on me.' But nothing

happened. At first he thought that the tunnel must have collapsed, burying the spade; then, that some of the snow blocks over the tent had given way. Whatever it was, and whatever the consequences, there was nothing he could do except wait and see: 'Hope nothing further happens tonight.' Coolly he went on to speculate when the expedition would get back to England and where they would land; if it was Harwich, he would get Mollie to meet him. Then, in Chapman's atlas, he studied a map of Scotland: 'It is quite obvious I must do another cruise on the west coast.'

On New Year's Eve, half an hour before midnight, he wrote, 'It is certainly quiet.' Any day now he was expecting to see the sun again and had done some spring cleaning in honour of the season. Now he made a list of the books he wanted to read and wrote down his New Year resolutions. The first was to mend his moccasins and sleeping-bag. The second, to get home and ask Mollie to marry him, though in fact they were already engaged. The third, to find a house, a boat and a job. The fourth, to give up exploring. The fifth, to collect a library and study literature, poetry, music and polar exploration.

The year 1930 ended with August wishing he could send a wireless message to Mollie and wondering how they were getting on down at the base: 'Finishing up the last of the good eats and drinks, I suppose.'

Since August Courtauld's winter alone on the Greenland ice cap in 1930–1931, other men have written about their solitary confinement: Arthur Koestler who spent three months under sentence of death during the Spanish Civil War; Christopher Burney who was caught by the Gestapo in Paris in the Second World War and held for eighteen months; Anthony Grey, the journalist who was a hostage in his own house in Peking for more than two years; and Geoffrey Jackson, the British ambassador to Uruguay who was kidnapped and kept for eight months by urban guerrillas. But few men, however unpleasant and dangerous their situation, have been so totally severed from human contact as he was. Through their guards and interrogators and occasionally through visitors, prisoners have had access to a world inhabited by others. Messages can be tapped out on the walls, water pipes can become speaking tubes. In a Spanish death-cell Arthur Koestler could climb up to the window and watch his fellow prisoners exercising in the yard. Evidence of continuing life (the legendary spider in the corner) can be comforting; and though Koestler said that the only consolation you can give a condemned man on his way to execution is to tell him that a comet is on its way and the world will be destroyed tomorrow, a man locked up in prison may find hope, however frail, in the merest snatch of birdsong through the bars or the shadow of a leaf growing on a twig outside.

August was quite alone, cut off from every symptom of other life as few men have been: no blade of grass and, after he killed the bugs in his underclothes, no insect for company. Anthony Grey, the Peking hostage, became completely and happily absorbed watching a colony of ants at work. August's solitude was enhanced by the vacuum, the total biological emptiness around him. But unlike most prisoners he chose the ordeal for himself. He even wrote afterwards that his one serious dread was that somebody would send an aeroplane to land on the ice cap near him; it might be unable to take off again and the crew would be stranded, his uninvited guests.

On 1 January 1931 he noted that there were only fourteen gallons of paraffin left. With toes and fingers still in pain, he got no pleasure from digging his way out to reach the instruments, but on fine moonlit nights he would go for a short walk and he took an observation of Mars to check his watch again.

On 4 January there was a gale raging when he woke up, the tunnel was already blocked and he had to dig himself out to take the first weather reading. Outside in the solid stream of wind and snow his face got plastered up and he could hardly see his hands. When he came back into the tent a lump of snow fell off his clothes inside the lamp and broke the mantle. He dug himself out four more times but by the afternoon, as the gale increased, the back of the tunnel was so piled with snow that he could only just wriggle through, and by the evening it was completely choked. Blocked in, he had to give up the observations for the first time in nearly a month and lie in his sleeping-bag till the storm passed; then he would find some way of getting out. Meanwhile, with fumes from the broken lamp getting thicker in the tent and snow getting deeper on top, he could only hope that the air would stay breathable and the roof hold up. If not, there was only one certain event. But August could see consolations: 'My end should be peaceful enough and I have four slabs of chocolate to eat during it. Anyhow it won't be attended by the fuss and frills of pegging out at home.'

Next morning he decided that it was impossible to try using the tunnel any more, so he dug his way into one of the two snow igloos and cut a hole up through the roof. It didn't collapse and he managed to get out. 'THANK GOD,' he wrote. Later the gale calmed down and in the peace of evening—in the exhaustion and relief—he made notes for his ideal yacht. She should be fifty feet long, built of pitch pine planking on an oak frame with teak decks, rigged as a ketch with a squaresail and raffee topsail, designed for seaworthiness rather than speed, easily handled by two people but with room for four in comfort and six at a pinch. She was his dream ship and after designing her he made plans for a dream cruise round Scotland. During these fantasies, late at night, he had another jolt. Twice, quite distinctly, he heard his name being called; the voice was Mollie's.

The tent was almost buried, but though he heard cracks and groans and the walls bulged inwards, nothing gave way. And he was pleased with the hole in the roof of the igloo. Unlike the tunnel entrance it was above the level of the snow, above the yard walls, and didn't get blocked by drifts. For a hatch he used an empty ration box, sealed round with snow. But there was still spadework to be done. Most of the spare food and paraffin had been left outside for lack of room in the tent, though he didn't know exactly where. The whole station was now blanketed with deep snow and he would spend days probing for more supplies, then dig six feet down to reach them.

On 10 January the sun made a more convincing appearance and the winter seemed to be broken. For a week or two August's laconic diary notes reflected the benumbed, patient mood of that time:

Filled up pemmican bag . . . Nothing much has happened the last few days. Rather beastly weather . . . Signs of easterly fornicator . . . Still as death and dark as pitch. Barometer dropping like a stone. Suppose something pretty unpleasant is about to happen . . . Reading *Guy Mannering*. V.V.G. Descriptions of food make me writhe, worse than *Forsyte Saga*, but I like reading about it . . . Felt rather faint yesterday . . . Heart beating very fast . . . House showing signs of collapsing. Wish I could get snow dug off roof. Would have done so yesterday if I hadn't felt so bad . . . Can't stay out for more than a few minutes as feet freeze up. Finished *Guy Mannering*. Jolly good book . . . Just finished *Jane Eyre*. It is a great book, one of the best I have ever read . . . The sun came up yesterday and today. It is grand to see it casting its rose-pink light along the snow and making shadows and bright places so that one's eyes blink . . . Only ten gallons of paraffin left . . . Finished *Wuthering Heights* . . . Now reading Pepys and *Vanity Fair* . . . A foul gale is blowing at present and nearly succeeded, the night before last, in blocking up the snow house bolt-hole which is my only exit . . . No sign of the aeroplane. I very much doubt if it will come now. Probably it can't take off, so I suppose I shall have to wait a few more months until someone can sledge here.

Ten days after designing a boat, he turned to meteorological instruments. They hadn't changed for hundreds of years; surely they could be improved by modern techniques—electricity for instance. Barometers, thermometers and hypsometers might all be electrified and made more accurate. 'One must get personally organized,' Geoffrey Jackson, the kidnapped ambassador, told a journalist who came to interview him in his cell. 'God has given me a very active and positive type of mind and imagination. I plan my day; I spend a lot of time thinking. I try to imagine what goes on in the world. I don't dwell too much on my own case, otherwise I would go crazy.' And Anthony Grey, organizing races for his ants and looking at his watch, was surprised to find that an hour had passed without thinking of himself and his plight. So with August Courtauld: in a small tent in the middle of the Greenland ice cap, besieged by one of the world's worst climates, his engineering studies at Cambridge and his experience of fieldwork combined in a burst of scientific invention. Unluckily two of his own instruments were soon to be broken; he dropped a cooking pot on a barometer, and cracked a thermometer while wiping the snow off it.

By 1 February he was longing for something better. Even when the sun shone it was too cold to stay outside for long, and sometimes the storms were so strong that he could only stagger backwards against them. The attacks came from all directions; soon after a south-east gale ended another started up from the northwest. During a particularly nerve-racking one the paraffin in the tent nearly ran out and he began digging for more, but whenever he stopped the hole filled up and it was three days before he struck a tin. Both the snow igloos had partly caved in under the weight and any day he was expecting the tent to fall on him. He wondered when, if ever, he would get away and noticed that his legs were thinner. Christopher Burney, in a Gestapo prison, remarked the same: 'I noticed, too, for the first time how thin I was becoming. My arms, for all the exercises I forced on them, were mere sticks, and I could already without difficulty pass my whole hand between my neck and the shirt collar which had once fitted.' If he went on losing weight and strength, August would have difficulty in travelling unless he could ride out on a sledge.

He wasn't bored, there was too much going on: 'One can't be bored living an entirely novel life under such interesting conditions.' Even when he had no work he could invent his own diversion, and his thoughts were not just of his predicament. 'What a hopeless fool Charles II seems to have been,' he wrote after finishing Pepys's diary. 'Not only by his effeminacy and incompetence did he let down the Country' (the capital C was still important, as it had been four years ago in Nigeria) 'but he broke people's faith in kings for ever . . . He deserved the block fully as much if not more than his father.' Another time he worked out an elaborate duodecimal system of measurements, weights, angles and money.

His ability to adapt to circumstances—itself a kind of modesty —was one of the qualities most needed to bring him through, as important as self-discipline, emotional stability and courage. Freddy Chapman, himself a famous survivor of the Second World War who lived on his wits for three years in Malaya under the Japanese, said that British soldiers who died in the jungle only succumbed because they couldn't adapt to a new way of life and diet; they expected to be dead within a few weeks, and usually were. Anticipation can be a killer. And hope diminishes as the fact of abandonment grows. In stories of survival Wilfrid Noyce noted a common element, 'a sense of self in community', a belief in the encouragement and cooperation of others, that buoyed a man's spirit. So it was with August Courtauld. Always, to supplement his capacity for endurance, there was a feeling of belonging to the expedition, of community with his friends, as if a thin connection ran back like a vein down the line of half-mile flags from the ice-cap station to the coast. Knowing that the others were at the base, and trusting them to come back for him as soon as they could, helped sustain him. Isolation was mitigated by its very opposite, like weights delicately balanced. 'No man is an island, entire of itself'—even in the middle of the Greenland ice cap.

Another factor, a form of his adaptability, was at work. Just as at times a sailor can become one with the sea or a climber one with a mountain, August achieved a kind of absorption into his surroundings, a sense of identifying with the force that might have destroyed him but instead gave him strength. Antagonism between man and element, figure and landscape, yielded to an implicit partnership. It could only have happened when he was alone and free to respond to the changing demands on him; a companion, requiring attention, would have been a distraction from the wider relationship. As it was, he could make his own terms with the ice cap in the knowledge that somehow, indefinably, the contract was mutual. He sympathized, he understood, he was in tune.

But like a schoolboy ticking off the weeks of term—except that August didn't know when the holidays would come—he couldn't help recording the passing time: 'Now been alone here just two months . . . Have now been ten weeks alone . . . Now been here three months alone and away from home eight months . . . Been here a hundred days alone.' He noted his father's birthday, which he celebrated with boiled rice and home-made toffee, and his brother's twenty-first birthday: 'Wish I had something to drink his health in. Must remember to get him a present when I get back.'

In the middle of February the temperature outside fell to fifty degrees below zero. In the tent the food was running out, but searching for another ration box was unthinkable in such cold. A rise in temperature brought a gale and because the hatch over the hole in the igloo roof didn't fit well the igloo filled up with snow. After August had dug it out and fixed the hatch the gale swung round and blew in from the other side, filling the igloo again. Now there was only one day's food left. Though digging the igloo out once more meant filling the passage with snow, he somehow managed to crawl out, but when he foraged for a ration box his fingers and toes froze up before he found anything. He gave up and spent a hungry night longing for chocolate. Next day he remembered there was a ration box in one of the igloos, now buried. He chipped away with a knife at the rock-hard snow, loading it into biscuit tins to be emptied outside, and after two hours uncovered the box. With a screwdriver he broke it open, to find that it was one of the plundered boxes and all the chocolate was gone.

He wasn't daunted: 'Read *Master of Ballantrae*. V.G.' But more and more he thought about his eventual release and the general fortunes of the expedition. 'Hope the chaps haven't set out from the base yet. This weather is impossible for sledging. As far as I can see, six months of the expedition will be a complete waste of time. All the proposed long sledge journeys will go to pot.'

The British Arctic Air Route Expedition, and August in particular, had a great advantage—luck. Unknown to any of them, the ice cap had already claimed two lives that winter. Three hundred miles further north and a hundred miles further inland, on the other side of Greenland, a German expedition had also set up a weather station and hoped to maintain it through the seasons. Their leader was more than twice Gino Watkins's age, they carried more equipment and scientific instruments than the Englishmen, they used Eskimo porters and Icelandic ponies and motor sledges as well as dogs, they established their ice-cap station several weeks earlier in the autumn, but they had no luck. One of the three men at the station, badly frostbitten, had to have all his toes amputated with a pocket knife by a companion, without anaesthetic. In October the expedition leader, with a faithful Eskimo, had carried supplies up to the station, but not enough for the two to stay the winter with the other three. They had started back to the coast, but never reached it. Their fate was not to be discovered until next spring. The German had died first and was buried by the Eskimo; the Eskimo struggled on for a few days and was buried by the snow. Thus when August was left alone at the beginning of December the bodies of two other men were lying on the ice cap. It was as well he didn't know.

On 19 February he had his worst fright:

Terrifying thing happened at five-thirty this evening. I was reading in here as usual when I heard a rushing sound seeming to come from behind, and increasing in a second to a roar like an avalanche. It ended suddenly with a crash like thunder. I thought at first I was going to be overwhelmed in some sort of snow whirlwind, then as nothing happened I thought one of the snow houses had fallen in and I should be imprisoned, but there seemed too much noise for that.

It vanished as quickly as it came. Nothing more happened and when he ventured out an hour or so later, everything was just as it had been before: 'What it was I can't think, unless some chasm forming in the ice underneath. It sounded like thousands of tons of snow falling in an avalanche.'

He never found an explanation. The ice below him was a mile and a half thick and under vast strain. It wasn't living—nothing could be more hostile to any kind of life—but it wasn't static either. With the creeping slowness of a geological age it was being compressed and pushed outwards, shifting inch by inch towards the sea. Movement was imperceptible but could be audible. A crack of any size in that immense block, far or near, could have made just such a terrifying noise. It could have been a fault resolving itself, a weakness settling after a thousand years, a mere splinter in the scale of eternity, a bubble in time. Or it could have been the snow. Other polar explorers have spoken of a distant roar rushing towards them, louder every second, tearing over the surface, surrounding and overwhelming them, passing on and disappearing, with nothing to be seen. Something like that might have been what August heard. The soft snow, under wind and sun and frost, had formed a crust; more snow, another crust, more snow—making in time a deep, many-layered sandwich. In one place a lower crust had broken under the weight and the rot had started, spreading outwards with terrific speed and noise.

He wrote nothing in his diary for a week, and resumed in a more melancholy mood. He was fed up with going out to take weather readings every three hours and getting snow all over his clothes, which never dried: 'If ever I get back to the base nothing will induce me to go on the ice cap again. When the others will come, God knows.' By the beginning of March he was down to only four gallons of paraffin. To conserve what was left he lay half the day in darkness, lit the primus only for porridge at breakfast, and gave up having a hot supper. He also gave up his morning tea and sucked a lump of ice instead. But he was convinced that the relief party was on its way and would reach him before the end of the month. More than anything it was the thought of real food that excited him: 'What wouldn't I give for a basin of green peas, new potatoes and brussels sprouts?' Other prisoners have been troubled by thoughts of food. Arthur Koestler had daydreams of steaks, potatoes and cheese. Christopher Burney too: 'I would drift into daydreams, mixtures of memory and desire . . . At the end of everything there was a meal . . . The journey's end was its chief delight, and my imagined steps were guiding me surely to supper, with pies and porridge and all the other things that fill you to a stupor.'

Then August turned to something more momentous:

Why is it that men come to these places? So many reasons have been ascribed for it. In the old days it was thought to be lust for treasure, but the treasure is gone and still men wander. Then it was a craving for adventure. There is precious little adventure in sledging or in sitting on an ice cap. Is it curiosity, a yearning to look behind the veil on to the mysteries and desolations of nature in her forlorn places? Perhaps, but that is not all. Why leave all whom we love, all good friends, all creature comforts, all mindly joys, to collect a little academic knowledge about this queer old earth of ours? What do we gain?

What would he have gained, he might have asked, by remaining as a stockbroker in the City or following his father and grand-father into the family firm? He knew the answer—nobody knew it more clearly—but he was testing his faith in the knowledge. The test was grim enough. It had taken him three months of solitude to reach this point. Now he was lying most of the time in

The ice-cap station before the winter storms began

Digging out the tent
after the winter: the
ventilator shaft is only
just visible above
the snow

August emerging after
five months buried
in the snow

darkness, becoming thinner and more feeble, with only a daily
plate of porridge for warmth, with no certainty that relief was on
its way or would ever come. He was getting near the limit,
though he would still get closer. But he wasn't doing it merely
because it was a job; not only for the British Arctic Air Route
Expedition, or for his Country, or for Mollie. Still less was he
here for empty, negative reasons. He may have had an ascetic
streak in him, a touch of self-denial, a relic of his Calvinist
ancestors perhaps. Remotely he could have seen the ice-cap
station as a penance, an antidote to the easy life, a rejection of
luxury and wealth, a private way of escaping the security he had
inherited and—if it must, or could, be done—salving the
Courtauld conscience. 'If only I could rake up some of its slimy
past and do some subtle blackmail on it,' he had written not long
ago, disgusted with his family's complacency. At least he would
show that one member could break from the rut and strip to the
barest minimum. Yet he wasn't spurning life. The explorer who
first crossed the Greenland ice cap, Nansen, said that without
privation there would be no struggle, and without struggle no
life. Another polar man, Cherry-Garrard, described exploring as
the physical expression of the intellectual passion. August was
no abject hermit, no drop-out lapsing into a state of purposeless,
mindless passivity. Actively, obstinately, his faith in a slender
idea defied the vast cold death-mass of the ice cap. And his
questions, though framed in doubt because he was not a dogmatic
man, gave their own answers.

Do we in fact morally bury ourselves in fleeing from the world?
Do we simply rot or grow rank like some plant thrown over the
garden wall? Or do we rather come nearer to reality, see more
clearly the great purpose behind it all, in stripping our souls of
the protection of our friends and in putting from us the
pleasures of the body? How little the worries of the world
seem to one in such a situation as this; how grand and awful
the things that are here, the things that grip the heart with
fear, the forces that spin the universe through space. In leaving

6

behind the transitory hopes and fears of pathetic humanity,
does one come closer to the things that abide, the forces which
endure?

On 7 March he returned to more pressing things: 'I reckon,
unless something has gone wrong, the relief should arrive
between the 15th and the end of the month. One can only trust
in God.' By 15 March, with less than two gallons of paraffin left,
he had reduced his food to less than a pound a day, which he
found sufficient as he took no exercise and had little appetite,
and allowed himself the lamp for only brief periods: 'In short
lighted intervals am reading *Forsyte Saga* again. Extremely
good.' But the winter was passing and at midday the sun was
now so bright outside that he had to wear dark glasses. The relief
party must surely be approaching. At pessimistic moments he
thought of the things that might go wrong to stop them—they
had all fallen into a crevasse, an epidemic had killed the dogs, a
fire at the hut had destroyed the sledges and harness—but he
knew it was irrational and that as soon as the weather allowed
they would come.

On the night of 17 March the snow forced its way through the
hatch in the roof of the igloo and filled it again. He tried to burrow
through but failed. He thought of cutting a hole up through the
roof of the tunnel, but the snow on top was probably eight feet
deep and he knew he could never do it. He tried to clear the
entrance to the second igloo, blocked by snow from his diggings,
and escape that way. Scraping and squirming he reached the
igloo and started to cut a shaft up towards the surface. There was
a deep drift above and he began to wonder if he would be able to
reach high enough, but after five feet he cut through into daylight and scrambled out. It was good to be in the open air. The
next problem was how to close the shaft. It was too high to be
stopped up with an empty ration box, like the other, and if he
dug the snow away at the top to shorten it a hollow would be left
to form a snow trap: 'Then I shall be sealed in for good.'

Somehow with a ration box he made a makeshift hatch that

worked for a while. But on 22 March as he feared—as he expected, perhaps—the worst happened: a gale blew, the snow drifted, the hole was covered. Soon there was such a weight of frozen snow on top of the box that he could no longer push it up: 'So I am completely buried. Paraffin has v. nearly run out and things are generally pretty dismal.' It made things no better that, so far as he could tell, the weather was bright and fine on top.

When he realized he couldn't get out there were three things that frightened him: the accumulation of snow on the roof, now that he could no longer clear it off, would crush the tent; the air would become fouled, with nothing but the ventilator pipe at the top of the tent, and eventually poison him; and the relief party, as he couldn't keep a look out for them, might never find the station.

Soon he was reassured. The tent didn't collapse, though it creaked and sagged; the snow outside was almost up to the top and he believed that once the surface was level any further drifts would blow straight past. Nor was he being poisoned, perhaps due to a down-draught in the ventilator or to fresh air seeping through the snow. As to being missed by the relief party, he trusted to their navigation and to the Union Jack on its pole. So there was nothing to worry about: 'It was clearly futile to get anxious, when by no possible endeavour on my part could I make any difference to the course of events.'

His thoughts turned to home and family; he wished he knew how they all were. Once again he took out Mollie's last letter to read: 'It is the only thing left to do that gives me real pleasure.' Had he known he was to be entombed like this he would have brought all her letters and photographs with him to the ice cap. Now the prospect of getting back and seeing her again seemed too heavenly an event to ever happen: 'However, God has kept me going so far, so perhaps He will see me the rest of the way.'

The most annoying part of being buried was that he had to give up the weather observations. Who would ever get another chance like this? It was nice to be spared the three-hourly battles to reach the instruments and instead to lie listening to a blizzard

raging above, knowing there was no need to dress up and go
into it and undress and thaw out afterwards, but the observations
were the whole object of the ice-cap station. They had imposed
an external function on him which now was missing. To stop
them meant that all the efforts of hauling supplies up on to the
ice cap were wasted, and his own struggles pointless. Without
a job he had no purpose; the sense of uselessness returned.
The best he could do was estimate the wind force from the
noise overhead and take readings from the barometer in the
tent.

Men in confinement have found comfort and stability in
routine. With no clear future to focus on, with the time dimension
lost, a prisoner's horizon shrinks to the small-scale pattern of his
daily life. Each brief incident is followed by a long empty interval
of expectation before the next. Geoffrey Jackson wrote,

> The captive requires two classes of routine, corresponding to
> two distinct human needs—the need to break up his day and
> the need to fill up his day . . . Just as the traveller in a snow-
> storm survives the mortal danger of wandering in a circle by
> taking even the shortest bearings from one visible tree to the
> next, so the captive must break up his day into stages from
> one to the other of which he can progress without vertigo,
> emotional, intellectual, even spiritual.

Meals, Jackson found, were very important but not only for the
food. The pain of an empty stomach was nothing to the pain of
an empty mind or an empty space of time.

For August the blank hours ahead must have become more
desolate now that they were no longer marked by a regular time-
table. The observations had been landmarks in time, the central
habits of his life which now he would have to do without. But
though he possessed great self-control and mental energy, he
wasn't a methodical man. Any form of discipline cut against his
nature. He didn't plan his days, he could be disorganized, forget-
ful, unpractical. Afterwards it was suggested by other explorers

that he need never have got snowed up, or anyway with a daily spell of digging he could have kept an exit open—even if he had left his spade outside and however weak he was—if he had really wanted to. Anyone else, they said, would have somehow fought his way out. But he simply didn't bother. How else explain a man of such ingenuity resigning himself to a dark little hole in the ice, risking unnecessary anguish and danger? Yet perhaps the truth wasn't so simple; perhaps the test, to be fully valid, had to have another twist.

Occasionally he crawled through the tunnel, now choked with compressed snow, and scratched away at the roof of one of the igloos with a knife. Vaguely he had an idea that if the relief didn't arrive before his food ran out he would have to excavate himself and walk back to the base alone. But soon the snow became as hard as concrete and he couldn't work for more than an hour or so at a time; cutting a hole out would have been a long job and he was optimistic if he thought he could ever reach the coast. Gradually, with inactivity and undernourishment, he was gripped by an inertia as relentless as the cold. He could only lie in the darkness imagining what was going on in the world and waiting for release. Sometimes to cheer himself he sang snatches of Gilbert and Sullivan and songs he had learnt with Mollie. In his Gestapo cell Christopher Burney had done the same: 'As a rule, unless I was too interested in my own thoughts, I embarked on a musical programme to conclude the day. Being no singer, even to my own taste, I whistled every tune I could remember.'

One day August kept the lamp burning long enough to write the most yearning, wistful page of his whole diary:

The following pleasures I should like to have granted most, if wishing were any good. One: sitting in an armchair before dinner, in front of a roaring fire, listening to Mollie playing and singing. Two: eight o'clock on a fine summer morning at sea, at the helm of a small boat, a fresh breeze blowing, all sail set, with Mollie and a smell of breakfast coming up to say good morning. Three: just having got into bed with clean sheets and ditto pyjamas. Four: bright autumn morning, eating an apple in the garden before breakfast (an enormous one—kippers, poached eggs, kidneys and mushrooms, cold partridge). Five: getting into a hot bath.

On Easter Sunday he wrote, 'Now been here alone four months. No sign of relief. Only about a cupful of paraffin left and one or two candles. Have to lie in darkness almost all the time. Chocolate finished and tobacco almost. What a change from last Easter.' Knowing too well the details of his own day, he tried to picture Mollie's—walking, living, sleeping—and for the first time addressed her direct: 'If it were not for having you to think about as I lie in the dark and can't sleep, life would be intolerable. I wonder what you are doing. If I could be sure you were happy I wouldn't mind. But I trust in God absolutely. I am sure He doesn't mean me to die alone here.'

Eight days later, on 13 April, he finished his last pipeful of tobacco: 'There is now precious little left to live for.' Conditions in the tent had become rapidly more unpleasant. He could only afford to light the lamp for meals—porridge just warmed up for breakfast, biscuits and margarine and uncooked pemmican for lunch and supper—and the tent was now very cold. The walls, bulging inwards from the weight of snow, were lined with hoar frost that hung in icicles, reducing the space still further; they dripped, or pieces dropped on him in the dark. Condensation turned to ice in his sleeping-bag, so that his feet froze and he had to take off his socks and warm them with his hands. The lamp, when he lit it, smoked because of its broken mantle and everything was covered in a film of grime. He could no longer dispose of his own rubbish, and he hadn't had a bath or clean clothes for many months. When he first took over the station he had put it into a shipshape order which had already yielded to chaos and was now giving way to squalor. 'The comfort of the house,' as he put it, 'was much reduced.'

Yet far from despairing, he was sustained by 'a curious growing feeling of security'. At the beginning there had been obvious doubts and dangers, and over the weeks fresh ones had appeared.

> But as each month passed without relief, I felt more and more certain of its arrival. By the time I was snowed in I had no doubts on the matter, which was a great comfort to my mind. I will not attempt any explanation of this, but leave it as a fact, which was very clear to me during that time, that while power-less to help myself, some outer force was in action on my side and I wasn't fated to leave my bones on the Greenland ice cap.

As at other uneasy moments of his life, he found relief in the sea, this time in his imagination and confined to a line or two of his diary: 'I wonder if *Cariad* is cruising now. What wouldn't I give to be aboard her and eating a beef and onion pudding.' But he ached for Mollie: 'I would give an eye to be home now and with you, my own, and see you yourself instead of only your poor old pipe, for which I have no tobacco.' He clutched the pipe, her present, as a fetish. Likewise Geoffrey Jackson would put his hand under his mattress to feel the shoes that had once stood on a carpet beside his wife and one day, he was sure, would walk down a London street with her again.

In a typically modest and understated chapter of *Northern Lights*, the expedition book, August said there was nothing against leaving a man alone provided that he volunteered for it himself, that he was certain of his shelter and food and ultimate relief, and that he had plenty to occupy his mind. He saw no reason why a normal man, with every element of doubt removed, shouldn't live indefinitely in perfect peace and calm. But he warned that the remotest risks, by being brooded on, can become grave dangers; so the man should have 'an active, imaginative mind, but not be of a nervous disposition'. It was a fair prescrip-tion for himself.

Nobody has done quite the same as August Courtauld but another polar explorer, three years later, came near it and for similar reasons. In the Antarctic winter of 1934 when Richard

Byrd, leader of an American expedition, was faced with having to close a remote weather station on an ice shelf or leave one man alone in it, he decided to stay himself. 'I really wanted to go for the experience's sake,' he admitted, and spoke of 'one man's desire to know that kind of experience to the full, to be by himself for a while and to taste peace and quiet and solitude long enough to find out how good they really are.' He was alone for four and a half months, but though he came nearer to death than August, the conditions he lived in were very different. His hut was palatial in comparison with the Greenland tent. He had a gramophone on which he played Beethoven symphonies and a wireless on which he kept contact with his base. He received a personal message direct from President Roosevelt in the White House, and when he was cooking flapjacks which kept sticking to the pan he asked for advice by wireless and it came back from the chef at the Waldorf in New York.

On 20 April, with almost no paraffin, only one candle left and one of his feet swelling up ('hope it isn't scurvy'), August lay in the dark planning the perfect yacht and the perfect meal. On 26 April ('everything running out') he was down to his last two biscuits, wondering what he would do for water when he had no paraffin for melting snow, and filling his pipe with tea leaves to smoke what he could no longer drink. On 1 May ('no sign of relief') he had finished the biscuits and candles. When he tried to make a lamp with a tin of ski wax and a piece of string it only burnt for a few minutes, giving more smoke than light. By all reckoning, the rest of his food should have given out too, but he still had a little pemmican and margarine and a few drops of lemon juice. Soon, as he wrote in his last diary entry before the long solitude was broken, he would have to think of trying to get out and walking to the coast.

Perhaps he really thought he could have got there; he didn't know about the German and the Eskimo who had failed. Probably it was a warning to himself, an expression of the futility; even a reminder, unconscious or not, of a famous sacrifice less than twenty years earlier at the other end of the world. Captain Oates, that gallant officer and English gentleman, had left the tent, telling his companions, 'I'm just going outside and may be some time,' and had walked away into the blizzard. August must have known that he wouldn't have got very far either.

Chapter 8

Rescue

CHAPMAN'S PARTY that left August at the ice-cap station in December had had a terrible journey back to the base. After that, as August well realized, all ice-cap travel was impossible for the rest of the winter. Plans for sledge journeys along the coast were also given up; the pack ice in the sea never froze firmly enough to the new ice in the fjords.

The long months—the short twilit days—were spent waiting for the spring; making hunting trips, training dog teams, studying geology, ornithology, meteorology and a pleasant form of anthropology among the Eskimos. Lemon kept his regular wireless watch, Riley conducted a church service on Sundays, Chapman fell through a hole in the frozen sea, D'Aeth broke his arm in an aeroplane propeller, Lindsay's bathtub was blown away in a gale, a troublesome dog was butchered and eaten (which made a nice change from seal meat and tinned beef) and the aerial masts fell down and were put up and fell down again. In the hut the men played bridge and poker, listened to the wireless, read, smoked, argued, laid bets on almost every trivial event of the day, and ran a perpetual house-party for visiting Eskimos.

At Christmas, feasting more lavishly than August, they toasted his health, sang carols and danced with the girls. They opened a surprise parcel from the Professor of Geography at Cambridge, containing fresh gramophone records and novels, and received wireless messages from their families and the Prince of Wales. On New Year's Eve, while August was making his list of resolutions, another party in the hut was brightened by special greetings from the BBC. A few days later one of the aeroplanes was smashed by a gale. Soon afterwards, as daylight grew longer, stores were taken up to the Big Flag in preparation for ice-cap journeys in the spring.

On 8 February, when August was celebrating his father's birthday with boiled rice and toffee, D'Aeth and Chapman tied a sack of letters, books and assorted luxuries for him between the skis of the second aeroplane. They took off from the frozen fjord, climbed all too easily over Buggery Bank and set course for the ice-cap station. Looking down they saw the surface flecked with the shadows of drifts formed by winds and crosswinds, in which the flags marking the route, even if they were not already snowed over, were hidden. They wondered what the station would look like, but never discovered; a band of thick cloud, too high to fly over, forced them back. On their return they sighted a sledge party that had gone up to retrieve the wireless abandoned three months earlier; the dump had been four feet high and well flagged, but it was lost for ever.

On 25 February Cozens and Scott made a second flight to look for the ice-cap station. After flying what they thought was the right distance inland they saw nothing, but the return took only a third as long and they realized they had been flying against a strong headwind; they hadn't nearly reached the station. Next day that aeroplane too was badly damaged when the ski under-carriage hit an ice hummock. Both planes were eventually repaired but the trial flight to Canada and back, which was to be the climax of the expedition, never happened.

In *Northern Lights* Chapman wrote:

By this time Courtauld's parents and others at home were getting rather worried, and not realizing what the conditions were like in Greenland were naturally wondering why no one was being sent up to relieve him. In consequence of this a relief party set off somewhat earlier than they would otherwise have started, as the gales had by no means abated. On March 1st Scott and Riley left for the ice-cap station.

The ground beyond the Big Flag was more difficult than ever; the first day's travel was like sledging up and down stairs. After only a mile, with one sledge wrecked, Scott and Riley gave up and next day were back in the hut. They started again with Lindsay and a third sledge, but almost at once ran into a blizzard and couldn't even find the Big Flag. They searched for three days, sinking waist deep in soft snow, then retreated.

On 9 March Scott started a third time for the ice-cap station with Riley and Lindsay. To save weight they carried a minimum of food and fuel and took no wireless time-signal set; though they could find their latitude with theodolite or sextant, they couldn't check their watches for an accurate longitude. By dead reckoning, using compass and sledge wheel, they would aim for the latitude of the station at a point to the east, then steer due west until they hit it.

They were treated to gales, blizzards and surface conditions of every adverse kind. For the last volleys of winter the ice cap had saved all its tricks and it wasn't till 26 March that the three men reached the latitude they wanted. Now at last they were approaching the station. But what state would they find August in—for surely they couldn't miss him altogether? One night, at about the time he was finally snowed up, Scott had a dream of August arriving alone at the base; at first he seemed perfectly all right, but he turned out to be mad.

For more than a fortnight, backwards and forwards, east and west, along the latitude of the station, they hunted for the Union Jack that marked the tent and its lone occupant. It was a miserable, heart-breaking time. One man's life depended on three men's courage and skill and judgement, as well as on their luck. For days on end they were held immobile by storms, unable to search; to save paraffin for the station they spared none for their own warmth and often lay in their tents in a temperature of forty degrees below zero. Sometimes, encouraged by better weather, they would dig out the sledges and strike camp, to find that by the time they got going the weather had changed again and they couldn't see a dozen yards. Even when they could get an observation of the sun it was an uncertain business; fingers froze to the metal of the theodolite unless they were covered in clumsy gloves, breath turned to frost on the lens, and the mercury bowl for the sextant developed a scum of ice. Methodically, stopping often and standing on a sledge to scan the limits of visibility, they travelled twenty miles along the latitude, then back again a mile to the north, and once more a mile to the south. There was nothing in sight but the endless blankness of the ice cap. Some-where—somewhere very close—was the station, but it never showed itself. August Courtauld, though at one moment perhaps no further than the other side of the nearest snowdrift and singing Gilbert and Sullivan to himself as he waited for them in his smothered tent, might as well have been at the South Pole.

On Easter Sunday, when Scott and his two men believed they were within four miles of August (when he wrote in his diary that there was no sign of relief and his chocolate was finished), they opened a tin of marmalade for their Easter tea. But already they were losing hope. Lindsay confessed he couldn't under-stand why they hadn't seen the station, Riley comforted himself by reading the Communion service in his prayer book, Scott killed the first dog to feed to the rest. They could kill them all one by one, then haul the sledges themselves. They could stay another fortnight quartering the ground and in time would probably find the station. If not, August's food might run out before they could get back to the base to organize another relief party, and it would be too late. Blindly they went on for five more days, but on 10 April, with nerves and muscles wrung out, they admitted they were beaten. In an agony of conflicting doubts Scott decided to retreat while there was still time. 'If we can get back quickly now,' he wrote in his diary, 'there may be another chance.' At midnight a week later they stumbled into the hut to be greeted by the dreaded question: 'Have you got August?'

Watkins listened to their story, told them they were right to come back, then at once made plans to set off again. The winter was nearly over, the weather was already better, they would take a wireless time-signal set and find the station by exact navigation. The three men who had come back after forty days on the ice cap, climbing dizzy with fatigue into their bunks, were not so hopeful.

> Gino would find the station [Scott wrote], but would he find Courtauld alive and sane? When I shut my eyes I saw the ice cap as it had been while we were hunting up and down. The shadows of the snowdrifts had been as confusing as camouflage. But we must have passed close to the station. We would have seen it if it were still above the surface. Therefore the tent with August Courtauld in it must be buried. And people who are buried are generally dead.

On 21 April, with Chapman and Rymill and three sledges, Watkins started for the ice-cap station. Before leaving the base he sent a wireless message to the Royal Geographical Society in London reporting that Scott's party had failed to find the station due to the weather, that August still had plenty of food, that there was no reason to suspect disaster and that another relief party led by himself was on its way, with sledging rations for five weeks. Watkins ended the message: 'There is always the possibility that Courtauld is not alive, or unwell, in which case the station is probably completely covered.' In his kitbag he packed a prayer book—in the same way, as Scott said, that he would carry an umbrella in London on cloudless summer days. He left Lemon in charge of the base and told him that if there was any sign of a relief expedition being sent from home, to try and stop it, and to assure everybody that nothing could be done that wasn't already being done in Greenland.

They travelled as fast as they could, checking their course by sun and stars. At first the weather was brilliant—too brilliant, and Chapman found that sunburn was even more painful than frostbite. When the temperature dropped and a freezing wind blew on their raw lips and peeling faces the degree of torture rose. On 4 May, the thirteenth day from the base, they knew they were close to the station but a gale made it impossible to search or take sights. On the 5th—that bright spring morning—they got a fix with theodolite and wireless time-signal that put them one mile north-west of the tent. Spreading out on skis, each with a dog on a lead, the three men approached their buried friend.

On 22 April, the day after Watkins left the base and just as he had feared, a wireless message came from London conveying the anxiety of the Royal Geographical Society. Lemon replied, as coolly as he could, that Watkins didn't consider the position desperate and everything possible was being done. Two days later *The Times* carried a report, solemn and restrained, under the headline, 'Anxiety For Safety Of Mr. Courtauld'.

August's parents were on board a liner returning from America. Though they knew their son too well to be alarmed, they cabled to Captain Rayner, secretary of the expedition committee and soon to be married to August's sister, to arrange a relief expedition, whatever the cost. Rayner first tried Canada and the United States, inquiring about aeroplanes capable of flying over Greenland and petrol supplies in the far north. The answer came that the perils of Arctic flying were extreme and there was no plane to make such a flight. So Rayner went to Sweden where he chartered a special plane with skis as well as floats, fitted with wireless and piloted by a famous Arctic airman.

The world loves a hero. Taking their cue from *The Times*, and weary with the budget and the King's bronchitis, other papers grabbed the chance of lurid journalism and irresistible clichés. Greenland's icy mountain at last made news, every day for a fortnight. Chilling in a way, it was a story to warm an editor's heart. 'Millionaire's Son Alone On Ice', the *Daily Express* announced, and was echoed by the *Evening Stardard*: 'Marooned In An Arctic Waste'. The *Daily Mail* knew when it had a lucky break in a dull season: 'Few stories of Arctic endeavour have combined so many elements of drama,' and it tried to put its readers in the picture: 'The long night of the north fell and froze the whole land in its impenetrable grip.' The *Sunday Dispatch* spoke of 'Father's SOS From Liner—No Expense To Be Spared'. The *Evening Standard* interviewed Mrs Courtauld soon after she disembarked: 'Mother Says, I Have No Fear'. The *Daily Express* discovered that the marooned explorer had a sweetheart: 'Meanwhile there is a girl waiting in an Essex village'. The *Daily Telegraph* also pounced on Mollie: 'The Woman Who Waits . . . Mr. Courtauld has always been keen on exploring, she said.' (A French paper—apocryphally or not—is said to have sighed over Mademoiselle Augustine Courtauld, the only woman on the expedition, deserted by the men.) When the story flagged the *Evening Standard*, forgetting that their hero had no wireless, invented three desperate words tapped out by him into the ether: 'Absolutely Without Food'.

It was an agonizing fortnight for August's family, worst of all for Mollie. A few papers tried to rectify Fleet Street's excesses. *The Times* said, 'It is to be regretted that such irresponsible reports should be circulated, as they must add to the distress of Mr. Courtauld's relatives and friends.' The *Daily Telegraph* reported the opinion of a veteran Arctic explorer: 'I do not share the view that Mr. Courtauld is in imminent danger of starvation . . . Far be it from me to raise false hopes for his safety, but explorers facing worse odds have come through with flying colours. Mr. Courtauld, imperturbable as ever, will, I think, turn up safely.' The same belief was held by most of August's friends. They knew the danger he was in; they also knew August. He had been in scrapes before, he could look after himself, he was the one man who would be sure to survive. He would be found by Watkins, they had no doubt, smoking his filthy pipe and asking what the fuss was about. Their confidence was some comfort to Mollie. Letters poured in, many from strangers offering help and suggestions and telling of their dreams and prayers. But some people, including James Wordie and Francis Rodd, privately believed there was no hope.

For the greater public the drama had to be played to the bitter end. But rescue was on its way. 'Airman To Dare Arctic Seas', the *Daily Herald* cried. 'On Friday or Saturday the eyes of a starving man, marooned alone in his tiny snow-hut on the lofty ice cap of Greenland, may be gladdened by the sight of an aeroplane swooping from the east.'

The brave Swedish airman wasn't the only rescuer. August's father bought a second plane and engaged an ex-officer of the Royal Air Force to join the hunt. (When the officer was prosecuted for speeding through London he explained in court that he was on his way to rescue Mr Courtauld and was given a mitigated fine of £1—but still he reached the Arctic too late.) The Danish government, which already had a ship cruising off Iceland to give wireless directions to the Swede, sent another to the edge of the Greenland pack ice with a professor and a seaplane on board. (When the professor took off in the plane he crashed after a flight of four minutes.) At the same time one of the British Arctic Air Route Expedition's own Gypsy Moths, repaired with spare parts, driftwood, shirt cloth and some clever needlework by the Eskimo women, was in the air again. Thus, unknown to the man at the centre of the clamour and to his subsequent fury, but to the newspapers' delight, two ships and four aeroplanes were involved in his relief.

Since Watkins had set off from the base with Chapman and Rymill nothing had been heard of them. On 4 May (when the Swede, having landed on the Greenland coast, was changing his floats for skis before making his first flight over the ice cap) the three explorers were already camped close to the place where the station ought to be, hoping for clear weather next morning.

That day, as ignorant of his friends' closeness as of the London headlines, and lying in the tent with nothing better to do, August found that his thoughts kept returning to tomorrow's date. All day he wondered what it was about 5 May that made it so famous, but he couldn't think of anything that had happened on it—it wasn't a battle or anybody's birthday. Had he counted up he would have found that it was going to be the 150th day since beginning his long lone watch on 6 December. It was also to be the day when the paraffin finally ran dry. The greatest day of his life, he called it later.

But he didn't know about it yet. And the world too was in ignorance, if not suspense. No news was bad news; and bad news, in Fleet Street, was good. That same day, while *The Times* said there was no cause for alarm, the *Evening Stardard* announced, 'There are now *four* Englishmen lost in the icy wastes of Greenland.'

The primus gave its last gasp as I was melting water for the morning meal. I was lying in my bag after this so-called meal of a bit of pemmican and margarine and had just decided that I should have to start to walk back on June 1st if I could get out, when suddenly there was an appalling noise like a bus going by, followed by confused yelling. I nearly jumped out of my skin. Was it the house falling in at last?

5 May 1931: the greatest day of August's life. His account of it bears the flavour of the moment, dazed but exuberant:

A second later I realized the truth. It was somebody, some real human voice, calling down the ventilator. It was a very wonderful moment. I couldn't think what to do or say. I yelled back some stuttering remarks that seemed quite futile for the occasion. 'Hooray!' they shouted. 'Are you all right?' 'Yes, thank God you've come, I'm perfectly fit.' 'Thank God,' they said.

The three young men on top, standing in that desolate spot on that bright May morning and hearing the voice of their friend below, didn't hide their gladness. The voice was tremulous, according to Chapman, and no wonder: for five months it had been used only for occasional private song recitals, it was out of practice, and it was taken by surprise. But to dispel their most dreadful fears, it was the voice of a normal man. And he, so

stunningly rescued and restored to normality, found that his joy
was shared: 'They were as relieved as I was. The whole world
seemed turned inside out. At one moment I was lying in the dark
wondering how ever I was going to see anybody again or ever
get home, and the next, home was in sight. It was bright sunshine outside, they said.'

After taking photographs of the smothered station—the
tattered flag and the tops of a few instruments sticking above the
endless plateau where, last time they saw it, there had been a
tent and two igloos ringed by a high snow wall—they began
digging with a spade. The level of the snow at the top of the
tent, beside the life-saving stump of pipe, was only a foot or
two thick and soon they were through the snow blocks of the
outer shell. With a few slashes of his knife, Watkins ripped open
the two layers of canvas.

Looking down, they saw a bearded man in a sleeping-bag,
long-haired, hollow-cheeked, smoke-stained. Round him were
the remains of his food and the debris of his cramped home.
More cramped than they remembered it; the original tent, ten
feet across, had shrunk to an eight-foot hole lined with ice.

Looking up, August was blinded by the light. He had last
been outside in a winter blizzard and for six weeks his eyes had
focused on nothing further than the dark frozen walls of his cell.
All at once, in an explosion of brilliance, the spring broke from
a dazzling sky, almost too much to bear. Watkins and Chapman
and Rymill—a sudden shock of company—were bursting from
above: 'The next moment they had dropped through the hole and
we were grasping hands and thanking God that the job was done.'

They put a pair of the darkest goggles on him and hauled him
up through the hole. He wobbled on his feet a little and began
staggering on skis towards the three men's camp, until Rymill
went ahead to fetch a sledge for him. A warm dry tent, a roaring
primus, hot food, a bright lamp, three friends who seemed nearly
as happy as he was, with so much to tell and be told—it was all
too suddenly and wonderfully overwhelming. He could hardly
eat and didn't sleep at all.

Next morning they treated him to a big bowl of porridge and went back to the buried tent to collect the weather records and instruments (fifty-three degrees below zero was the lowest temperature recorded during the winter). Many things—clothes and books that had been precious companions—had to be left behind. Even food was abandoned, to August's distress. They had brought five weeks' rations, they had taken only two weeks to reach the station, they were in a hurry to get back to the base, they wanted to lighten the loads and give him a ride all the way. But it was no fun watching them make a bonfire of all the rubbish and set fire to it with a tin of paraffin, a tin he would yesterday have given a fortune for.

Then they started for the base, in cloudless weather. August, whose feet were still painful, sat on a pile of sleeping-bags writing his diary and reading *The Count of Monte Cristo* as he was pulled over the brilliant ice cap: 'It is more wonderful than words can express to be free, out of that dark place under the snow and to be really going home.' The line of flags was totally buried, so one man went ahead on skis and the last man took compass bearings on him to check the course. August said it was like sailing across a dead white sea, but it must also have re-minded him of riding a camel across the Sahara. All day they travelled under a blazing sun, the endless horizon sometimes broken by fantastic mirages—castles, bridges, mountains that didn't exist. Their faces were blistered with sunburn and their eyes ached with the glare of blue sky and dazzling snow. At night they pitched their tents, and over unlimited food and tobacco talked of the winter's events and planned the summer journeys.

August, who recovered quickly and seemed to forget—or never mentioned—how near the limit he had been, had no doubt what he would do next: 'Once I get to the base I shall stay there. I have had enough of sledging, ice caps and boat journeys.' He didn't know how soon he would change his mind.

At midday on 7 May, the second day of their journey to the coast, the astonished explorers heard the noise of an engine and a big Swedish aeroplane swooped over them. It dropped a load of food which they didn't need, though the chocolate and fresh ptarmigan were welcome, and also some letters. Then it flew back towards the coast.

From the letters they learnt for the first time about the fuss. August was disgusted: 'We gather that the most frightful chaos is taking place . . . Aeroplanes, icebreakers, patrol boats of all sorts and nationalities are pouring in with the idea of rescuing me. Nothing can stop this absurd hysteria . . . It really is too ridiculous.' He particularly hoped that his parents had had nothing to do with it.

They pressed on as quickly as they could. On the fourth day the coast mountains rose above the horizon ahead, the first solid land August had seen for nearly seven months: 'Grand sight to see the old mountain tops coming up above the snow.' That evening they passed the Big Flag: 'Dumped all the food there and then started off at the gallop for HOME.' It was dark but they couldn't stop, whipping the dogs down the glacier till at last through the mountains they saw the frozen sea. The winter journey up to the station had taken thirty-nine days, the return took only five. They had to slide backwards down Buggery Bank. August's sledge broke through a snow bridge and he got his foot soaked in an icy stream, but it felt hot after anything on the ice cap. The sun was coming up when they reached the edge of the fjord, the winter snow was melting off the southern slopes of the hills, there were wheatears and snow buntings singing for the four explorers—especially for the one who for so long had seen no living thing.

They sledged quietly up to the door of the hut and burst in, demanding breakfast. The others rolled out of their bunks and grabbed August's hand: 'It was indeed a great moment . . . I was seized by the photographic fiends and filmed, snapped and close-upped until I was giddy.' He shouldn't have been surprised by the spontaneous gladness of his friends, but they could hardly have expected his own self-effacement. As soon as he saw Scott, Lindsay and Riley he apologized for having dragged them out on to the ice cap, searching for him. He was sorry to have caused so much trouble. It was typical of the view he took of the long winter's vigil, typical of his efforts to minimize the achievement —'to dispel the strange ideas of danger and risk in leaving a man in such a situation,' as he put it. He had done nothing unusual, he was perfectly sane: 'There are many men, trappers and the like, who live by themselves for most of the year. An accident is very rare among these men, nor are their minds usually deranged.'

At the base he heard in detail about the rescue. It was ironic that it should all end in a way so repugnant to his taste. The last five months, despite their pain, were unique and precious. Solitude had become a personal possession, almost a friend. Confinement had brought freedom. In that tiny ice-hole, stripped of the common demands of society, his vision had reached farther than ever before, to the frontier of the mind and spirit. Knowing himself better, he was free of illusions, free of past unconfidence and future uncertainty. He belonged out there, pushing beyond trodden ground, carrying experience into the unknown, not stopping at the ordinary boundary or caring whether his adventure was any use to anybody else. As an explorer, he had expressed himself on the Greenland ice cap as fully as a painter on canvas, a musician in sound, or a poet with words. He had passed the test, he had done 'something really big', he would have nothing more to fear from life. Henceforth he could claim a new wisdom and a new humility. The feeling that he had once been to the limit and glimpsed the other side would always stay with him, lodged in his spirit and inducing tolerance, generosity, love.

The Englishman kept his emotions submerged. The American, Richard Byrd, was more voluble about his winter alone and probably spoke for them both: 'I did take away something that I had not fully possessed before: appreciation of the sheer beauty and miracle of being alive, and a humbler set of values . . . A man doesn't begin to attain wisdom until he recognizes that he is no longer indispensable.' But for August it was sickening that such an intensely private experience should now be turned into a public triumph. After the isolation the contrast of his return must have sharply recalled his feelings of last autumn. The crowded base was noisy, oppressive, disturbing. Solitude had gone, abandoned in the little tent in that Arctic desert with the other remnants of the winter.

Another Englishman, in other circumstances, put it as August might have done if he could have found the words. On being released from the Gestapo prison and sent to a concentration camp after eighteen months in solitary confinement, Christopher Burney wrote,

I was reluctant to leave. If my door was opened and I was told that I could go quietly wherever I liked, I would have gone with joy, but probably to some place where I knew nobody and would be able to remain aloof. But I could imagine the noise and promiscuity of a camp, and it repelled me. I knew that so many months of solitude, though I had allowed them to torment me at times, had been in a sense an exercise in liberty. For, by absolving me from the need either to consider practical problems of living or to maintain the many unquestioned assumptions which cannot conveniently be abandoned in social life, I had been left free to drop the spectacles of the near-sighted and to scan the horizon of existence. And I believed that I had seen something there. But it was only a glimpse, a remote and tenuous apprehension of what lay behind the variety and activity of life, and I was afraid that I would lose sight of it as soon as I was forced to turn my attention back to my immediate surroundings. Also I had built up a kind of security. The cell door was a battlement behind which I practised habits, and however futile they were they had become familiar from long and unvaried usage and represented an element of stability which was more desirable than even a hopeful hazard.

Burney was taken from his cell and put with three other prisoners who plied him with questions. He could hardly speak, but listened to their chatter and tried to recapture normality. From a bus, being herded to a town, he gazed at great spaces of land-scape, beautiful fields and trees and sky; bewildered by the vast and wonderful scene, troubled at this new test put upon the thin faith he had acquired in confinement, and paralysed by shock:

> We arrived at Compiègne near nightfall and were crowded together in a shed to spend the night there on the floor. The heaped and jostling bodies oppressed me, and the shouting and singing made me long for silence. But silence and privacy were gone; an episode was ended. Solitude, with its mysteries and adventures, had passed over me like a wave and washed back into the spreading ocean of the past, while the next sea, cold and clamorous, already mounted.

After breakfast in the hut ('hot porridge, real white bread and marmalade served by the women who all seemed frightfully pleased to see me') August washed and shaved off his beard and sent a wireless message to Mollie: 'Got back from ice cap today. Fit as an orchestra. Terribly sorry kept you so long without news. How are you? Send me long wire with news of you and family. Take no notice hysterical rescue nonsense. Relief carried out as part of ordinary programme. No danger. Love.'

Then he went out with Scott to shoot ptarmigan on the dark hills that kept the ice cap back.

Chapter 9

Return

'MY IDEAS are completely liquid,' he wrote to Mollie two days after getting back from the ice cap; liquid perhaps, but pouring into his letters during the summer weeks at the base. He was still sickened by the publicity of his rescue: 'This press rot is all completely obscene . . . The incident was very mere.' He only hoped that Mollie thought no worse of him because of it. Alone at the station he had been all too aware what a rotten time it was for her and considered himself an utter cad for letting her in for it. But from friends he heard that in the panic she had behaved impeccably: 'If you don't mind my saying so, they tell me that you alone kept your head when the papers were trying to frighten everybody and that you had the guts to say that I was all right.' The reason was plain: 'It is because you, like me, without "having religion", know when God doesn't mean to do us down.'

From the chilly tone of a telegram from his parents, he guessed he was in bad odour at home: 'I have been so very rude to everybody about this absurd relief—and I gather the family have spent thousands on it and being in the wrong must make them all angrier—that I don't suppose they will speak to me again.'

He expected to be back in England in three months, by the end of August. If Mollie couldn't meet him off the boat he would invite Mildred Flint instead, an unknown lady from Margate who had sent a telegram saying that she had seen his picture in the *Daily Mirror* and had lost her heart. All her life, Miss Flint said, she had been looking for a husband who didn't mind being left alone to mind the baby, and she would be waiting on the quayside to greet her Arctic hero. (It was some time before he found out that the telegram was sent by members of the expedition.)

By the time he got back, unless Mollie had found somebody better, he expected her to have everything planned for them. His ideas for a house in Suffolk had been modified to a flat in London and 'a really marvellous boat which I am busy designing as a country house'. As for a trip abroad (perhaps he meant a honeymoon), Austria sounded fascinating and he asked Mollie to fix it up. Meanwhile there were things she could send him from London: a decent collar, shirt and tie, some oranges, gramophone records ('fairly highbrow'), sherry, brandy, gym shoes, a photograph of herself and the suet he still craved for, instead of the unwanted suit. If she had time she might look at the new cars, 'the sensible ordinary sorts' like Wolseley, Rover and Humber. But there was a problem: he had read in a paper that the Courtauld firm had crashed, 'so now that the family has poured its money down the drain over this absurd rescue panic I don't suppose we shall have any'.

August's father, not for the first time, was hinting at jobs: 'He always does, poor man, and I always reply by finding some absurd job in Yucatan.' The only thing that briefly attracted him was a partnership in Lloyd's, 'unless anything more amusing turns up,' but he couldn't seriously have considered a life in insurance: 'Jobs seem to me to entail a far greater expenditure of money than they bring in, for which one is expected to get a great kick out of being one of the world's workers. I think the only unselfish thing is not to have a job, thereby allowing someone else to fill a place which one might fill oneself with less efficiency.' When he got home he vaguely intended to start work on a history of Arctic exploration.

On one point, in case rumours had reached Mollie of the goings-on with Eskimo girls at the base, he wanted to reassure her: 'My moral state is of unsullied purity, unblemished even when I was presented with a pair of sealskin slippers to welcome me back.' Rather less gallantly he explained that he had no opportunity for anything else, all the women being already booked. As for Mollie he wrote, 'I hope you are still a good girl and all that sort of thing, though I don't suppose you are.' In her reply ('my precious prawn, I'm so happy now that you have been taken out of your aspic'), Mollie affirmed that her own moral state was as pure as forty snowdrifts.

The early summer passed pleasantly at the base. Azaleas and lilies of the valley and sea pinks flowered among the rocks, Arctic terns whistled over the fjord, and the expedition divided into small survey and exploring parties. Some of them had kayaks made for them, which they launched as soon as the ice melted. A few learnt to roll as expertly as the Eskimos, the others hung upside down in the water until they were rescued.

In July, with the doctor, August went off for a week to finish the map of the fjord and catch fish for the base. It was hard to believe he was in the same land as the ice cap:

> The country is very lovely just now. One walks in valleys deep with moss and grasses, with thick patches of harebells in full bloom and saxifrages of many sorts. All round are the soaring peaks standing clear against the blue unclouded sky, while between them wind the many arms of deep fjords studded with fantastically shaped icebergs. To seaward the pack ice gleams white to the horizon, an occasional great berg, larger than fifty liners, relieving its level expanse. When we feel hungry the Doc goes out with his rod and brings back a fish which is soon sizzling in the frying pan.

For variety they also had tins of Fortnum and Mason soup sent by August's mother.

'Been in Greenland just a year,' he wrote in his diary on 21 July; and a few days later, 'Shall be twenty-seven in a month.' Watkins was now busy with plans for summer journeys before the expedition left for England. One party had already climbed Mount Forel to within a few hundred feet of the top, walking 350 miles on snow shoes. Another was to cross the ice cap to the west coast of Greenland, a third was to sledge down the centre of the ice cap to the south-west coast. Watkins himself, with two others, planned a prodigious journey by open boat from the base to Julianehaab, a port round the southern tip of Greenland 600 miles away.

When August first heard of 'that wonderful boat journey' as Wordie called it—taking an eighteen-foot whaleboat with a three horse-power outboard engine down an unmapped, almost unin-habited, coast that had only once been traversed by a European—he thought it was a mad idea. Fuel for the engine would take up so much room that there would be none left for food; and if the boat was wrecked they would be marooned with no hope of rescue and the choice of wintering on the coast or trying to cross the ice cap at the end of the season, without dogs or proper equipment. Watkins's answer was that they would take hunting kayaks and live off the country like Eskimos, and he practised for weeks in his own kayak until he was confident he could support three men. Then he decided to take two boats and the idea—the adventure—began to seem less crazy; while more and more, instead of merely mapping the coast, the object became to try a novel kind of Arctic travel. Watkins was plausible and persuasive. Lemon agreed to join him; and though August had written in his diary that he had had enough of sledging, ice caps and boat journeys he couldn't refuse, or resist, when Watkins asked him to go too. But he admitted afterwards that he would never have gone with anybody else. 'He could plan with care and execute with audacity,' August once wrote, 'and could not only lead men by the force of his personality but with his charm inspire them to do more than ever they knew was in them.'

It was hard to tell Mollie that he wouldn't be back as soon as she expected: 'It is utterly bloody, I know, but what else can I do? Gino wants another man for his journey, so how can I get out of it on the plea that I want to go home? I feel a frightful rotter about it, but I know what you would have me do in your heart of hearts. You wouldn't have me run out before the show is over.' He tried to convince her that there was no danger:

'Various things may go wrong, but they can only cause delay and not disaster'—which was the nearest he got to warning her that they might not finish the journey before the ice closed in again.

By the middle of August 1931 the expedition was breaking up. Three members had already reached south-west Greenland after a dazzling journey down the ice cap, sometimes hoisting sails on their sledges and skimming over the summer ice; they had then taken a cargo boat for England. Six others had departed direct from the base in the annual ship from Denmark that brought the first stores and mail through the melting pack ice. On the 13th Rymill and Hampton started on their crossing of the ice cap to the west coast of Greenland. Two days later the last three— Watkins, Lemon and August—left the hut they had built a year ago on a little promontory in a lonely fjord; left their Eskimo friends too, sitting on the rocks and weeping.

A journey is like the life of a man [August wrote later]. The labours of its birth are heavy, its youth is full of ideals and hopes, its main course leads swiftly to hard reality and its end, whether of failure or success, is bitter . . . It is here that we realize the futility of our endeavour and the smallness of our achievement . . . For this is the time of parting from the fellow-sharers of our joys and disappointments, parting from the life of grand uncertainty . . . In looking back on a journey, as with the retrospect of our lives, we have a hazy memory of good times, good fellows and bright sunshine . . . One has forgotten, until referring to the diary written up every night in the friendly tent, about the untimely breakdown, the leaky boat, the just-avoided calving of the iceberg, the all but unweathered storm.

He was saying, more or less, that a published account of that boat journey down the Greenland coast with Watkins and Lemon— 600 miles in eight weeks—must separate the achievement from the experience, the triumph from the agony. So far from being a story of 'good times, good fellows and bright sunshine', it was one of near-calamities, strained friendships and terrible weather. The events so sharply recorded in his diary can never have been quite as forgotten as he claimed.

On board the two whaleboats they took three kayaks, three sledges with man harness for crossing the ice cap if necessary, tools, guns and rifles, survey instruments and a wireless transmitter. August also packed Mollie's supply of suet which had at last arrived from England, and soon his puddings became as famous as they were familiar.

For ten days all went well. In warm sunny weather they motored down the coast between islands and icebergs, landing occasionally to set up their instruments and draw their map. While Lemon and August surveyed, Watkins hunted in his kayak, bringing back gulls, ducks, guillemots or with luck a seal. 'At night we would pitch our little tent on some mossy ledge, tying up the boats in a cranny of the rocks.' Then they were stormbound on an island while a fierce wind swooped down from the ice cap and the floes tossed in the sea. It was a week before they got away.

The next delay, in a fjord where an Eskimo family was spending the summer, was due not to the weather but to the charms of local society. Hunting by day—astonishing the Eskimos by his handling of a frail unsteady kayak and his knowledge of the ways of seals—and telling stories by night, Watkins couldn't be dragged away. August grew impatient: 'He said we were going to stay here two days and we have been five already. It is very pleasant but I want to get home.' They stayed more than a week and by the time they moved on the fine weather had broken, never to return. The sea was rough, the rocks and icebergs hazardous: 'The remainder of the journey was a tale of tip and run with the weather.' They had hoped to find a belt of pack ice protecting the coast from the Atlantic Ocean; instead they had only icebergs drifting in from the sea which cut the swell into confused tumbling waves, and floes broken from the glaciers which clogged the coast.

Two days after leaving the Eskimos they woke to heavy rain and a strong wind. August advised waiting for something better but he was overruled. The outboard engines were wet and wouldn't work. After two hours August had one running and towed the second boat with Watkins and Lemon in it. Out of the lee of the islands, with both boats overloaded and rolling dangerously, the rain beating and the wind rising, the engine stopped. They drifted between icebergs and the shore while the sea broke heavily on both sides. Watkins shouted from the other boat and August struggled with the engine. He got it going on one cylinder and they turned back, making for shelter, but it stopped again. Watkins and Lemon rowed and August wrestled with sparking plugs and carburettor, the waves slopping over into his boat. He started the engine and they hobbled past the icebergs. In calmer water he went forward for a bucket to bail out the boat, now half full. At that moment the engine sprang from its bracket and fell into the sea. He saved it but it never worked again. The tow was reversed, Watkins and Lemon rowing furiously and August directing. They passed downwind through a gap between the icebergs and behind an island to the head of a small creek where they camped, 'only just in time, as it then came on to blow properly'. It was Mollie's birthday and August wished he was at home: 'Celebrated by eating her health in suet'—or rather in a suet pudding made with cranberries and porridge.

For three days it rained harder than he had ever seen in Greenland. Whipped by the gale, the sea thundered on icebergs and rocks alike. The boats, already smashed and leaking, tossed and banged at their moorings and filled with water. Everything was drenched, including the instruments. Films were ruined, the wireless seemed unlikely to work again, the bag of porridge oats was under water. New streams plunged down the mountains. It looked like the end of summer.

Watkins talked of abandoning one boat and pressing on with the other, then of giving up the journey and staying there for the winter. On the fourth day, with the storm dying down, he and Lemon went up a hill to look at the sea, leaving August to ruminate and write his diary: 'Gino and Lemon talk of nothing now but plans for wintering.' He believed Watkins had lost his nerve last time they put to sea and didn't want to go on; anyway the other two seemed keener on hunting seals and learning about Eskimos than getting home:

> This is bad news for me. It is the last thing I want to do, but Gino seems to want any excuse for staying and Lemon backs him up. I have said nothing yet, but my opinion is never consulted . . . Why I ever said I would come on this journey I don't know, after my solemn resolve to do no more journeys . . . Those lucky devils who are now at home! So far it has been just as I thought it would be. A continual nervous strain of keeping Lemon in a good temper . . . Reading *Moby Dick* again. V.G.

If they stayed for the winter on the Greenland coast he would have no suitable clothes, few books, no writing materials, no tobacco. Seal meat was their only hope of lasting till next summer. But nothing was as bad as having to wait a year before getting home and thus, as he saw it, letting down his parents and Mollie: 'I broke my word to them all by coming on this journey and I shall feel I can never look any of them in the face again.'

The weather cleared and they spent two days drying out. Once more Watkins wanted to move on, leaving one boat and the wireless behind. Lemon transmitted a last signal saying they might try to cross the ice cap or spend the winter on the coast, carefully not giving their position in case of attracting rescue parties, but the receiver was broken and they never knew whether the message was picked up. Then they found that neither of the outboard engines would work.

Next day August got an engine going and after rough repairs they set off in one boat, more overloaded than ever. To avoid stopping and being unable to start, they kept the fuel tank filled up with a teapot. The boat shipped half a bucketful of water at the slightest wave. Watkins became alarmed, Lemon wanted

The expedition team: Gino Watkins is centre front, with August on his right

Mollie

Mollie and the children

to turn back. August drove on and in calmer weather they made good progress:

> We are well over halfway now. If we can only get half a dozen more good travelling days we shall be there. Lemon gets more impossible every day. He is continuously raising objections to going on . . . Gino said tonight he was going to have a row if he continued. This is amusing, after warning me repeatedly before we started on no account to have any row.

With signs of another storm, they camped in a cove near an abandoned Eskimo settlement and fitted canvas screens to the sides of the boat. 'Fornicator continued all night. Tent flapping and shaking.' At two in the morning Watkins whispered that he could hear a bear outside the tent. Unluckily they had left the guns in the boat. Further gloom fell at breakfast when the last of the sugar ran out, but August found that the others disliked sugarless porridge so much that he could eat their second helpings.

They were now at the critical point of the journey. The hunting was poor, which could mean starvation if they had to stay the winter. They had gone too far and it was too late in the season to go all the way back. The first snow had already fallen. The mountains here were impossible to get over with sledges for crossing the ice cap, whereas further south towards the tip of Greenland they would find the mountains easier and the ice cap narrower; further south, for that matter, they might finish the journey by kayak. But the next stretch of coast was the most difficult of all—thirty miles with no shelter and a reputation for pieces of underwater ice breaking from the glaciers and shooting like torpedoes out to sea. A small boat, if it got past without being sunk, could have a lively time.

It was the moment for a decision and they agreed that if they could get no further by the beginning of October, in a fortnight, they would stop for the winter. At dawn on 19 September they started in fine weather but soon ran into thick ice and had to

7

steer out to sea in the hope of getting round it. After twelve miles, with a threatening storm and no sign of a break in the ice, they turned back to the same camping place—a wasted day. That evening August finished his suet in a final pudding, and that night they learnt the folly of pitching the tent on moss rather than stones; it was flooded out and Watkins woke half under water.

They moved the tent to stony ground, but it was the beginning of ten terrible days. For the first two they were held up by rain or fog. On the third night the boat chafed through one of the mooring ropes and smashed against the rocks which ripped off the copper sheathing and holed the bottom. They repaired it with pieces of floorboard and on 22 September made another attempt to travel. 'Bright sunshine and everything seemed auspicious'— though the kayaks kept falling overboard and fresh leaks appeared where nails had worked loose. They plugged them with matches, but after a mile, when the engine stopped, they couldn't start it and had to row back. By now they had run out of fresh food and were living on pemmican.

They beached the boat and in heavy rain August worked on the damage while the other two went hunting. On the 23rd and 24th it rained and a strong onshore wind began to blow. They moored the boat with an anchor, but it dragged; every two hours, day and night, someone had to go out into the rain to lay it again. Twice the boat was blown on to the rocks and once into an iceberg. Clothes and sleeping-bags got soaked and, after a tarpaulin was torn off the pile of baggage, all spare clothes too. 'We don't mind this if we can get away. It is sickening to be stuck here, only five days from civilization with the year getting more and more advanced and the weather worse and worse, able to do nothing. Still, the seal Gino shot the other day being young, one eats very well.' Even when things went wrong—sometimes, perhaps, because they did—August could see the glories of what he called a life of grand uncertainty.

The rain wouldn't stop. On the 26th, when he had put on a pair of new trousers which he was keeping for Julianehaab, August had to go out knee-deep into the sea to save the boat. On the 27th, with the boat full of water from rain and leaks, they couldn't reach it to bail it out because an iceberg had settled on the mooring rope. 'It is sickening to the point of desperation.' But though the seal meat was finished they still had some gulls to eat. On the 28th, the first clear morning for more than a week, they struck camp and loaded the boat. Watkins walked up a hill to prospect and reported that there was thick fog down the coast and the ice was worse than ever; there was no point in trying to press on, so he went hunting instead. 'It really begins to look like having to winter,' August wrote in his diary. 'If so, it isn't too good as the kayaks are getting rotten with all this wet, and if they become unusable we haven't a hope of being able to feed ourselves.'

Watkins came back with a seal which cheered them up, and next day, in brilliant weather, they escaped from the place where they had been kept ten days. Half an hour later, when the engine stopped, Lemon began the familiar struggle to get it going. 'Gino and I then spent the most agonizing hour of the expedition waiting to see if it would start. Lemon was feeling sick and losing his temper at the same time.' They all knew that if they had to go back once more it would be for the winter. Eventually Lemon coaxed the engine into life and they went on, hardly expecting the luck to last. Somehow, steering far out to sea, they got round the dangerous stretch and with a good moon hoped to continue all night. But the engine began to limp, the wind rose, the sky clouded over. In such an unseaworthy boat there was no chance of riding out a storm and it was hard to navigate through the ice in the dark, so Watkins decided to camp. On a little island, after the tensions of the day, tempers finally broke. Watkins and Lemon had their row while August kept clear, glad to be out of it. Faintly, from an age ago, he may have been reminded of another quarrel in another desert—between the Rodd brothers over the time of breakfast.

After an hour's sleep they tried to get going again. The engine wouldn't start. They worked on it all day—wasting bright weather, though they could get their kayaks and bedding dry—

and in the end decided to take it to pieces. Lemon said he would need a week to file down their spanners for the job. Watkins brooded grimly, glowering at the engine and at the sea. They had never seen him so depressed; even his hair, usually so sleek, was in a mess. Then August had an idea—disconnect the silencer and run it with an open exhaust: 'This I felt was the last hope. I tried it and immediately the engine went full speed. Our spirits rose vertically . . . We really were going to get there.'

Next day, 1 October, with the engine roaring and one man bailing all the time, they covered fifty miles. The nights were getting longer, ice was already forming on the water, they would have to race to reach Prince Christian Sound—the channel through to the west coast, cutting off the southern tip of Greenland—before it froze up. On 2 October the sunrise touched the mountains with crimson, the wild scenery making up for the crippled boat, but later a heavy swell drove them for shelter. Then new hope appeared. Entering a fjord in search of somewhere to camp they met three men in a rowing boat—Norwegians who had been left to spend the winter there, hunting bears and foxes, and were glad to have visitors. Coffee, real bread and butter, fish cakes, the first potatoes for a year, a full night's sleep on the floor of a dry hut—hospitality was never more warmly accepted.

The first snowstorm and a rough sea outside the fjord, as well as the Norwegians' kindness and the need for rest, kept them for three days. They hauled the boat out of the water and were appalled at the damage; it would never survive the fresh ice they were certain to meet. One of the Norwegians repaired the broken wood, caulked the planks and fitted new copper sheathing. When they launched the boat again the water mostly stayed out. 'Meeting these people,' August wrote, 'has definitely been a godsend.' The Norwegians, faced with a year in that bleak place, wanted the Englishmen to stay with them and hoped the fjord might freeze over to stop them leaving. But the travellers got away, taking a sackful of tinned food in exchange for some unwanted skis, and headed for Prince Christian Sound: 'Everything going splendidly, engine roaring, nice long swell, bright sunshine.'

On the afternoon of 6 October they entered the sound and went on into the night. Ice floes held them up, the first bumps re-opened some of the leaks, the moon wasn't bright enough to steer by, so they drifted till the sun came up. With the new ice already half an inch thick, they were lucky to get through before the winter.

At the first Danish settlement on the west side they were greeted by hundreds of people; treated to coffee by the school-master and a glass of port by the headman's wife. August had mixed feelings about 'civilization, its comforts and horrors', but rejoiced at the sight of acres of green grass and a flock of sheep. 'The journey has been very successful and not at all unpleasant,' he wrote in his diary while they travelled up the coast to Juliane-haab. 'We certainly had bad weather but the many disasters that might have happened were all, by God's good grace, averted.' The anxiety and frustration of the last long weeks soon dissolved.

Not so good was the news that Rymill and Hampton, who had set off from the base on the east coast to cross the ice cap, hadn't arrived on the west coast. Lemon, an army officer who had to return to duty, took a cargo ship for England but Watkins and August had to go by boat 500 miles up the coast to wait for their missing friends at Holsteinsborg. 'There have been some hard things to bear in the last year,' August wrote to Mollie, 'but the hardest of all was this last happening—to see the ship sail for home and not be able to go in her.' They might be delayed several weeks, they might have to start a search party on to the ice cap, and once again it looked as if they were unlikely to leave Greenland before the winter. August was miserable and told Mollie so: 'It's a bit of typical irony that we should ever have met. If we never had, you would now be happy with someone else and I should be content to follow my fate. As it is, I don't know how it fares with you, but for me it's a wretched state of kicking against the pricks in this revolting Greenland . . . By the way, your suet was a wonderful thing.'

Slowly Watkins and August made their way north in local

boats from settlement to settlement. They got involved in a
wedding party ('these Scandinavians don't seem to be able to
hold their liquor'), went to a cinema ('nothing but a stream of
sob') and were entertained by dignitaries all up the coast
('extremely hospitable but would not stop making speeches'). To
August, going for ever north when he longed to be going south,
it seemed that Greenland was like some mythical island which
seduced and imprisoned a traveller; he would never get away.
'You had better forget me,' he wrote to Mollie. 'But *you* know
that if it wasn't a matter of honour and of life and death, nothing
could stop me coming back.' On 24 October they heard that
Rymill and Hampton had reached Holsteinsborg: 'THANK
GOD. Now we shall not have to do that ghastly search in this
appalling weather.'

The two explorers, with kayaks lashed on top of their sledges,
had taken ten weeks over the journey instead of the six they had
expected. They had been held up by crevasses, ice streams and
lakes. Hampton's boots fell to bits and he had to repair them daily
with empty tins. Equipment and instruments were abandoned,
food ran out, the dogs all had to be shot and the two men
struggled on, carrying their kayaks, tents, bedding, fuel, rifles
and hunting gear—loads of a hundred pounds over the most
difficult Arctic country. When they reached a river on the west
coast they found it already frozen over, so couldn't use their
kayaks. When they came to open water and launched their
kayaks they were carried swiftly down on the current, over-
turned and both nearly drowned when they were swept under
the ice. It was remarkable that they survived to meet the party
of Eskimos sent up to look for them by the Danish governor.

The meeting of the last four members of the British Arctic Air
Route Expedition at Holsteinsborg was a happy event. A Danish
ship came in, bound for Copenhagen, and with charm and
cajolery Watkins talked the captain into taking more passengers.
By the end of October they were away from Greenland and in a
fortnight, after a good voyage, they reached Denmark.

To be met by Mollie on the quay had been one of August's

ice-cap dreams. But before sailing he had sent her a warning: 'There is to be some awful sort of reception in Copenhagen for us, so I should keep clear as these Danes are such fans at formal entertainment.' He promised not to get held up too long, but to take the first boat home. Now, on the eve of arrival, he wrote in his diary, 'There is to be an appalling official welcome. Bands playing, national anthems, Prince Christian, British ambassador . . . There is a rumour I may have to say something. Heaven forbid! It is going to be a horrible show.'

It was every bit as bad as he feared. Watkins, who had arranged for a suitcase of clothes to be smuggled aboard with the pilot, went ashore looking as dapper as ever, with bowler hat and umbrella, but the other three still looked like explorers. At a quayside ceremony, quite unlike the departure from St Katherine's dock sixteen and a half months earlier, Watkins made a short speech. Then a man from the British embassy took the microphone and said that everyone should be grateful to Denmark for rescuing Mr Courtauld, whom he invited to say a few words. August obliged: 'I only want to say that everything the last speaker has told you is entirely wrong. I wasn't rescued by anyone.'

He was almost as terse, but with more courtesy, a month later at the Royal Geographical Society after Watkins had given a lecture on the expedition. Though there were famous explorers waiting to make speeches the president, Admiral Goodenough, gave priority to 'one who undertook and underwent a somewhat unique and unusual experience, from whom I am sure you would like to hear a word or two'. August said, 'You have heard far too much about my little part in the expedition, so I'm not going to say anything further about that.' Instead he spoke of the Danish administrators in Greenland—not only of their generosity to the expedition but of their way of running the country for the benefit of its rightful people: 'I have seen one or two peoples administered in different parts of the world by white races, but I have never seen a race administered so disinterestedly and so unselfishly for their own good as the Eskimos in Greenland.'

Finally he felt that as an ordinary member of the expedition he ought to say something about the man who did all the work: 'To be an Arctic explorer now means no more than to be a tube train traveller. We who went with Watkins were fortunate in not being tied, that we could just go and do what we were told . . . To be the leader of an Arctic expedition is quite another matter. I wouldn't care for it if I had the opportunity.'

Chapter 10

The Last Fling

O N 2 JANUARY 1932, six weeks after August got back from Greenland—a year and a day after his ice-cap resolutions—he was married. 'Mollie and I decided to get it done at Southwark Cathedral,' he wrote many years later, unable to be sentimental about such events. The night before the wedding he gave a bachelors' party which ended up at the fun-fair at Olympia where the bridegroom's black eye was not the only damage. Afterwards he took his bride for a wedding trip (honeymoon was a word he didn't like), travelling from Dover to the Continent, then by way of Sicily and Egypt to the Sudan where his friend Charles de Bunsen was a government administrator.

As a tourist August usually made a point of visiting at least the most famous local attraction, but this wasn't the time for strenuous sightseeing. Cairo was no good, he told his mother. He refused to look at the pyramids, but luckily for Mollie their hotel balcony had a splendid view of them, so he had to give in and be dragged off for a closer look. The steamer up the Nile wasn't bad and, though Khartoum was stuffy with officials, they got some sailing on the river and a dance at the club. The best part was staying with de Bunsen in the province of Kordofan, 1,500 miles across the Sahara from the mountains of Air where August had explored with the Rodd brothers:

It is exceedingly pleasant being in such a peaceful place where there are no hotels, trippers or sights . . . We sit on the verandah most of the day while Charles is working. In the evening we go for a ride. The country is open bush and sand, dull but pleasant. Mollie has only fallen off once . . . It is rather good to be in a place where it is a known certainty that every day is going to be cloudless and hot.

Much the same could be said, in a sense, of most of his life. Ever since the first decision to go to the Arctic, he could be sure that every day was to be free of the worries that generally troubled people's lives—not just from the advantage of inherited wealth but from the possession of an inner, more personal fortune, an ease of living, a privilege of nature that had nothing to do with money. But a clear sky, like the landscape of bush and sand, could be dull as well as pleasant. To be certain about the climate, with no risks or even surprises, was too monotonous for a man who relished the unexpected and the improbable. August's choice of career, his opting for 'the life of grand uncertainty', while depending on a sort of moral solvency as much as on any credit at the bank, could be seen as a reaction to the conditions that made it possible, an improvement on the calm weather that each day always brought. Clouds were needed to enliven the steady prospect ahead, and would sometimes have to be invented. Confident in himself, he found that the security required by others was superfluous; though for the moment, with Mollie in the Sudan, the reliable climate was rather good.

They ended with a fortnight's trek on camels through the southern part of the district, with a train of servants and an escort of native police. For a man so susceptible to contrast it must have given extra pleasure to reflect on last winter's solitary ice-cap vigil and compare it with the present leisurely safari through Africa, in the company of an old friend and a new wife, attended by the best comforts available in such corners of the British Empire. A war dance put on for them by Sudanese tribesmen could scarcely have been more unlike the crowded parties in the expedition hut, with Eskimo girls and a battered gramophone. And for further contrast, on the way home, August and

Mollie stayed with her uncle, the British consul in Venice: 'We had a splendid time gondoling about the canals.'

Contrast, with the contradiction that it implied, was always a feature of August's character as of his life. He sought peace and quiet, yet strove to fill them with excitement and incident. He could seem harsh, rigorous, austere—perhaps through a strain of Huguenot influence, though it was marked not by gloomy puritan attitudes but by a genuine ability to do without luxury—yet he could equally revel in the good things of life. He might appear disorganized, inefficient in practical matters that didn't interest him, unable to look after himself properly, yet few men have been so totally thrown on their own resources and survived so well. He was both innocent and experienced, immature and wise, ingenuous and philosophical, light-hearted and earnest, unconventional and conservative.

He would never violate decorum or propriety except when he felt the need to shock somebody. With friends at a restaurant, during a lapse in conversation he could turn without a blink to a very proper-minded stockbroker and ask loudly, 'I say, what d'you think of buggery?' And staying once with Launcelot Fleming, a bishop as well as polar explorer, he alarmed his host at dinner by telling another guest, a young man who was thinking of ordination, 'There are far too many parsons already.' August expanded the theme outrageously before saying that being ordained was the best thing the young man could do (which he later did) and the bishop was soothed. But he had a strict code of his own, and though not exactly prudish he drew the line at the first hint of anything remotely lewd. In a letter to him in Greenland Mollie passed on a story that a friend had told her, hoping it wouldn't shock him. August couldn't even understand it and had to have it explained; then wrote back to Mollie saying he wasn't a bit shocked, he only wished that people wouldn't tell her such stories: 'They aren't nearly nice enough for you and I don't like you knowing them, but if you *do* know them I don't mind you telling them to me.'

All his friends agreed that August's marriage was one of the happiest they knew, but perversely one of them also believed that he should never have got married at all. Having done so, he turned to another of his ice-cap dreams—the ideal yacht. He found her at Burnham-on-Crouch, a gaff-rigged yawl of twenty-two tons, fifty feet long, built of English oak and elm and, though already twenty years old, as near as possible to the design he had lovingly sketched in his Greenland diary. As if to reassure his wife he changed the name to that of his first boat, *Duet*, and six months after getting married they were cruising together again on the west coast of Scotland, fulfilling yet another dream. August wrote to his father, '*Duet* is a very perfect ship and I am lucky to have got hold of her. She sails like a witch and is a fine sea boat, a very rare combination.' The words could be true for more than his new ship. Good fortune was piling up.

With Mollie expecting a baby and getting a new house ready, August was left to sail home down the Irish Sea with his father-in-law. At Penzance he heard that Gino Watkins, who had gone back to Greenland, was dead. 'This news about Gino is so awful,' he wrote to Mollie. 'He was the only really brilliant traveller that has appeared since the war. That he should be dead now, quite apart from personal considerations, is the worst blow for England that I can think of.' What Watkins might have done for England was something his friends went on guessing for years, but August's hyperbole, natural at the moment of first grief, expressed more than his own loss. Watkins, volatile as a god, entered the mythology of a generation.

August and Mollie settled into a house in Chelsea Square, where their first child was born and where August performed revolver practice in his study, pinning the target to the London telephone directory to spare the wallpaper. Later when they moved to a house in Tite Street, he used his revolver to silence the crickets that chattered under the stairs. For a time they also rented a farmhouse for holidays, close to the shores of the Solent facing the Isle of Wight, and *Duet* was moored nearby in the river Hamble.

Sailing became one of the principal pleasures of his life, in which Mollie happily shared. During the twenty-seven years of his ownership, in the darkening days of peace before the Second World War and in the bleak times afterwards, *Duet* made long voyages in the waters of north-west Europe and won several races. Even in the thirties she was not a modern yacht—she belonged to a more robust, more elegant age—but under August's command, sailed in a style suited to the man and to the ship, she often came home ahead of more up-to-date competitors. Generally it was cruising, not racing, that August preferred—to Brittany, the Baltic and Scandinavia, round the north of Scotland to the western isles, to Holland, Spain and lastly through the Straits of Gibraltar into the Mediterranean.

On such passages he showed skill not just as a fine navigator. 'As a seaman he was fearless and undefeated,' Freddy Chapman wrote, 'and frequently frightened his friends.' *Duet* at sea was seldom allowed to ride the wind except with every thread and fibre straining, and her master's nerves were tuned to match. He made few concessions to the weather or to his crew, and though he didn't take needless risks he earned a name for driving his ship harder than most men, for carrying canvas when others would have shortened sail, and for performing manoeuvres— such as steering under full sail through a crowded anchorage— which nobody else could have hoped to get away with. There were no near misses and no fumbling, sometimes to other people's alarm but always to their admiration. In the summer of 1939, after a cruise up the Norwegian coast, *Duet* crossed the North Sea to Shetland in fast time, making a perfect landfall despite thick fog and sailing through the entrance of Lerwick harbour as if she had been out for a short trip on a sunny afternoon. Not many men, as August wrote in an introduction to a book of sailing photographs, were unmoved by the sight of a ship under sail, and he made sure there were none at all if *Duet* was anywhere in view.

A sense of romance and momentousness as well as of adventure pervaded his voyages and he shared it with everybody on board. He liked best to sail with Mollie, which wasn't always possible.

Without her it wasn't enough to write a letter or postcard from every port, but signals were made to the coastguard on Flamborough Head or St Catherine's Point or whatever headland had just been rounded, requesting *Duet*'s position to be reported home.

Most of his many friends at one time or another sailed with him, though not all could spare the time for a long cruise and at least one, on occasion, was worried by the expense of joining him in some distant foreign port; '*Duet* will pay' was August's way of saving embarrassment and disguising his generosity. He tended to pick his companions for the pleasure of having them on board rather than for their knowledge of sheets and halyards, and in his memoirs wrote of a spring cruise with Peter Rodd and Evelyn Waugh, neither of whom had much claim to yachtsmanship. (Peter Rodd wrote that it was probably among those whose walk in life departed far from his own, but who from time to time stood watch in *Duet*, that August formed his most devoted friends.) They sailed from Burnham-on-Crouch bound for the Irish Sea but were soon confined to harbour by storms, first in Dover, then in Boulogne, though with such a crew it couldn't have been dull. At last they reached Teignmouth in Devon, where Evelyn Waugh went ashore and sent himself a telegram saying that he was needed elsewhere on urgent business. August didn't blame him.

Another memory was of a day in the Solent watching a race of the biggest class of yachts, among them the King's cutter, *Britannia*. To keep out of their way August steered close to a battleship anchored off Cowes, but the huge racing schooner *Westward* altered course and followed *Duet*.

We pulled in our sheets and sailed as close to the battleship as we could without fouling . . . *Westward* came tearing astern of us, her immense mainboom squared right off. It seemed inevitable that it would strike our starboard shrouds, in which case we would certainly have been dismasted. The faces of rows of men lying on her decks peered at us over the bulwarks. Not a word was spoken. At last, when there seemed a mere matter of inches to go, a voice sang out from for'ard, 'Luff sir, for God's sake, luff!' Her steersman moved the wheel one spoke, *Westward*'s boom drew out a foot and she rushed by.

Besides sailing and the occasional engagement to lecture there were other things that took August away—the call of hills, the love of shooting, the craving for escape from London where, much as there was to enjoy, he had no reason for lingering and soon felt stifled. Often, if Mollie had to stay behind, a tormenting ambivalence ruled his feelings as if the momentum of a long-planned, much-desired journey was nearly defeated by the pull of home and family. In March 1933 he was on his way to Scotland for a walking tour with J. M. Scott. 'Why we are going I don't know,' he wrote to Mollie who was at home with their new baby. 'Please don't push me off any more in future.' If Mollie had done any pushing, it was only because she knew how deeply he needed wild places for a time, though she was afraid Scott might make it a tough holiday: 'I *won't* have him making my husband a flat-outer,' she wrote. Her fears came true, whether through Scott's doing or not, and August's letters recited the painful progress of their tour: 'Here we are after our first bit of walking with sore feet and aching muscles . . . It hailed at first, then rained and then snowed . . . My feet are rotting and all blistered, my limbs all stiff . . . Nothing to do except walk up these foul mountains . . . All very nearly vertical.'

In the summer of 1934, after racing *Duet* in Denmark, he was off to Scotland for the grouse-shooting with only his dog for company. Mollie was expecting their second child, and soon August was fretting at their separation, kept indoors by bad weather while the rest of the house party happily did crossword puzzles. Two years later, again in Scotland without Mollie, it was no better: 'Just come in from a very stupid day's shooting. Wind put all the birds wrong and nobody seemed to have the sense to do anything to alter matters to suit. What shooting there was I didn't get. House v. dull.'

Early in 1937 he went to Uist in the Hebrides with Scott to shoot wildfowl. 'Have you ever had really well cooked widgeon?' he asked Mollie. 'They are incredibly good, much better than ordinary wild duck.' Tramping over the hills after woodcock, or sitting alone before dawn on an islet in the Sound of Harris, being visited by an otter and reading Mollie's last letter while he waited for the geese—these were very special pleasures. But not unmixed. Some of the delight of solitude had faded: 'If ever I say I'm going away from you again, will you stop me, because I don't like it.' That summer he went down to Dartmouth to sail with Quintin Riley, leaving Mollie who was expecting their third child: '*Duet* seems absolutely empty without you, it really is frightfully sad and I can't think why I came all this way.' And at sea off Cornwall: 'It is disgusting you aren't here . . . An absolute waste being on board.'

The following spring August went to ski in Switzerland but a letter from Mollie, at home with the children, made him wish he had never gone: 'It makes everything here, however good it is, not worth having. The snow is good, the sun shines all day long, everything for skiing is perfect but I'm not liking it a bit. All day we go up to the top and I fall down to the bottom and get thoroughly bad-tempered and tired . . . I want to come back so much, but I suppose I must stick it out.' Two forces conflicted— the yearning for exploration, solitude, adventure and sport in the wide empty spaces, and his love for Mollie, family life, friends and the multifarious interests that kept him happy at home.

The year 1931, though more than midway between two world wars, can be seen to divide the post-war from the pre-war years. It marked the point when Britain slid into an apparently chronic economic depression, while from abroad came the first rumbles of violence and disorder—the Japanese invasion of China, the revolution in Spain, the growing danger in Germany. The mood of the '30s settled in. For many young men the war-to-end-wars, fought by an earlier generation, had destroyed the old ideals of honour and glory on the battlefield and they looked elsewhere for their heroics. By 1933, a few weeks after Hitler came to power, the Oxford Union could pass its famous motion that in no circumstances would it fight for king and country. Action needn't mean only battle. Exploring was a natural alternative and it spilled into contemporary literature. While Evelyn Waugh was making fun of the tinsel foolishness of society life, Auden and Spender, who in another age might have praised famous men-at-arms, turned to the deeds of such men as mountaineers. Several poets took to climbing. But the old explorers' motives of scientific discovery and commercial enterprise were superseded. Captain Scott and Shackleton already seemed as old-fashioned as Stanley and Livingstone. Writers as different as Louis MacNeice and Peter Fleming described their journeys in books that were equally distant from the classics of their predecessors. Travelling became a private quest, a romantic metaphor, a parable for the times.

August Courtauld belonged to his generation, yet also stood apart. For him 1931 was the year whose beginning he had watched alone on the Greenland ice cap—the year of his most intimate journey, his deepest exploration. Nothing could ever be quite like it again. 'Although he wouldn't have spoken of this in theological or religious terms,' Bishop Fleming wrote, 'it was evidently a spiritual experience as if he had been an ascetic meditating in the desert, which is very much what he was.' He emerged from it, at the time of his relief, sane and unperturbed and cheerful, but also subtly changed. Henceforth life would be different. He had reached the utmost—or anyway got as close as most men would care to go—and come back. He was only twenty-seven in 1931 but there was no need to explore any more, if only because he could never travel quite so far again.

In the five years since 1926 he had joined four expeditions. In the rest of his life he went on only one more.

The lure of the Arctic was as potent as ever, particularly the unknown mountains in Greenland which Watkins and D'Aeth,

flying their Gypsy Moth in 1930, had seen in the distance. They
had been found to be the highest north of the Arctic circle and
were now named the Watkins Mountains, but nobody had
climbed them. Danish, French and Italian expeditions had all
failed. To August, the chance of exploring his friend's own range
was too tempting and in 1935, in his inimitable way, 'I thought I
would get up an expedition to have a stab at the mountains Gino
had discovered.'

The party was to consist of seven Englishmen and three Danes.
Among them were Lawrence Wager, the geologist on the British
Arctic Air Route Expedition who had since been to Mount
Everest, and another Everest man, Jack Longland. Then August,
seeing no reason why marriage should clash with exploration, had
another idea: 'I thought it would be nice for Mollie to see Greenland, so I asked the married men to bring their wives . . . Everybody said it was bound to be an appalling failure.' But as he
knew himself—though others often didn't—anything that he set
his mind to, if it excited his imagination, could also catch his
talent for improvising. When he cared enough he would make it
work; otherwise he had no interest. Afterwards he declared the
experiment a success: 'The four girls survived all right and I
think they enjoyed it; they certainly made themselves very
useful.'

He chartered the *Quest*, the Norwegian sealer that had carried
Watkins's expedition in 1930, and on 4 July they left Aberdeen.
On the 15th they reached the pack ice, close to the Greenland
coast and very dense. To Mollie, her Arctic initiation was
astonishingly beautiful. Coming on deck on a brilliant sunny
morning after days of rough grey seas and fog, she found a
fairyland of sparkling ice, with a miraculous line of snow
mountains ahead. To seasoned polar men the situation was grim.
By midday the *Quest* was stuck fast and by evening so tightly
gripped that there was a risk of the propeller being snapped.
Dynamite proved useless; a hole could be blasted in the ice to
relieve the pressure but straightaway it closed up. Within sight
were forty giant icebergs, one of them more than 200 feet high.

For the imprisoned ship, being lifted and dropped on the swell, to strike a berg would be disaster. At midnight the captain came down from the crow's nest and said he could do no more, they must get ready to abandon ship. The cargo was broken into and stores were got up and stacked on deck, but the prospect of camping on one of those tossing little rafts of ice, after watching the *Quest* being smashed and sent to the bottom, was hardly cheerful. Helplessly they looked on, as they were taken within a few yards of one iceberg, then of another—their voices echoing off the terrible cliffs—and next day drifted into clearer water.

A band of Eskimos came out in kayaks and soon August was ashore and in the midst of a boisterous welcome from old friends. 'Civilization,' he wrote, 'had made unfortunate progress in the last four years,' but it was good to be back in Greenland. Days and nights were filled with feasts and dancing before the *Quest* was allowed to continue up the coast.

The ice made their passage northwards dangerous and slow. The Englishmen organized sports on the floes and the women went for walks. In time they reached the fjord where Watkins had been drowned—where the huge wooden cross erected on the shore by his companions now carried the claw marks of a polar bear that had climbed to the top. Sailing away, the *Quest* stopped her engine and dipped her flag before turning north again. More ice and strong currents delayed them. Sometimes they were held up by fog, more often they lay for brilliant, windless, wasted days locked in the ice, staring at the mountains that glistened in the distance. It was no comfort to hear on the wireless that four other sealers off the Greenland coast had been crushed and sunk.

On 5 August, a month after leaving Aberdeen, the *Quest* entered Irminger Fjord, an inlet with a good anchorage that would have to do for the expedition base. They were still a hundred miles from the Watkins Mountains but the ice prevented them sailing further up the coast and it was too late in the season to wait for better weather. Equipment and stores were landed at the foot of a glacier and on the 7th, leaving the four women to return to the ship, the six men of the climbing party began the long march across difficult, unknown country towards the mountains.

Because of crevasses they had decided against using dogs. Instead they took two sledges fitted with harness for man-hauling, three men to each, as Captain Scott and Shackleton had done in the Antarctic. On the second evening after strenuous climbing over soft snow, like a mixture of sand and glue, they had their first view of the goal. The tops were in cloud but the precipices were spectacular—the finest mountain wall that Wager, who had not long returned from the Himalayas, had ever seen.

Each stage of the journey had to be prospected in advance. Sometimes, climbing to a pass, they had to double-haul the sledges one at a time. Sometimes they could descend on skis or ride on the sledges. Sometimes they travelled in the rain, sometimes they slogged through deep wet snow surfaced with a crust too thin to take the weight of man or sledge. Always they advanced through a marvellous wilderness of peaks, passes and glaciers that nobody had seen before; and always far ahead, but daily getting closer, was the shimmering range that had brought them there.

After five days, having climbed an icefall where thin bridges spanned the crevasses and fantastic towers tottered overhead, August reckoned they were halfway. They abandoned one sledge with a dump of unnecessary baggage and pressed on towards the King Christian Glacier, a mighty stream twelve miles wide and more than a hundred long, one of the biggest in the world. On the far side, magnificent above their neighbours, rose the Watkins Mountains.

A week after leaving Irminger Fjord the six men pitched their tents in the middle of the great glacier. With only a few hours' sleep, they struck camp soon after midnight to catch the snow before the sun had softened it. The dawn came up through a screen of haze, painting the glacier pinkish-mauve, then yellow like a field of buttercups, but mercifully for the state of the snow and the climbers' burnt skin the sun remained clouded all day.

They set course for a small glacier that gave a promising lead into the mountains and camped that night high under their chosen summit.

'Got peak yesterday,' August wrote in his diary on 17 August. The climb took thirteen hours, first up the small glacier and then up steep ice which, with the rarefied air and their heavy loads, almost defeated them. The two Everest men carried the day, Wager by setting a fast pace to reach the top in daylight and Longland by finding and leading up the last narrow ridge. Photographs were taken, thermometers boiled, aneroids read, and August took an azimuth and a round of angles with the theodolite he had laboriously brought up. Then the only Dane in the party pulled out his national flag and to everyone's applause planted it on the summit, the highest point in Danish territory as well as in the Arctic—12,250 feet above the sea, 3,000 feet higher than Petermann Peak. For their descent the sunset turned green and orange, and the shadows of men and mountains the deepest blue. Silence, but for the swish of skis, fell again on Gino Watkins's conquered range.

For nearly a week they explored in the mountains—a delectable time for everyone. The scientists observed rocks and signs of precarious life—a rare lichen, a caterpillar feeding on an Arctic poppy, a trio of inquisitive gulls far from their habitat—and the mountaineers climbed new peaks, and surveyed. The main object had been won, there was no pressure for further great achievement, but there was much to enjoy. To the others August, the originator of the expedition, imparted his own delight at simply being in one of the beautiful wild places of the world. Much of his pleasure was shown in his energy and thoroughness; he would carry his instruments up to yet another point, or climb again to a pass they had already crossed, if he thought he might get better readings.

In time they returned to Irminger Fjord. As they descended from the mountains and high glaciers the going became worse— pot-holes in the ice, ditches full of water, fields of glutinous snow. When they reached the coast they had covered more than

200 miles in a fortnight. The *Quest* had also been away, unloading stores, coal, timber and materials for a hut; five members of the expedition, with the wives of two of them, were to spend the winter in Greenland and be picked up next summer. 'Ship got in half an hour before we did,' August wrote when they were all back on board. 'Very satisfactory . . . Excellent meal and everyone very happy.'

Four years earlier he had said that he wouldn't care to be leader of an Arctic expedition. Now he had become one, almost unconsciously. Months later, after the ritual lecture he gave to the Royal Geographical Society in London, it was left to his old leader James Wordie to comment on his courage, philosophic calm, self-effacing spirit and modest way of putting himself in the background, giving the credit for success to his companions. The hopes and fears of a leader, the responsibility and uncertainty of decisions, were August's alone. All he chose to share was the enjoyment.

Another week was spent on botany, geology and archaeology along the coast. Then one morning the winter party—seven English figures with dogs and attendant Eskimos, all dwarfed by the mountains behind them—were abandoned in their lonely fjord. With a parting hoot, the *Quest* sailed away. It was August's fourth departure from Greenland, and to be his last. The pack ice had vanished; by evening only a few floes dotted the calm sea, pink in the pale green water. Astern the land darkened under a golden sky and then the northern lights shone in their finest way, an apt farewell.

That expedition to Greenland was August's last fling as an explorer. He was elected to the council of the Royal Geographical Society, and on the committee in charge of expeditions and instruments he had a hand in other men's travels, but his own were limited to ordinary tourism and the voyages of *Duet*. If Gino Watkins hadn't died they might have gone together to the Arctic again. During the boat journey in 1931, Watkins had talked of a long voyage he wanted to make by kayak and August had suggested sailing north with him in the yacht he planned to buy. Some years later he had *Duet*'s bottom sheathed in copper in preparation for the Arctic, but he never went. An expedition to the Himalayas was another dream, and in 1938 he got as far as talking of the Karakoram. Mollie would come too and they might have a look at Kashmir: 'I don't see why the delectable spots of the British Empire should be left entirely to colonels and their wives to recover their livers in . . . Actually the Poona and tiffin stuff would be rather amusing.' That plan too, if it was ever serious, was stopped by the coming war.

In 1934, asked by Freddy Chapman to write an introduction to *Watkins' Last Expedition*, August turned out an essay that was as near as he ever got to a private testament. Reading the book was for him a sentimental journey in itself, a test of nostalgia: 'One lives again under the clear skies and among the happy people of that gaunt land.' (No longer 'this revolting Greenland' as he had called it once.) What do explorers go for? he asked. What was the use? Why waste a young life like Gino's on such a fruitless task? 'If there is an answer one must look in the eyes and know the hearts of those "who have done and must do more." ' Watkins hadn't gone for fame or science but because he wanted to, because he had to. It was the life he loved, and August implied that the same was true of Chapman and himself and every other young explorer:

In this book you will find enough of risk and danger—not sought for but accepted when it came, and dealt with calmly. Of fear too there was enough. Many times it must have taken their hearts in its cold grip, though afterwards they would laugh it out of sight. [So much for the contention that August didn't know what fear was.] Read this book and you will know something of the life of that fantastic land, of its ascetic naked-ness, of its strong weather, of its laughing people, and of the feelings of an impetuous Englishman who has lived there. To know more, throw away your job, your friends, your cares . . .

and go there, not as a great white man to teach, but as an inferior to learn.

It was an ardent call, coming from the heart; and perhaps in his heart August knew that it was one he would never heed again.

Soon after their return from Greenland Mollie asked her husband, now aged thirty-one, what he was going to do with his life. 'Nothing,' he told her, forgetting one of his ice-cap resolutions—to find a job. But he contradicted himself once more; and although his private wealth meant that he didn't have to earn a living (in 1938 he had investments worth more than half a million pounds and a large country house) and for the rest of his life couldn't seriously be accused of working in any conventional way, he never interrupted his constant diversity of doing things. Activity of a quiet, untrumpeted kind, ruled by the values that had sustained him in his tent alone, was his lifelong theme. Just how he filled his time, to men who would have been lost without an office or bored without a profession, might have seemed a puzzle, yet he was never short of something to do, never in need of a purpose. One way or another, pursuing the many objects of his own invention, he contrived to busy himself as thoroughly as most people with more ordinary careers. 'He did the jobs,' his old sailing friend Frank Carr said, 'that needed doing but nobody else would do.' He did them with the inspiration of a true amateur.

In 1937 August and Mollie left London and bought a large Georgian house, Spencers, at Great Yeldham in Essex, not far from where they had both been born, in the heart of the Courtauld country; and there, in a changing ominous world they somehow preserved the style of living that August had been brought up to, adjusted to his special taste.

Children (the third was born in 1938), servants, dogs, ponies, cars, sailing days in *Duet*, holidays in Scotland, all formed part of a pattern that was repeated with variations across the households of English upper-class society. August's version was marked by his own idiosyncrasies. Guests at Spencers could sometimes detect a whiff of astringency in the atmosphere, as if their host disapproved of too much fun and wanted to show there was a limit. He read books as well as shot pheasants. He entertained well and told good stories, but seldom about his own achievements. At times he could be high-spirited to the point of gaiety, at others he was taciturn to the point of gloom. The changes could be baffling. Some people, sharing his laughter or subdued by his reserve, suspected that he had never felt so much at home as when he was alone on the Greenland ice cap. Yet with the explorer's rough habits went something of a squire's high standards. More than one of his friends remembered August's claret as being the best in Essex; and Peter Rodd, a connoisseur of such things, noted 'a certain fastidiousness about the conduct of his house, which was the reverse of the Polar Medal whose obverse showed him unwashed and unlaundered for months on end in the deserts of sand or snow'. (Mollie remarked that the fastidiousness mainly applied to the wine.) Another friend who often stayed there believed that Spencers was comfortable and pleasant only because Mollie made it so, and that on his own August would have had one bath a month and lived on pemmican. But in all things August paid the piper, and in most of them Mollie liked the tune he called. Spencers may have been ruled by her hand, but family life was dominated by his vision.

From Spencers, where he watched the events that led to war, August conducted various one-man campaigns. He had already made a nuisance of himself at the Board of Trade by interviewing officials and tackling them about the hazards that beset the country's shipping. 'British ships were sinking all over the place for no apparent reason,' he wrote. 'It seemed to me that things were very bad indeed.' But it didn't seem so to anybody else. Nothing he could do would open official eyes, though he badgered Members of Parliament and Lloyd's about it and sent a letter to *The Times*. The spirit of appeasement, the ostrich attitudes of the government, appeared to infect civil servants and everyone in authority. To them this tiresome individual, coming in with his odd alarmist theories, was to be listened to and soothed and ushered out.

Next he tried the navy. His experience as a boy at the hands of the old gentlemen of the Admiralty might have put him off for life, but as long ago as 1930 he had tried to enlist in the Royal Naval Volunteer Reserve, to be told there were no vacancies. Now in 1935, with Fascist Italy invading Abyssinia, and Nazi Germany making predatory noises in Europe, he thought of something else: 'It seemed to me that men who knew a bit about the sea ought to be allowed to give a hand in the navy. I got out a scheme whereby we might help, using our own ships.' He took it to the Admiralty, where his childhood hopes had once been wrecked, and came up against the same disdain that he had found in other Whitehall offices. Small ships, he was told, would have no part in modern war. Britain was building battle-ships and August was treated as a boy playing war-games with his model yacht.

With some sailing friends he persisted and eventually the RNVSR (S for Supplementary) was formed, though with only the meanest blessing from the Admiralty. Its members were to have no uniform, no pay, no instructors; the best they could do was sort themselves into regional groups and invent their own training. August, given command of a group in East Anglia, arranged classes in seamanship and signalling and navigation; and later these part-time mariners, rehearsing naval exercises in boats of all rigs and sizes, were allowed to sit for a yachtmaster's certificate. Thus, under sail and at weekends with nothing to help them but their own skill and energy, a few defiant English-men faced the war which they saw ahead. Patriotism was not enough; they needed greater scorn for their rulers than their rulers showed for them.

In the last year before the war, August got involved in an organization which he called, cryptically and dubiously, 'the crooked people'. Who they were, beyond being one of the prolifer-ating and semi-autonomous arms of British intelligence, he was probably never clear. A colonel came to stay at Spencers (he left a revolver under his pillow, which frightened the housemaid) and a conference was held behind the locked door of the billiard room. Superficially the work was what August liked doing anyway. With a number of other yachtsmen he was required to survey the coasts of northern Europe and collect information about harbours which, in case of war, might be useful. He and his friends covered parts of Norway, Sweden, Denmark, Holland and Belgium, and sent in their reports. So perhaps *Duet*'s cruises were not always the innocent affairs they seemed. But if there was a touch of *The Riddle of the Sands* on board, it would have been borne in a spirit of unorthodoxy, serious but not solemn. The job was a mission to be achieved but also an adventure to be enjoyed and August, master of the unmissed chance, would get all the fun he could; though whether any use was made of his work in the summer of 1939 he never knew. Yet however intense his love for England he couldn't have been happy among 'the crooked people' and possibly they never felt at ease with him. Deviousness was as alien to his nature as deception.

Meanwhile life at Spencers, those last peacetime months, rolled smoothly on. It was discovered that the house had been built for the Duke of Marlborough's grand-daughter, so the names of his battles were painted on the bedroom doors—Blenheim, Ramillies, Oudenarde, Malplaquet. Out in the garden, among the trees and flowers, the children played. It was a lovely summer, as August recalled afterwards: 'We sat on the lawn listening to the war starting up on the wireless.' The gathering storm hardly spoilt the sunshine that fell on the unemployed, if never idle, rich. Sometimes the family had tea sitting up in the branches of an enormous oak tree in the park. On fine nights they would sleep out under the whispering cedars, watching the stars go wheeling by.

Chapter 11

War

THE WAR STARTED a week after August's thirty-fifth birthday. Like many others of his age who believed that their talents and experiences would be useful, he found he wasn't needed. The RNVSR, the band of amateur sailors who had trained themselves in readiness, was ignored or forgotten. Members of August's group, expecting urgent instructions that never came, telephoned each other for news. Nothing happened. Better to join the army, some thought, than sit waiting. August sent a telegram to the Admiralty suggesting that his men should be signalled to stand by, if only to discourage them from slipping off to the other services, and got a reply telling him he could resign if he wanted to. In the time of the 'phoney' war before the action began, he wasn't the only loyal Englishman frustrated by the apathy he met.

During the first winter, through his connections with 'the crooked people', he found himself making improbable journeys across England on business that had the faintly theatrical flavour of the period. Almost anything in those jumpy days, however innocent, was labelled hush-hush and treated with reverence. Of the secret bomb he claimed to have carried to Swansea in a suit-case, August afterwards wrote with mystification verging on contempt. But somebody was pleased, for early in 1940 he was hauled into the Admiralty itself and given a job in the Naval Intelligence Division. It didn't fit his own ideas of waging war against the enemy.

The Admiralty, in a word, embodied all that he felt about

authority. It had been the Admiralty that had dashed his hopes as a boy, that wouldn't let him join the RNVR, that begrudged every penny for the RNVSR, that refused to train it properly and rejected it when war was declared. Now here he was, sitting at a desk in the Admiralty like a schoolboy being kept under the head-master's eye, though he had done nothing wrong. It was as if the Old Men had appropriated him for their own use. It was a betrayal, in a way, of himself.

The Naval Intelligence Division, growing quickly from almost nothing into an efficient and vital department, soon collected a motley crew—a journalist, a barrister, a stockbroker, a classics don, a poet, an insurance agent, an artist, a marine biologist, a schoolmaster, an antiquarian book collector, an archaeologist, a novelist, a royal duke and, to keep them all in mind of their link with the navy, a sprinkling of regular RN officers. In such company even a Greenland explorer could hardly feel too odd a fish.

Room 39, where August worked among a dozen other people, was the intelligence headquarters, the brain-box of the navy. It has been likened to the newsroom of a daily paper, with some-times the air of a club smoking-room, though among its junior staff it was known as the Zoo. In the next room behind a green baize door sat Admiral Godfrey, who had recently commanded a great cruiser and a still greater battlecruiser and had a name for his exacting energy, quick mind, impatience, and occasional ruthlessness. Anyone who couldn't keep up with him, or didn't match his own meticulousness, or bothered him with delays and mistakes and trivialities concerning yesterday's problem when he himself had already moved on to tomorrow's, could expect little help. Outside his door sat his personal assistant, a RNVR officer later to become famous for his novels of the secret service, Ian Fleming.

Paper poured in and out of Room 39—signals, reports, maps, orders, minutes, all marked according to strict categories of secrecy. Far from being a sailor, August was a pen-pusher, a filing clerk, a janitor with a bunch of keys who went round locking and unlocking safes. The horizon was confined to the dismal London view, the storms and calms were conditioned by the moods coming from behind the green baize door. Anyone who applied to go to sea and take part in the fighting was liable to be told by Admiral Godfrey that it was just what he wanted to do himself.

August was moved to the Balkan and then to the Scandinavian section which was controlled, in the peculiar way of the Admiralty, by an expert on Egypt. 'Everything is stupid here,' he wrote in January 1940. 'A hectic buzz all the time, while I try and do six or seven jobs at once and act as errand boy for two or three different people.' The hours were long even when he wasn't on duty all night, so he lived at his father's house in Palace Green, as he had during that unhappy time in the Stock Exchange, and joined Mollie and the children at Spencers when he could.

The work was not only hard and dull but, to August, futile and remote. In the weeks before the Norway campaign the Scandinavian section feverishly collected and distributed information about traffic from neutral ports to Germany and other northern routes used by the enemy; and when the fighting began the work multiplied. A temporary commission in the RNVR came through at last, but gave small hope of being released from the Admiralty. To be summoned by some obscure but important person and asked about ice conditions between Greenland and Iceland, or told to plot a track for ships down the Norwegian coast, was tantalizing to anyone in a bleak office, longing to be in a ship and wallowing instead in a sea of ignorance and muddle: 'This chair-borne work might be all very interesting but it wasn't what I joined the navy for. I must get out somehow, I thought.' Requests for transfer had no effect. Eventually, by displeasing his senior officers sufficiently, he escaped.

In June 1940, after volunteering to help at Dunkirk but being turned down, he was sent on an executive officers' course at Greenwich naval college: 'All Christopher Wren and Inigo Jones,' he wrote to Mollie, 'and we dine in the Painted Hall.' But life at Greenwich, though more elegant than at the Admiralty and brightened by parcels of strawberries from Spencers, was almost as frustrating: 'This war doesn't seem to be half as much fun as the last.' France collapsed, bombing raids began in earnest, a German invasion threatened the country, while August sat in stuffy classrooms or drilled on the parade ground in a gas mask or scuttled down into the shelters when the air-raid siren went.

As pupil he was no easier to handle than as desk man. The training was designed to turn him and a bunch of other men ('rather the sort of people who come to see to the drains') into temporary naval officers and with luck, in the scoffing RN phrase, into temporary gentlemen too. Most of the things August was taught, he knew already. Some things he knew much better than his instructors; the navigation lectures were considered too elementary, so he was allowed to sit in the library. A few things, the favourite lessons of small-minded men, he would never learn. Nor was he much given to the kind of veneration expected by officers on the strength of the gold lace round their sleeves. Rank meant nothing unless it went with some other reason for respect. Out in the Thames with his class in a motor yacht, under instruction on ship-handling by a retired commander with memories of long-scrapped battleships, August tripped the old man with awkward questions and pointed out errors and hazards that nobody had noticed; and during a lecture on pilotage he didn't hesitate to correct a point that was being wrongly taught. Often he fell conspicuously asleep. It hardly raised his opinion of senior officers to be told, as if in retaliation, that his shoes were not the proper naval pattern. He felt he was wasting his time: 'I have come to the conclusion that the Admiralty invented this course to serve as a dustbin to put inconvenient people in. Once dumped here they can be forgotten.'

At the end of a month he was promoted to temporary lieutenant RNVR—one of the rare men in the navy to wear the white ribbon of the King's Polar Medal on his uniform—and asked what appointment he would like. Navigator in a cruiser, he replied. With his experience of the perverse official mind, he could have expected the result. He was sent on a Coastal Forces course at

HMS *Hornet*, a collection of huts beside a creek in Portsmouth harbour, and told that within three weeks he would be given command of a motor torpedo-boat.

At the beginning of the war Britain had twenty-eight coastal craft; by the end, more than 1,500 had been built—motor torpedo-boats, motor gun-boats and motor launches. But though Coastal Forces—nicknamed costly farces—were still treated rather as a joke by men in the big ships, the jibe was aimed not so much at their strategic value as their unconventional manner. Partly because the crews usually lived ashore, only taking to their boats for an operation, and partly because their skirmishes could be sudden and violent and fought at close quarters with the enemy, a Coastal Forces flotilla acquired something of the character of an air squadron; and an MTB commander, seen as a swashbuckling piratical figure with no time for the punctilios of regular service, was the nearest thing at sea to a fighter pilot. Their unorthodoxy may have raised a few admirals' eyebrows but their courage was unquestioned and by the end of the war they had fought many hundreds of naval actions, mostly in the English Channel, the Straits of Dover and the North Sea.

When August arrived at *Hornet* in July 1940 he found an atmosphere of excitement and novelty overlaid with a welter of naval procedure. New tactics had to be invented for new boats, manned by new officers and crew, to meet a new situation. Across the Channel the coast was in enemy hands, the German navy was working from harbours close to British convoys, an invasion was expected daily. Life at *Hornet* was very different from the dry intangibles of Room 39 or the drowsy classrooms of Greenwich. Yet even here there were things to irk a man itching for action and appalled by the unreality of life around him. He wrote to Mollie soon after arriving, 'The game here appears to be croquet which I believe gets dangerous at times.' There were aspects of the Drake myth that could be carried too far.

Many of his colleagues, RNVR officers like himself, had already been on active service and he was impatient to make up for lost sea time: 'I feel very small, having done nothing the whole war.'

He had no scruples about cutting a lecture if there was a chance to go out in one of the boats—'grand little craft', he called them. But a number of RN officers had found their way into Coastal Forces and when he was posted to an MTB it was as first lieutenant to an elderly lieutenant-commander who had come back from retirement and had a low opinion of the temporary officer under him. In return August didn't think much of the way his captain handled the boat. Though they went out on trials in the Solent and even out to sea on patrol, August spent most of his time copying out tide-tables and Admiralty orders, correcting charts and signal books, writing up the log and paying the men.

> This life is really rather rot [he wrote after less than a month at *Hornet*]. I thought I was coming to something warlike and find everyone living a more or less peacetime life of nine-thirty to four-thirty with an hour for lunch. Nowhere have I seen any really hard work being done. The thing seems to be to get a nice job and sit in it. Suggestions for doing anything above the minimum are treated with derision.

His MTB went on patrol ('the same old routine of going in and out') and sometimes spent all night at sea, but when August asked why they didn't try new tactics he was ignored: 'One isn't encouraged to have ideas.'

In his free time he was confined to a ten-mile limit from *Hornet*, but found that he could take the paddle-steamer across to the Isle of Wight without breaking bounds. There, on a hot summer afternoon, he walked through the countryside: 'So close yet so completely out of the war. Just quiet valleys and green downs and cows and nobody about.' Later, Mollie came to stay in a guest-house, bringing the new baby, their fourth child, and watched the MTBs pirouetting, as August called it, in the Solent.

In September 1940 he was given command of MAC 2, a pre-war MTB stripped of one of her engines and both torpedo tubes, and sent on air-sea rescue duty to Dover. Since the fall of France it was in the front battle-line and frequently under shellfire from across the straits. August was billeted in the hotel where he and Mollie had stayed on their wedding night, now converted into a Coastal Forces base called HMS *Wasp*—a much nicer insect than *Hornet*, he thought. There was a majority of RNVR officers and an informal atmosphere, with sweaters worn at dinner and no King's health drunk afterwards. It seemed that he was going to see the kind of active service he had been hoping for.

The work was tedious and dangerous. Through the autumn of 1940 the German air force pounded England with the most savage bombing yet known, and every time an enemy bomber or a British fighter crashed in the sea the rescue boats were sent out to look for the wreck. Sometimes there was a British airman or a German prisoner to bring home, sometimes a corpse. Often there was merely wreckage or nothing in sight at all.

Before long August was having trouble with his senior officers. When MAC 2 needed a new part for her engines he sent a signal direct to the admiral without getting consent from the vice-admiral first, and made it worse by sending two more signals to hurry things up. In the fit of counter-orders that broke out the engine part was lost, putting the boat out of action and causing more fury. Another time he was given a reprimand for bringing MAC 2 into harbour without permission from Dover Castle. And ashore one day, walking into the town, he was stopped by a captain in a car, apoplectic because he was carrying his gas mask the wrong way. Pettiness pervaded too much of naval life, but August couldn't accept rules and habits which made no sense to him. It was a relief to get to sea, driving at thirty knots down Channel or through the straits into the North Sea. He and his crew liked each other, sharing danger, boredom, frustration, exhaustion and every possible scrap of fun in a vessel not much bigger than *Duet*; and his little cabin, with books and gramophone and family photos and a Greenland sealskin on the floor, was a sanctuary from the idiocies of HMS *Wasp*.

With winter and worse weather the air raids dwindled, and the rescue boats spent days, weeks, in harbour. Occasionally MAC 2 was ordered to sea for other tasks—to sink a drifting mine or relight a buoy that had gone out or retrieve a barrage balloon that had broken loose—but it wasn't enough for August. He wrote to the Admiralty asking for another posting. Nothing happened. Later, 'to stop us going to rot', he was sent out to escort mine-sweepers at work in the channels through the minefields, going ahead in foggy weather to find the marker buoys and generally helping to keep the convoy routes open. To Mollie he called the job 'really very mere', a favourite word which he hoped would conceal the peril.

They wrote to each other almost every day and telephoned often. While August spoke of 'this dull hole' and apologized for having so little to say, Mollie told him in detail about life at Spencers, a life with as much incident as his own. Through the dark months of 1940 and 1941 she tended the family and house-hold, adjusting to each new phase of total war as she knew her husband would expect. She started a knitting-party and a savings group, she collected for the Red Cross, she held a whist-drive in the garden, she attended jam-making classes, she scrubbed hospital floors. The children slept in the cellar, the chauffeur drilled the Home Guard on the tennis court, soldiers camped in the park, and the white walls of the house ('it shines like a lamp in the moon') were painted brown to hide it from enemy planes—not before a bomb had landed on the lawn and blown the windows in. Essex was in the front line no less than Dover, but Mollie spurned the chance of moving to a safer place and stuck to Spencers, the home she had made and shared with August. Looking back on that idyllic pre-war time she was thankful they had spent so much of it together, though she wondered if to him they now seemed wasted, unexciting years: 'Look at all the expeditions you might have had,' she wrote, 'and didn't, for my sake.' The present awful separation was a chance for gratitude.

For August she sometimes stirred an old ambivalence. It was nice to be sent flowers and fruit and jam and *Country Life*, yet too many luxuries could be embarrassing and he never enjoyed a fuss being made. He felt the same about excessive adoration. But Mollie knew him well enough and at the end of a letter filled with more than the usual amount of love she added, 'I can see you making a face and thinking what rot the woman writes.'

News of the children was another matter and August could never have too much. He sent back fatherly advice on their care. If they were out in the garden when a plane came over, they were not to make easy targets by running across the lawn into the house, but must get under the trees. He hoped they were looking after their own little gardens, their part in the war, and getting on with their lessons. The governess should concentrate on a proper grounding of English, with a little Latin and arithmetic and music later: 'If they don't learn the elements in the right way they will find the next twelve years a pain and grief, as I did . . . Home education should be the best sort of all but frequently isn't, due to indifferent and ignorant governesses who don't know their stuff and haven't sufficient *character*.' When he heard that rationing was to be stricter and meat might be abolished altogether, he told Mollie to give the family a good plate of porridge and milk every morning. For a sick child he recommended lightly cooked liver or kidneys, underdone cutlets, rabbit pie, suet (with his Greenland puddings in mind) and tongue. The leader of an Arctic expedition, he said, had saved the lives of several men in the last stages of scurvy by giving them raw musk-ox tongue.

Exasperated by being kept idle in harbour, he became obsessed with the national war effort. Everybody must pull their weight. The boiler at Spencers should only be lit three days a week to save coke. Somebody should dig up the tins and old buckets buried behind the stables, and collect garden rollers and mowing machines and tools and iron gates and railings—even the legs of the baby's cot—for scrap. It was time the servants, instead of asking for more wages to keep up with munitions workers, woke up to the fact that they were in the war whether they liked it or not. It would be good for them to make a sacrifice, but how it was to be done he left to Mollie. She must give her orders and see they were carried out, allowing no arguments for the other side ('there are always twenty-four reasons why a thing can't be done and only one why it can') but if she turned out to be wrong she could repeal her orders later. She mustn't be unselfish or broad-minded; broad-mindedness was the worst sin. Single-minded, patriotic, decisive himself, he asked no less of others, especially his wife. But he was confident and proud of her: 'I know you are doing three times as much as anyone for the Country.'

As if being in the navy wasn't enough, he made small gestures in many ways, discreetly and with the least show. No sailors in Coastal Forces were so generously treated to extra food, jerseys, socks, mufflers and balaclavas as the crew of MAC 2, and when a huge parcel of cheese arrived August forwarded it at once to an old tenant at Spencers. On hearing that three army officers were to be billeted in the house, he told Mollie to give them a couple of bottles of port each week from his cellar. He asked her if a cheque for £100 was enough for the village War Weapons Week. He took his big astronomical telescope up to Dover Castle where the admiral, who had nothing so powerful for watching the French coast, gladly accepted it on loan for the rest of the war. And having plenty of money of his own, he quietly handed over his naval pay to the Chancellor of the Exchequer.

Occasionally Mollie stayed for a few days near Dover and even went out in MAC 2; and whenever possible August arranged for the boat to be overhauled at Felixstowe, not far from Spencers. But he couldn't get home for Christmas, and the round of jolly naval parties only increased his isolation. At moments he wished he had joined the army or the air force; it might have meant more action. Then he began to take a new view of the war. At first he had wanted every bit of his physical and mental ability to be used; now he saw that there were a number of jobs and a number of people and it didn't matter which were done by whom. Some jobs were more difficult or unpleasant or distinguished or dangerous than others; but what he called 'fielding in the deep' for crashed aeroplanes and 'plodding round with the sweepers' had to be done by someone, and if he had picked something that

kept him within reach of Mollie—as long as she didn't think it
too lowly or back-line—he was content.

During the winter and spring, for spells of a few weeks, MAC 2
was sent to Ramsgate to work off the North Foreland, in the
Thames estuary and in the wreck-strewn waters of Goodwin
Sands. To the crew it was a poor exchange for Dover, but for
August it had happy associations. From Ramsgate, after leaving
Cambridge, he had sailed on his first cruise abroad and had often
been back, racing in *Duet*. It was further from naval bureaucracy
and stuffiness, and improved still more by a great row with the
port commander—starting when MAC 2 was fouled by an un-
charted mooring chain across the channel. The commander told
August he ought to nurse his ship better, to which he replied
that it was the commander's harbour that needed nursing. Then,
one bright spring morning, he got a message from his coxswain
that MAC 2 was to shift to another berth. He refused. Presently
he was summoned to the commander, white with rage, and asked
to explain why he hadn't obeyed. He said he was a naval officer
and didn't take orders from his coxswain. The commander lost
his temper, to August's delight.

There were moments of great pleasure. One day a Thames
barge came bowling into Ramsgate harbour, a pretty sight for a
man who hadn't seen a sailing ship or real seamanship for too
long. And roaring in MAC 2 at full speed, spray-blown through
a fresh breeze, he could almost forget the extra joy it would have
been in *Duet*. Even when he was ordered out to a station at sea
instead of waiting on stand-by in harbour, and lolloped idly all
day with the gear smashing itself to pieces and the crew being
seasick, there were compensations. August bought fishing tackle
for his men, and if it wasn't too rough he played Handel and
Mendelssohn on his gramophone, glad to be beyond reach of the
authorities ashore.

MAC 2 was sent back to Dover and as the months passed,
though half resigned to what he considered an easy war—but
much less dull and safe than most people's—August felt more and
more sickened at the uselessness and incompetence he saw under

the comfortable roof of HMS *Wasp*. 'The usual lumps of crass stupidity sit in their offices and pass each other's babies round, and then go and drink it off.' In MAC 2 he was fairly independent and self-contained, but it was no fun to be controlled by people for whom pink gin and weekend golf and angling for soft jobs seemed to be the chief concern. Though there were kindred spirits in Coastal Forces, even a few friends, they too hated the stupefying air of the base. Many of them, like himself (and like many of the German E-boat commanders on the other side) were experienced peacetime yachtsmen and some of them were already naval heroes, but a few had found that as RNVR amateurs, though just as effective against the enemy as RN professionals, they were resented and sometimes snubbed. Meanwhile billiards, cinemas, variety shows, silly radio programmes, dances, Wrens—nothing could ease the boredom of war, except action. Drink was the commonest relief. August played patience, read novels, tried his hand at poetry and wrote some comic sketches for a concert party which were never put on. And though he shrank from sentimentality he sometimes walked, if he could bear it, along the harbour wall where he and Mollie had walked on the first evening of their marriage.

In London one day at the end of July 1941 he learnt from a friend at the Admiralty that he had been posted to another command, but the order had been cancelled on request from a senior officer at Dover. Though it couldn't have surprised him, it may have saddened him. A few weeks later, after he had been captain of MAC 2 for nearly a year and the war was nearly two years old, he was given command of a new motor gun-boat, MGB 20. He was pleased to find that most of his old crew wanted to go with him; pleased that there were men in the navy for whom he wasn't just someone who fitted in nowhere very neatly.

For three months he was at Portland, on trials in the new boat. Mollie came to stay at Weymouth and they snatched golden autumn walks through the Dorset countryside. Soon MGB 20 was 'running like a sewing-machine' at forty-five knots on her three immense engines, and at the end of November 1941 August took her up Channel and round into the North Sea, to be based first at Great Yarmouth and later at Lowestoft—two more naval insects, HMS *Midge* and HMS *Mantis*. He was second-in-command of an MGB flotilla, glad to be active on his own account and not just waiting in support of someone else. It seemed 'a well run show, the only one I have struck so far that is run for the boats instead of the boats for the base'. Occasionally, inevitably, there was a clash when some officer's behaviour transgressed August's minimal sense of rank, but there was nobody he disliked; and life could be exciting, though with long pauses between the bouts.

Convoys of British merchant ships passed up and down the east coast, supplying London. While German U-boats did their deadly work out in the Atlantic, trying to throttle Britain, E-boats played havoc in the North Sea. Coming in darkness and often lying stopped behind a lighted buoy, they would fire torpedoes at the leading ships of a convoy and be speeding for home before the escort knew it had been attacked. Until the arrival of the first MGBs the enemy had almost everything his own way, and the passage along the Norfolk and Suffolk coast, known as E-boat alley, was an uncomfortable place.

The MGBs' work was usually at night, patrolling out at sea beyond the convoy routes, and usually it was uneventful. Often the weather was the worst enemy. Rolling for hours in a steep swell with engines cut, or cruising at high speed through drenching rain and spray, could be more gruelling than the rare battles; tense and confusing too, and it was not unknown for friend to be attacked by friend. (The worst August ever did was to give chase to a suspicious light on the horizon, only to find it was Venus rising in the dawn.) The work needed patience, strong nerves, quick reactions. It also needed, for winter weather, tougher boats than the navy had. MGB 20 spent weeks in harbour for repairs, to August's disgust, and by Christmas he was in command of another boat, MGB 16, which, too often, was also broken down.

Life ashore, eating and sleeping in a hotel and rarely going to sea, suited many officers but not August, though he somehow made things tolerable for himself and his men. He bought an old motorcycle for exploring the countryside, he found friends in the neighbourhood who invited him to shoot their pheasants, he lectured to the troops on Greenland, and at Christmas when Mollie sent him a big pot of caviar—an astonishing luxury in the middle of the war—he gave a little party for chosen members of the flotilla. Even at sea he showed how life needn't be as bleak as some people made it. It was the coldest winter for years and the boats often got encrusted with ice, but in a blizzard August would stop and let the squalls drive past while captain and crew, dressed for the Arctic, brewed up cocoa in the wheelhouse. There were few occasions that couldn't be improved.

In the New Year with his boat out of action ('the whole thing is very enfeebling') there was some comfort when the senior officer of the flotilla went on leave and August took charge; took revenge too on the obstructivists, sending angry signals and banging rubber stamps. When he did go to sea, he went with appropriate panache. Officers in Coastal Forces, where legends bred easily, were expected to be dashing and elegant but August created a style that was like nobody else's—unintentionally, for he was the last man to strike a pose. At Lowestoft there was an Ordinary Seaman, half August's age, who was amazed that such an individualist could ever command one of His Majesty's ships; and over the years that young sailor, becoming a distinguished member of the House of Lords, kept a vision of the flotilla sailing at full throttle out through the harbour mouth where the port commander, a glass-eyed character known as One-fixed-one-flashing, stood to take the salute, while on the bridge of the leading boat Lieutenant Courtauld in a purple silk dressing-gown fired his Very pistol at the seagulls.

Two weeks in command of the flotilla convinced him that he didn't want one of his own, with untold paperwork and the responsibility for other people's sins. Instead, in February, he was appointed to command a 'B' motor launch, ML 152, and

after a torpedo course at Portland the new boat was sent for
convoy duty on the east coast. She was slower but bigger than
an MGB, comfortable enough for living aboard during several
days away from Lowestoft. The MLs worked in pairs as close
escort on the night passage between the Thames estuary and
Hull, trying to encourage the convoy to keep station, and picking
up survivors if a ship was torpedoed. It was a chance for good
seamanship, in which August revelled. On his first convoy,
having left the ships at dawn in the mouth of the Humber, he
found no difficulty and much pleasure in leading his companion
up river to Immingham in thick fog, taking soundings with a lead
line in the proper seaman's way. 'I'm very happy with my little
ship,' he wrote.

Through the spring and summer ML 152 continued her escort
duty. It was repetitive and never as free from naval red tape as
August would have liked, but while recognizing that there was
'practically no promotion except for bootlickers' it was good to be
doing something valuable that happened to be within reach of
home. Mollie recommended the bootlicking, for overdue leave
if not for a better job, but she knew it was useless; he would never
ask for anything for himself. Occasionally he got away for a day
or two at Spencers, and meanwhile was happy to be sent hampers
of spring vegetables, even if the naval cook treated asparagus like
cabbage.

August's mild eccentricities were noted by his colleagues as the
privilege of a man who knew more about his job than most of
them; and long after he left the flotilla—long after the war—he
was remembered not just as the ML captain who read books and
played the gramophone in his cabin, but as the one who, after a
convoy, would leave the routine job of bringing the boat back to
Lowestoft to his first lieutenant and only emerge on the bridge in
his pyjamas to bring her into harbour. There was nothing incom-
patible between the young man who had once told the Governor
of Nigeria that his Union Jack was upside-down and this older
one, the opposite of a stickler but still a fiercely loyal citizen, who
fought for England in the way that he preferred; and there was

no harm if, in doing so, he brightened one corner of a dismal war. Thirty-five years later another officer kept vivid the pleasure of meeting August in those grim wartime years and being able to talk all evening of mountains and expeditions and common friends—a happy, civilized moment 'before the world went mad'.

Then in June 1942 he startled even those who were used to his impulsive turns. There was to be a Parliamentary by-election at Maldon in Essex, and August offered himself as candidate to the local Conservative Association. They turned him down—'poor judgement', according to the admiral commanding Coastal Forces, who might have shown his high opinion by a gesture of promotion and may have been sorry not to see August disappear to Westminster. But nobody who ever heard August make a speech could have been surprised. He himself must have seen that he wasn't meant for politics, and, except to tell Mollie that he was glad to be out of it, he never mentioned the subject or tried again. Probably he would have lost at Maldon anyway. Though it was considered a safe Conservative seat, it was won with a big majority by an independent, Tom Driberg, who held it for many years.

In June the flotilla started a new base at Pin Mill, a village on the river Orwell below Ipswich consisting of a boatyard and a pub and not much else—the village where, on the ice cap, he had dreamed of living. It was an improvement on Lowestoft, closer to Spencers and a perfect haven after the rigours of a convoy: 'We are quite on our own and I think everything will be very happy and peaceful here. It all looks just the same as ever.' Mollie brought the children over for a picnic on ML 152 at her mooring. When they had gone, the captain sat on the bridge, the sun slanting down the river in a golden beam, the unrippled mauve-green water bright between glistening mud flats, the woods and fields untouched by war. It was the first of many pleasant summer evenings in a forgotten naval backwater. Often August slept on deck, sometimes he went sailing with two or three of his crew, and in the holidays Mollie came with the family to camp in a field—four children, nanny, tents and primuses. For fun as much as for training, August arranged a combined exercise with the army, ferrying 1,000 soldiers across the river in whalers and providing a landing-party of sailors with blackened faces and a barrage of shellfire. It suited his taste for the practical and the romantic. At Pin Mill the authorities could largely be ignored—a mutual wish perhaps, for when an admiral passed by in his barge and August lined up the crew to salute him, the great man looked the other way.

Life was as good as he could expect in wartime. Most heartening of all was the way Spencers was kept going by Mollie, who added the Women's Voluntary Service and the Soldiers', Sailors' and Airmen's Association to her other work, as well as taking cookery lessons in her own kitchen in case of emergency. Austerity and anxiety were absorbed into the household as if they were quite normal. Sometimes Spencers assumed the flavour of a novel by Evelyn Waugh. Homeless relations came to stay indefinitely, strangers were billeted in the house, tired air-raid workers from London were invited for a holiday, explorers disguised in uniform dropped in to talk of better times. A chestnut tree was planted in the bomb crater on the lawn, a generation of young rooks was shot by government request and the birds either sent to market or put in a pie, and half a pipe of port (fifty-six dozen bottles laid down at birth for the eldest son) was sold and national savings certificates bought instead. Conditions were disturbed, to a greater or less degree, by each new circumstance—whether merely inconvenient, like petrol rationing and the disappearance of bananas, or startling, like the building of an aerodrome at the edge of the village, from which American bombers were soon skimming the treetops in the park and American airmen were poaching rabbits. War could seem like a continuous demand for small adjustments. The wider aspect was never lost in the contracting focus, but the pain and horror were sometimes numbed by an unending stream of minor troubles.

Home and family, kept vivid by letters and occasional visits, were August's first concern. Without them war would have been

still more pointless; instead it was an interlude, a rude inter-
ruption in the pleasant business of life. The summer of 1942
passed into autumn, the season of raspberries and melons gave
way to nectarines and figs, the pheasant and partridge shooting
began again, and August might have settled down to a second
winter of east-coast convoys. But in October he was called
unexpectedly to the Admiralty.

Rolling a kayak was something he had never perfected in Greenland. After a short refresher course at a London swimming-pool
he was ordered to take a small landing-craft from Fort William,
on the west coast of Scotland, through the Caledonian canal and
up to Shetland. The job, as second-in-command of a commando
troop, was obscured by secrecy (August had to take off his Polar
Medal ribbon in case it gave anyone a clue), but it sounded
exciting and as the boat sailed slowly up the east coast it seemed
hardly different from a winter trip in *Duet*. At sea the skipper and
crew tucked into corned-beef stew together, and in port August,
who didn't see the point of hardship if it wasn't necessary, found
billets for his men and then made for the best hotel. Only the
distance between him and Spencers, the furthest since the
beginning of the war, darkened the prospect. 'How my love
stretches out to you,' he wrote to Mollie. 'Can you catch it, I
wonder?'

In Orkney the boat broke down. August was impatient to press
on but the local admiral, not fancying a helpless vessel adrift on
his waters, stopped him. Weeks passed with nothing to do—
short dark days of the northern winter, long nights alone and a
Christmas nearly as solitary as the one on the ice cap but far
more dismal—before August could get away and on with the
voyage.

In Shetland he was thrown straight into commando exercises,
carrying a heavy load on his back for the first time for years and
camping in terrible weather. Gales chased each other across the
islands, one after another. But though the training was tough and

he was alternately soaked and frozen, he admitted it was fun. The
unit, irregular and unique, was commanded by an old Arctic
friend, Andrew Croft, and contained several other explorers—'as
good a lot of chaps as one is likely to be with, so all unpleasant-
nesses are bearable'. Their purpose was to land on an island off
the Norwegian coast and harass the occupying Germans by sticking limpet mines to ships at anchor. But Shetland in midwinter,
racked by storms and deprived of daylight, was a poor place for
training, and soon they moved back to the west coast of Scotland,
to Loch Carron. There, in magnificent Highland country far
from any war, they practised with Bren guns, grenades, fuses,
knives and several kinds of canoe—sneaking up to ships, planting
dummy mines and making a getaway unseen. But it didn't last
much longer. In March 1943, with doubts afflicting the powers in
control, the unit was disbanded. Just as well, as it turned out;
later, when a party of commandos was put ashore in Norway
from an MTB, they were taken prisoner and executed in a
concentration camp.

For a while in early spring August was left almost alone at
Loch Carron, walking over the hills and wishing he were at home
or at least doing something more active. Once again the war
seemed to be passing him by. Most of the men who had joined
the navy with him had got their half-stripe and were now
lieutenant-commanders—a pretty bogus rank, he told himself,
without much comfort. Several of his friends, some of the best,
had been killed and it seemed that nobody was left but a lot of
rotters. But the end of the war, he felt, might be coming into
sight. Somehow he would get through the rest of it, without yet
seeing how. He would make no move himself, he would let the
navy use him as they wanted. When he heard that Ian Fleming,
still in the Naval Intelligence Division, wanted him back in the
Admiralty ('that expensive museum piece', August called it) he
lay low. He didn't care to be a Whitehall warrior again, he would
just wait and see.

Next time he went to sea it was as a passenger in the *Queen Mary* to New York. Also on board was Winston Churchill on the way to meet President Roosevelt, and August was banished to an eighteen-bunk cabin several decks down, where his ideas of luxury travel took some knocks. But he got a job as look-out on the bridge, and the Prime Minister occasionally climbed up there too, to watch his escort of cruisers ploughing at speed over the Atlantic.

In New York, after the black-out and rationing of England, August was amazed at the brilliant streets, aghast at being able to eat the fat of the land 'in miserable safety' and exhausted by hospitality. Nothing seemed quite real until he got a telegram from Mollie announcing the birth of their fifth child, a fourth son. 'When peace comes,' he wrote to his father, 'we shall have a good boat's crew.' Mollie sent another telegram with a string of possible names for the baby, but it was stopped by the censor who thought it must be a secret code. A few days later August went by train to Norfolk, Virginia, where he took command of an infantry landing-craft to be delivered across the Atlantic for the invasion of Sicily. He sailed in a fleet of others—a perfect summer passage, with a short stop in Bermuda and nothing to interrupt the sunbathing except some welcome deep-sea navigation—and in June reached Gibraltar. Waiting for a passage back to England in a troopship, he met some old friends and was nearly swept into the whirl of garrison society. He preferred to sit on his balcony with a book, watching the sun over the bay and listening to the bugle calls from ships and barracks.

A month later he was in a train to Sheerness on the Thames estuary to join HMS *Garth*, a destroyer working as convoy escort in the North Sea and English Channel. 'All rather high church,' he reported when he got on board. No more broken-down motor-boats or special operations that came to nothing or crusty old men who had never been much good at anything. This promised something more solid: 'A grand ship . . . An awfully good lot of officers . . . The best in the flotilla . . . A comfy cabin under the bridge . . . A bit strange and wildly complicated . . . The latest gadgets . . . Having great fun . . . Everybody is very pleasant and free and easy . . . The food is superb.' Though his signalling was rusty and his gunnery non-existent, he was in a proper ship at last, with plenty to do. Plenty to learn also, but that was the point. After a few months as watch-keeper in *Garth*, officer of the fo'c'sle in charge of the anchors, two four-inch guns, and the private affairs of thirty seamen, he would be sent as first lieutenant to a similar escort ship.

High time too, no doubt. The captain of *Garth* and all the others in the wardroom except the chief engineer were younger than himself. The first lieutenant was a keen RN officer of twenty-two, promoted from the lower deck, and it was hard to take a ticking-off from him for some trivial sin. But on his birthday a few weeks after joining the ship, starting his fortieth year, August confessed to Mollie, 'I am afraid I am very happy.'

It would have been even better if the work hadn't grown so monotonous. Life in an escort destroyer was pure routine. Convoys sailed slowly along regular channels with rare incidents and almost never a battle. On board *Garth* was a German dog that had swum from a sinking E-boat in more dramatic times, but now the passages were usually uneventful. The defences were stronger, the attackers stayed at home. Even when the ship was sent one night as a decoy off the French coast to entice enemy planes within range of British fighters, nothing happened. Planes did sometimes dive out of the sun, bringing everyone to action stations, but it was only the RAF using *Garth* for a practice target. And though August was enjoying himself, it was chastening to be reminded, when somebody mentioned Greenland, of his more illustrious life before the war: 'How much one feels descended in the scale of humanity since those days. Then, freedom and responsibility; now, narrow restriction and complete subordination of body and soul. The problem then was how to live, now it is how to kill.'

By December 1943 he was living in very different quarters—the state apartments of the royal yacht *Victoria and Albert* in Portsmouth harbour, a nice contrast to the naval gunnery school on Whale Island where he was doing a first lieutenant's course. Everyone else wore white trousers and canvas gaiters and had to move at the double, but elderly sailors were let off lightly and allowed to walk. Though incessant shouting and stamping and saluting turned the place into something like a guards' barracks, and though strict discipline and a chilling hierarchy were not August's favourite conditions, he was surprised how much he liked Whale Island. Such proficiency and purposefulness were impressive. And at the end of the course he would get some leave and spend his first Christmas for four years at home.

Early in 1944 he was appointed first lieutenant to a corvette that hadn't yet been built. He went to Troon in Ayrshire and for two months hung around a dockyard office while the last touches were made to convert an Admiralty contract, a hasty wartime job, into a fighting ship called HMS *Tintagel Castle*. August's task was to assemble 120 men straight from barracks, mostly young toughs from Liverpool and Glasgow, and turn them into something that hadn't existed before, a ship's company living and working and, one day, fighting together.

By mid-April, after sea trials, *Tintagel Castle* was ready for working-up—a month of rigorous training at Tobermory on the Isle of Mull for every destroyer and frigate and corvette that went into the Battle of the Atlantic. It was a non-stop treadmill of drills and exercises run by an old seadog of an admiral who took pleasure in keeping a ship for an extra fortnight if she didn't pass his inspection—and to August it wasn't improved by being in one of the most beautiful places he knew. There could be no fun, as he put a gang of uncouth seamen through some fatuous man-oeuvre under the admiral's withering eye, in catching sight of a loch where *Duet* had once lain at anchor, or a mountain path where he and Mollie had once walked. The working-up left everyone on board limp with exhaustion but in theory fit for the Atlantic, and by mid-May *Tintagel Castle* was on her way to America with a convoy. The first lieutenant, if nobody else, was thankful to get away. Many of the crew had never been afloat before, and seasickness at least put a stop to messdeck brawls.

Out in the Atlantic at last, zigzagging at slow speed to Newfoundland, August could rejoice in the open sea that stretched all round.

By mid-June they were back in Scotland with another convoy and the war had taken a turn for the better. The Allies had landed in Normandy, the second front had begun, the end was not far ahead. August would have liked to watch the last excitement, if only from a corvette in the back row, but there was little hope: 'We shall remain trundling back and forth with the convoys.' Sometimes they went down to Gibraltar, usually across to America. The Atlantic was already less dangerous. The U-boats were losing the long battle, but attacks still happened and the old vigilance had to be kept up; the old routine too, and it was galling to be swamped by the petty daily round—as policeman, magistrate, priest, impresario, captain's dogsbody, everybody's uncle—while the fighting was being carried across Europe. The best August could do was run a sweepstake on board for the dates when German cities fell.

Losing interest in the war, or anyway in the more boring aspects of it, wasn't a popular attitude. August was sent for by the captain, an ex-merchant navy officer ten years younger than himself, and told that his manner was too offhand. No doubt it was. But long after he had left *Tintagel Castle*, as if nobody had noticed how lucky they were until they saw the man who took his place, the captain wrote a fulsome letter to Mollie to say how much they missed him. For one thing the level of wardroom conversation, provoked and stimulated by August, had dropped sharply. But his good work—bringing the corvette up to pitch, tending her crew in his conscientious, unassuming way—had paid off. The captain was sorry that when they fought a brisk action in the Channel and earned the commander-in-chief's praise, August wasn't there to take any of the credit. Not that he ever would have.

With the war against Germany fizzling out and no wish to fight

Japan, with no hope of an active seagoing job and no prospect of quick release from the navy, August put out feelers towards possible work—vaguely something concerned with the political aftermath, something more interesting than just hanging around a harbour or Whitehall. Somewhere in the confusion ahead he felt sure he could be useful. Perhaps he hoped for too much. In its curious way, having taken him out of his corvette, the Admiralty sent him as watch-keeping officer to a requisitioned cargo liner, HMS *Agamemnon*, that was going to Vancouver for conversion into a canteen ship for the Pacific war. It wasn't what he had in mind. And Hitler's secret weapon, the flying bombs, had just arrived in England. Many had fallen in Essex and one had struck a tree in the park at Spencers, breaking all the windows again. A trip abroad was the last thing August wanted.

The long voyage across the Atlantic and through the Panama Canal and up the west coast of America, a comfortable winter cruise far from any war, was a mockery. He couldn't enjoy the Caribbean, the tropical nights, the idle life. The ship reached Vancouver in deep snow on Christmas Eve. Canada was on holiday. Irony turned more bitter still. Turkey and plum pudding on board, a carol service in the cathedral, a solemn walk to the naval cemetery to look at the graves of forgotten seamen, the King's speech relayed from London, party after party—none of it could raise August's humour and all of it stood between him and home. Spencers had never been so distant. At New Year another round of jollity thickened the gloom. 'The local hospitality is excellent for those who can take pleasure in it. I can't, I'm afraid, so I sit on board and become more impossible every day.' A letter came from Mollie but it had been written nearly two years before, when he was last in America, and had been following him ever since. It increased the sense of remoteness. Time seemed meaningless, or non-existent. Had the months in *Garth* and *Tintagel Castle* and *Agamemnon* really happened?

Having waited a fortnight for somebody to tell him what to do next, he took matters into his own hands. He stormed along to a senior officer who turned out to be a sailing man, a fellow member

of the Royal Cruising Club, and a few hours later he was crossing
America by train. In New York he went to a couple of concerts,
made a speech at a yacht-club dinner and celebrated five years'
seniority as a lieutenant ('a monumental disgrace, but I would
rather that than a lot of brass for being a base rat') by forgetting
all about the navy in the company of several Arctic explorers who
also happened to be in town. Then he got a passage back to
England in an elderly battleship, HMS *Nelson*.

A fortnight after Germany surrendered, in May 1945, August
was on his way to Copenhagen as first lieutenant of the naval
party in charge of disarmament in Denmark. He had come full
circle, taking five and a half years from the winter of the phoney
war to this bizarre experience of peace, and was back in the
muddle-headed world of naval bureaucrats. Nobody was sure
what he was supposed to be doing, but August knew that the
Danes could do it better. Most of his colleagues, thankful not to
have been drafted to the Pacific to fight Japan, were filling in
time before being released from the navy. Many of them, overtaken by their own survival, struck attitudes of inflated arrogance.
Some of them, so attuned to war, were terrified of peace. It
wasn't what they expected. Past hopes were irrelevant, future
needs would be different. Emptiness, purposelessness, uncertainty lay ahead. Old habits, dropped for so long, couldn't be
suddenly picked up. But for the moment this liberated northern
capital was glittering with distractions, an intoxicating contrast to
the danger and boredom of the long fight and the austerity of
England.

August's letters to Mollie during that summer rumbled with
frustration. He called it a housekeeper's job: 'At the barracks all
day, answering the telephone and seeing to the drains . . . The
work seems quite futile and the social life entirely fatuous.'
Welfare of the troops took up most of his time: 'Trying to get
something done for the sailors . . . No books, no beer, no clubs,
no games, no wireless.' The work of disarmament was soon

finished, the Germans disappeared and the naval party lapsed into the business of self-perpetuation, generating paper-work to justify itself. Trivialities cluttered the hot, unreal months:

'A mayor's reception for the allies . . . A victory ball . . . An official welcome ballet . . . Speeches in three languages as the Russians were there . . . Strawberries and cream for everyone . . . A dull dinner . . . An awful lunch . . . Everlasting eating-competitions . . . The usual quacking of Danish all evening . . . All I do is feel like a stuck pig and solemnly shake hands . . . My steward has been pinched by the admiral . . . I spent most of the time feeding decayed princesses . . . Like the old ladies of Essex . . . The admiral, when he had finished with them, kept parking them on me.'

The atmosphere was clouded by minor corruption and petty jealousies which August watched with distaste. Too much of Britain's post-war effort went into the admiral's yacht, he thought, though it was good to see the admiral's discomfiture at finding him, a mere RNVR lieutenant, on familiar terms with high society. And some of the parties were exotic:

'No end of people, most of them princesses and countesses, with a buffet supper, clowns and things performing on the lawn, and Chinese lanterns . . . In the middle the Queen came . . . Quite a nice old thing . . . I had to dance with the wallflowers . . . A bonfire and then an opera singer . . . I retired behind an apple tree.'

The endless social round would have been more fun with Mollie there to share it: 'A picnic in some little hills of heather and then on to a beach through a big wood . . . Very fine sand and a blazing hot sun . . . I felt rather out of it as everyone else had their pretty sweethearts or wives and I had nobody to bathe with . . . Montgomery has laid down no wives in north-west Europe . . . Most people seem to have their blondes and like it.'

It was a testing time in many ways, the longest August and Mollie had been apart since they were married. Early in the spring, before Germany surrendered, Mollie had remarked on her own lack of excitement at the news and wondered if August felt as depressed as she did:

> I just can't get up the slightest enthusiasm over the end of the war. It's the most extraordinary thing how little it seems to mean, when the BBC gives out that Mussolini is chopped up and Hitler gone mad and Himmler wants to give in. And yet this time last year, if we could have heard these tidings, how joyful we'd have been.

Now, when the war in Europe was over and she might have expected to see more of her husband, Mollie found he had gone away for longer than ever. 'How miserable this long-range marriage makes me,' she wrote. They had wasted enough precious time already without another separation—the worst one of all. Life at Spencers was no easier than it had been in the darkest days and it didn't cheer her to learn that in Copenhagen, after five years of enemy occupation, the bright lights were on again so soon: 'It shows how little Denmark has suffered, that they can now burst out into such a spate of gaiety . . . All these resistance women—I hope they still resist . . . These Ericsens that you see so much of—I hope she's about fifty and with a wall eye.' Mollie was tense, exhausted, resentful of the gap that seemed to have opened between them. 'Never in all the war years have I felt myself of so little importance to you—so little missed.' She couldn't sleep for worrying that they had fallen out of step, that August was leading a life she could never share; and it was no help when he wrote to say that he too was being kept awake at night—by the Copenhagen trams.

'Where do you get all these ideas about women from?' he asked, forgetting that it was from himself. 'One has to see something of some of them sometimes . . . I would much prefer to spend my free time with the Greenland people . . . As to amusing myself with these Danish females, far from it, they are mostly middle-aged.' But apart from social junkets there was less and less to write about, as the job slowly withered away.

In July came the British general election, the first for ten years. 'What a frightful election this seems to be,' August wrote. 'I suppose the only thing is to have the socialists in and let the Country find them out.' When Labour won with a huge majority, which Mollie found the most depressing thing since the fall of France, he called it 'a good thing probably—they can now go in to bat and make a mess of it'. A month later something more momentous occurred: 'We have just heard of the surrender of the Japs.' To Mollie the atomic bomb was a ghastly new discovery but August was matter-of-fact: 'This new bomb seems quite a good one. Let's hope the Yanks manage to keep it to themselves.' It put a stop to any risk of being sent to fight the Japanese. 'I hear that they have coughed up their emperor so I suppose the war actually is over . . . About time . . . Now we have to take the plunge into the cold and clammy peace . . . These hollow celebrations are completely meaningless.' But whatever else, it meant that release must come soon.

Meanwhile there was the daily cycle of duties to get through:

Just finished a mess dinner ending with an obstacle race over the tables . . . I have two funerals to arrange for Monday, with knobs on . . . Tomorrow there is a thanksgiving service, with more knobs on . . . The captain came to church and I tried to sell him the lesson which was a difficult one from Habakkuk, but he wouldn't buy it . . . I was told off to entertain two brigadiers . . . I have shut down on invitations.

Funerals gave an occasional antidote to parties. A stoker died of pneumonia, a seaman shot himself by mistake, and August had to arrange for a salute to be fired, and official mourners, messmates, flowers and letters of condolence. There was a problem when a petty officer who had committed suicide was forbidden to have naval honours, but conveniently another sailor died: 'It is very fortunate being able to do both together . . . He can come in on the other fellow's.'

While waiting in Copenhagen for his release August was offered a half-stripe—promotion to lieutenant-commander. Though pressed more than once by the admiral, he refused to take it. At the time he told Mollie it was because he had seen the frightful people who got promoted in shore jobs and he didn't want to join them. Years later he wrote that he simply couldn't be bothered to change his uniform.

In the mood of post-war doubts he wondered what he would do after leaving the navy. He even asked a cousin in the Courtauld firm if they wanted a commercial traveller or a bottle-washer. When Mollie tackled him about a rumour that he was planning an expedition to Greenland he denied it. She wished he would consider farming, but supposed he would be bored. She suggested buying a boatyard. All he could think of was getting home to Spencers. Mollie was making it ready. The huge dump of WVS clothing that had so long filled the drawing-room was carted away, the house was painted white again and the lawns were mown. At last the American aerodrome closed down, the bombers flew away and Spencers settled down to await the master who, since he bought it, had spent three-quarters of his time away.

So the last weeks of his naval career flickered past. In Copenhagen the RAF seemed to have taken over the best of the captured German yachts, but August got some good sailing and was glad to find that his pre-war membership of the Royal Danish Yacht Club hadn't lapsed. He bought presents to take back to his family and sent hams and cheeses and eggs in advance. And then, as a present for his forty-first birthday, a signal came from the Admiralty that Lieutenant Courtauld RNVR—who hoped and believed that he was the senior officer in the rank—was to go on leave awaiting release. He gave a party, his first and last, which to his delight was all over by midnight. From Spencers Mollie wrote that she felt like a hen on hot bricks, frightened at the thought of such happiness, and the children built a bonfire for their father's return. Then on 4 September he came home, six years and one day after the outbreak of war.

His last letter to Mollie written in the navy reached her a few hours before him. Since the winter of 1939, when he first went to work in the Admiralty, they had sent nearly 1,200 letters to each other, and kept them all. As a collection they give a clear picture of those years, a shrewd commentary, a lively chronicle. They show what war, for two people who would have claimed nothing unusual for themselves, was like. More than that: there is a touch of P. G. Wodehouse in August's letters and a tang of Jane Austen in Mollie's. They are very entertaining.

Chapter 12

Final Years

THE NEXT LETTER August wrote to Mollie was a year later in September 1946 when he took *Duet* on her first foreign cruise for seven years, after lying at a mooring all the war. He left Burnham-on-Crouch on the evening tide and sailed across the Thames estuary to the North Foreland, then on past the Goodwin Sands and across to Calais in time for breakfast. No matter that these were the bleak years of victory, the Attlee years, when British travellers were only allowed to take a few pounds abroad. It was a moonlit night with bright stars and a roaring wind—the topsail and mizzen were stowed, the mainsail was reefed—just the thing to drive out the taste of slow convoys plugging through those same waters or days of boredom in MAC 2.

The following summer he was sailing to Sweden again, and Holland and Scotland. Improvements were made to *Duet*—a hollow spruce mast, new decks and a new galley, a diesel engine, electric lights—but she went on being sailed as before, hard and often. If she could never beat her own pre-war record of 164 miles in twenty-four hours—almost seven knots—she made some fast passages, and in 1952 won a race from Dover to Sweden, leading the fleet most of the way though she was forty years old.

The children grew up and were enlisted as crew, willingly or not. It was on board *Duet* after a summer holiday on the west coast of Scotland in 1947 that the eldest son Christopher, aged twelve, became mysteriously ill. As they sailed home round the north of Scotland, through the Pentland Firth and down the east coast, he got worse and they put into Blyth in Northumberland for a doctor. Christopher was rushed to hospital where polio was diagnosed. There followed two years of severe paralysis, of plaster and surgery and physiotherapy, and then to help recovery a course of warm-water bathing was recommended. Ian Fleming, August's friend from naval intelligence days, offered him a house in Jamaica for the winter. August decided to sail *Duet* across the Atlantic to the West Indies where Mollie would join him with Christopher.

With three friends on board he left Teignmouth in Devon in October 1949, rather late in the year for an Atlantic crossing. Lisbon was to be the first stop. A violent rainstorm that broke over *Duet* as she sailed out into the Channel and headed for Start Point was a presage of things to come. The crew, clumsy in oilskins and not yet knowing their way about the boat, took time to settle down.

One of them was J. M. Scott. Later he wrote a novel which he dedicated to *Duet*, her skipper and his companions in the crew on that Atlantic voyage. The book concerns a man called Charrington, skipper of a yacht very similar to *Duet*, and although Charrington isn't Courtauld (like all characters in fiction, he is an invention of Scott's imagination and turns out to be a murderer) he behaves often enough as August did to suggest something of his origin.

August, as they rounded Start Point and set a course for Ushant, went below to his cabin and came up with a bottle of gin. His three friends in the cockpit brightened, but it wasn't for them. Under the glass of the steering compass was a bubble in the fluid. He turned the compass over, unscrewed the filler cap and topped it up with gin. Charrington, in Scott's novel, does the same. August, when his crew got constipation, made them drink mugs of seawater as a purge. So does Charrington. Like August, Charrington smokes a pipe, scraping out the bowl into an empty tin and jabbing more tobacco in. Charrington gives his crew mussels and roast goose for their first supper on board, but they get more ordinary food once they are at sea. August too, though he loved a feast, could be happy with a tin of bully beef and enraptured by a plate of sausages. ('Let's have a terrific sausage party,' he wrote to Mollie from Greenland.) Charrington, who is always alert for trouble—frayed ropes or chafing canvas—believes that half of seamanship is human understanding and that ships, like women, respect strength. He is more than master of his ship, he makes up for his companions' inefficiency. 'Charrington gave the orders, but from the start he had done everything himself . . . His voice, giving orders, was hard and sharp as a dog barking . . . He was everywhere at once . . . driving the crew with his tongue.' It is too harsh for a portrait of August but there are points of likeness, distorted by the writer's need for exaggeration and drama. Scott's narrator, who keeps on confusing Charrington with God, says that one has to admire him even if he is a bit of a sadist: 'How charming and interesting he could be . . . But when there is work to be done he doesn't care a damn what he says and can be abominably rude. "You bloody fool" is a form of endearment in comparison. But I am certain he is not merely a tough sailor. He is contradictory, hard to define.' Contradictory was a word that Scott used again, speaking of August long afterwards. But though he claimed that Mollie, when she read the book, felt uneasy at elements of her husband in the villain's character, nothing should be deduced except the risk of going to sea with a novelist on board.

On the second day they were twenty miles off the Lizard, bowling along at a good six knots with a rising wind, through rising waves. They reefed for the night, but next morning the sea was calm and *Duet* rocked on a wide ocean swell. When the wind got up again it came from the south-west, the direction they wanted to go. It blew steadily harder, waves came aboard, the sky was too overcast for August to get a fix. They changed the sails and tacked out into the Atlantic, then back towards France, hoping each time to have rounded Ushant, the corner of Brittany, but always the wind drove against them. In time it became a gale. The jaws of the wooden gaff were split, the staysail broke free, a basket of eggs crashed to the cabin floor, the generator packed up, the bilges had to be pumped out by hand, the lights fused, a

Stilton cheese was washed overboard, August lost a favourite pair of boots, everyone's clothes and bedding were drenched. All four men were cold and wet and tired, and when the gale blew itself out they hadn't begun to cross the Bay of Biscay.

Storm, calm, rain, head-wind—the weather rang the changes for a week. Hoist balloon staysail, change jib, hoist topsail, down topsail, down mainsail, hoist trysail—the crew were seldom idle, and even off watch there was a constant fight against the movement of the boat. Somewhere ahead was Finisterre, the corner of Spain, and then Lisbon, Madeira, the trade winds, the West Indies, but in this excessive weather it was hard to look beyond the bowsprit. They may have started too late, but the winter had come before its time. Other ships were occasionally sighted, sometimes too close, and one dark night a giant tanker gave August a few minutes' trouble. It was the size of Southend, he said, with a bunch of lights at each end and a mile of blackness in between, but he scared it off with a torch. When a cargo ship passed in daylight they signalled it to report *Duet*'s position, which reached Mollie at Spencers and drove her to the atlas to see how far they had got. Not as far as they would have liked.

Rounding Finisterre was as difficult as rounding Ushant. A fair wind was a dream that never came. Instead it blew from the Atlantic, piling waves towards the coast. *Duet*, battling to keep in open water, was pushed into the land. It was the slowest passage she had ever made. The mended staysail broke free again, the jib was ripped, the head of the mainsail came unstitched, the split gaff finally snapped, but waves washed over the deck and sometimes into the cabin and nothing could be repaired in such a sea. Fatigue assailed the crew. They saw the first Spanish fishing boats, and then the first Spanish rocks with bursting breakers and dark mountains beyond. With the engine they made a little headway, butting into the wind and inching towards Finisterre. But even when they got round it, unless the wind changed, they would be on a dangerous lee shore all down Portugal. They never did get round. A bigger wave than ever swamped the engine and stopped it, silencing the last hope of reaching the cape. They turned and ran for Corunna, the nearest port, chased by squalls and the furious waves. To seal their flight the topsail yard broke and they were reduced to jib and mizzen, a sorry rig. In harbour the exhaustion of eight Atlantic days caught up. After brief attention to a bottle of rum and a pot of soup, the crew collapsed.

They spent a week at Corunna, getting repairs done and waiting for better weather. The shipyard work cost more money than they had in Spanish currency—all Englishmen were poor abroad —but appeal to the British consul produced nothing and the port captain arrested *Duet*, forbidding her to leave until the bills were paid. August and his friends went off to dinner at the yacht club, came back to the harbour at midnight and slipped out to sea without waking the guard.

In the early hours, with a gentle south wind and a high barometer, they seemed set to get round Finisterre at last, but by dawn rainstorms hid the land and *Duet*'s old enemy from the south-west was driving her off course, out into the Atlantic. Before they were ready for them waves were coming on board and a big one found its way down into the cabin. Clothes and bedding, laboriously dried out, were drenched again. The chart table, screwed to the floor, broke loose. Matches wouldn't strike. The staysail split. All day and the next night the wind rose, creeping up from force six to force eight like a conspiracy of nature. They could make no headway.

Late on the second day August put the choice to the other three: push on or turn back. It was a matter of time. Already in the sixteen days since leaving England they were ten days behind. If they lost no more, which was unlikely, the crew would have to start for home as soon as they reached Jamaica. August gave no opinion, only the facts, and said he would do whatever the others wanted. They thrashed over the arguments as the waves flogged the boat and the wind tore the rigging; and at last, wearily and unhappily, they decided to run for home.

Turning north-east before the wind, they sped under trysail and storm jib over the ground they had won so agonizingly. Soon they were going too fast, seas were breaking over the stern and they had to stow the trysail and trail ropes astern, pumping the bilges all the time. The man at the helm needed every muscle to stay on course. On the third morning from Corunna, the wind rising to force nine and the barometer still falling, August ordered the last sail, the little storm jib, to be stowed. 'I didn't like the look of it,' he wrote, which was the worst he could say of the stormiest twenty-four hours any of them had known. With no canvas up they were still racing at six knots.

Then they were pooped. A monster wave caught *Duet*'s stern and slewed her round so that she lay broadside to the sea, her hull awash and listing with the wind on the bare masts. The mizzen boom was broken and August was washed out of the cockpit into the scuppers, almost overboard. The whole deck was under water and when it rose again anything not secured, like the lifebelt, had disappeared. Down below, to confound confusion, the heavy batteries broke loose. Wallowing helplessly across the waves *Duet* could have foundered; each towering ridge of sea might flip her over. They trailed ropes over the bows and tied a piece of canvas in the mizzen rigging, to drive her head a little into the wind. Later, they streamed a bag of oil over the side, hoping to subdue the wavecrests. (Not far away one of the navy's biggest aircraft carriers, sent to the aid of a steamer, was also pouring oil overboard.) The surface frothed like boiling milk, blown into a spume that hissed and boomed, yet the water that assaulted them, smashing the deck and swirling round their legs, felt hard and solid. They had to shout above the noise. In the log August recorded a force ten wind, a full gale.

All that day and night they rode it out. With no sails set and the helm lashed, the men stayed below, sometimes going up to look out for ships—a forlorn task in the fury of wind, sea and spindrift. The hatch got blocked by the sagging mainsail, furled along the boom and now filled with water, and they had to cut a hole in the canvas to empty it. The barometer reached the lowest point August had ever seen.

Storms were racking north-west Europe. At Spencers Mollie watched the tearing clouds and listened to the wind moaning in the trees and the torrents of rain lashing the windows. The wireless spoke of gale warnings, the papers printed pictures of wrecks and stories of lifeboats turning back, the liner *Queen Elizabeth* on her way from America had to reduce speed and reached Southampton twenty-four hours late—which wasn't good news to anyone interested in the yacht *Duet*, last heard of bound from Corunna to Lisbon on passage to Jamaica. Then a telegram came from Lloyd's; she had been sighted by a French steamer in the southern Bay of Biscay and had signalled that all was well and she was homeward bound.

The barometer touched bottom and began to rise, the gale to abate. The wind veered and moderated, the Atlantic mood changed from brutal to benign, and August set course for England. On the fifth day from leaving Corunna, *Duet* was becalmed in a dying swell, her rigging draped with clothes and bedding hung to dry. In time, with a pleasant breeze blowing up Channel, she made a landfall at Start Point which she had passed more than three weeks before, outward bound. Disappointment was mixed with relief. It was Sunday and the four men held a little thanksgiving service in the cockpit. August read a psalm— '*They that go down to the sea in ships and occupy their business in great waters, these men see the works of the Lord and his wonders in the deep*' (like Charrington in the novel he could turn an occasion into something peculiarly his own, without ever acknowledging how much was owed to his seamanship)—and then they sang the hymn, *For those in peril on the sea*. Scott wrote that they didn't sing very well but the words meant more than usual.

The sea had become for August what the ice cap once was: his painter's canvas, his sculptor's block of stone. In *Duet*, for want of another instrument, he expressed something both private and universal. But though sailing was his ruling passion in the post-war years, it was far from being his only one. If he had seemed too old at the beginning of the war, he was six years older at the beginning of the peace and on coming home to Spencers, which he also loved, he might have lapsed into the life of an Essex squire, content with nothing more. Instead he settled for a typical mixture of activities, partly self-indulgent and partly patrician, combining the pursuit of his own interests with a stern observance of his public duty.

When he was still in the navy Mollie, herself a justice of the peace, was asked if her husband would stand for the county council. She couldn't answer for him but said that he might, and was surprised to read in the local paper that he had been elected unopposed. For ten years he was a conscientious councillor, needling the people who he thought deserved it and usually getting what he wanted. In debates he would pick on some tiresome detail, and if sometimes he seemed to do it only out of mischief it often meant that a point which nobody had bothered about was properly considered. He could disarm or deflate, exasperate or expose, provoke or praise, always to make life a little better. Once, when the Conservatives' courage was questioned by a socialist, August challenged him to meet outside in the car-park, to test it. But nobody ever doubted that Councillor Courtauld was a force for good. His performance in local politics, welcome for originality of style, was marked by his concern; and his private generosity—liable to move stealthily and in disguise, long known to his friends and already felt among his neighbours at Spencers—began to stretch further, even into public view.

Perhaps it was odd that someone who had restlessly sought the deserts of the world should confine himself so narrowly; that a man who hated authority should become Deputy Lieutenant of a county. Limits that might have been intolerable, and officialdom that had always been anathema, now seemed to be accepted. Romance, as well as a need to bestow his influence more widely, must have been at work. Birthplace and home were the complement to ice cap and sea, the nourishment to sustain solitude. In 1955, in his farewell speech to the council, stricken by the disease that was slowly killing him and pushed into the hall in a wheelchair, he saluted Essex and its people: 'What a county! There's no doubt that it's the best in Britain.'

9

As was expected of him—as he expected of himself, no doubt, for it was the tradition of a Courtauld, even such an unusual one —he spent more and more time on public service. 'I naturally couldn't help collecting committees,' he wrote. Though most of the collection was concerned with Essex—education, hospitals, rural community work, boys' clubs—he also sat on the committees of the Scott Polar Research Institute at Cambridge, the Royal National Lifeboat Institution and the Cruising Association, as well as being an honorary secretary of the Royal Geographical Society. Later, equally expectedly, he decided that committees were a waste of time and resigned from them all except his two favourites, lifeboats and boys' clubs. He founded the Augustine Courtauld Do-Good fund to be used for any purpose the trustees wished, and installed oak panelling in the village church in gratitude for his rescue from the ice cap and his son's escape from polio. When his mother died (leaving £200,000) he presented a new lifeboat named after her to the station at Walton-on-the-Naze in Essex. When his father died (leaving half a million pounds) he absorbed the responsibilities of owning 2,000 acres of land in the same unperturbed way that he had volunteered for the ice cap, and found much pleasure in running one of his own farms. The gates, as Peter Rodd noticed with approval, were always in good repair. 'It is a good thing,' August wrote, 'to have this farm for any of the boys who may want it in the future'—which in time one of them did. When his turn came up for High Sheriff, following his father and grandfather, he took on the duties calmly: 'One man was sentenced to death and we had to hang him. I didn't go to the execution.' Ceremonial had never been much to his taste, but it was part of English pageantry and so to be condoned; and he showed that he could wear a top hat or carry a sword as correctly (or not—his schoolboy's haphazard appearance lasted all his life) as if they were balaclava and ice axe. Underneath, rarely in public view, was always the solitary, questing explorer. The guests at a Coronation garden party might have been surprised to learn that their host, an impressive civic dignitary, happened to be editing an erudite anthology of polar writing.

The idea of the book had come to him on the ice cap, where one of his New Year resolutions had been to study the history of polar discovery and write about it. Slowly over the years the plan had been modified. Faced with a library of fat exploration books, mostly inaccessible if not intimidating to ordinary readers, he decided on a selection from the best—a string of extracts picked from his own wide reading to illustrate not just the long epic of Arctic and Antarctic travel but his sharp and intensely humane view of it. The compiling and editing of thirty centuries of literature took several years but eventually *From the Ends of the Earth* was published in 1958 by the Oxford University Press and declared 'a most satisfying anthology' by *The Times Literary Supplement*.

It is a delightful book, telling the story of the men who were impelled towards the poles—their vision, their moments of comedy and tragedy and in some cases their hour of death. Thus Homer writes of the world's brink, a dim country of melancholy people and everlasting night. An early Irish monk, on the contrary, reports that it is a land of endless day where at midnight a man can see to remove lice from his shirt. The Vikings make their astonishing voyages, followed by the merchant adventurers of the Renaissance and later by the scientific navigators. Hudson is set adrift in a small boat by his mutinous crew. Cook sails in one immense cruise from the Antarctic to the Arctic circle. Franklin vanishes on his search for the North-West Passage. Nansen makes the first crossing of the Greenland ice cap. The balloonist Andrée reflects, as he floats to his death over the pack ice, that it may be mad but it's better than dying forgotten like less adventurous men. Peary, the first man at the North Pole, finds it all so simple and commonplace. Shackleton, crossing unknown mountains in South Georgia after his prodigious journey in an open boat, speaks of the invisible stranger travelling at his elbow. Scott, beaten to the South Pole by Amundsen, writes his famous, hopeless, brave messages in his diary. And

Oates walks out of his tent into the blizzard and isn't seen again.

August included two pieces by explorer friends—Rymill returning with some of the secrets of the Antarctic and wondering what to tell anyone who asks why he went there, and Haig-Thomas sledging wearily through the Arctic towards a food cache only to find it has been raided by wolves. He even let in a passage of his own—the account of the boat journey down the east coast of Greenland with Gino Watkins and Lemon—but he put it under the name of Watkins and only mentioned in small print that he had written it himself.

Modesty was always the screen behind which he sheltered from any hint of his own achievement. It was a matter of shyness, of embarrassment, of disbelief that anything he had done was in the least important to anybody else or worth talking about. Even from his children he naturally concealed a past that might bring admiration which he felt he didn't deserve or didn't want, and it was from their mother that they first learned about what he called 'my little escapade' in Greenland. Afterwards he was touched, moved to tears, to hear from Mollie that they had been so interested.

The last of six children (four sons and two daughters—Perina, Christopher, Julien, Stephen, William and Susanna) was born in 1950. August was a loving father but inclined to stay aloof, letting nobody get very close, keeping his distance even in the family, suggesting that personalities were irrelevant and confidences too private to be shared. He could be stern in an old-fashioned way, bringing up the children to the kind of life he had himself inherited. He launched arguments, he talked of ships, stars, trees, Vikings, mathematical puzzles, odd scientific theories, family history—whatever struck him at the moment—and was pleased if a child's interest seemed to stir. He liked to read aloud the same books he had enjoyed as a boy, and would start great games, rather in the spirit of arranging entertainment for a ship's crew. When tents were put up, or in snow when sledges and skis were brought out, everything had to be done in the proper explorer's way. There was no nonsense, no slacking and not much sympathy for anyone who couldn't keep up or didn't enter into the general fun. He had definite ideas about childhood, as if he had never quite forsaken his own, which in a sense was so.

The family went for holidays in Switzerland and France and Spain, a little dutifully as something that was expected and would therefore be enjoyed or at least endured:

> We did a bit of climbing with the children . . . We thought we would like to have a look at the pictures and old towns . . . We inspected the stained glass through binoculars . . . We took in a visit to the Ile d'Oléron where my Huguenot ancestors had lived . . . We liked Segovia and Toledo best . . . What specially impressed us were the El Grecos . . . We had an introduction to the Duke of Alba and lunched with him, finding him most charming . . . Very fine, especially the Alhambra . . . The cathedral looked magnificent in the early light.

Tourism was no substitute for travelling; August was never much good at it and his perfunctory comments read like those of a man who had nothing more to say on the subject. Words came more happily when they came from the heart.

He never lost interest in the navy, staying on in the RNVR and occasionally putting on his uniform again. In 1952 he was back at HMS *Hornet*, the Coastal Forces base in Portsmouth harbour, for a reserve officers' course on the modern navy:

> How funny this is . . . We are a queer lot, all ages and sizes . . . Everything has changed—signals, alphabet, guns, wireless . . . They keep us on the hop pretty much all day . . . You have no idea how much saluting one has to do. One's arm nearly falls off . . . I am to be captain of one of the small fast boats . . . All very good fun . . . It was a bit bumpy going out through the Needles. The senior officer might have reduced speed for the tide rip but went through it at about thirty-five knots. I was driving and we hit one or two bumps pretty hard. The boat was leaking rather badly . . . On Sunday night we go out for a

sham battle against another lot from Dartmouth . . . We have
just drunk a silent toast to our late King and then to 'the
King is dead, God bless our new Queen' . . . It's all very
hoity-toity but very inefficient . . . We had a very uppy-
downy night out and got in at six this morning. As an exercise
it was a flop . . . We couldn't find the enemy . . . Very good for
our souls, no doubt.

The man who had spent five months alone in an ice hole without
getting bored had no difficulty filling the decade of his forties.
But watching the new explorers—more technical, more brash,
less romantic but no tougher or braver than he and his friends
had been—he may have felt that he belonged to another age.
Though others of his generation were still making difficult
journeys, their style of travel was getting out of fashion. An
expedition's manner, like its motive, was different now. The man
who had been so uncomfortable in the headlines back in 1931,
might applaud but never envy an adventure of the noisy modern
kind. He had claimed nothing for himself and never would.
'We started at A,' he once wrote, comparing a journey to the life
of a man, 'and after X days arrived at B. There was nothing in it.'
Conservative, philistine, generous, socially awkward, personally
intimidating and even frightening, intolerant of anyone who
didn't match his standards of integrity, impatient of any restric-
tions on his own individualism, single-minded to the point of
perversity, self-effacing in public, absurdly modest in private,
youthful, even boyish in his enthusiasms—August Courtauld
was precisely (to himself, anyway) just the ordinary chap he said
he was.

That ordinary chap—the 'normal man' whose voice had come up
the ventilator pipe at the ice-cap station and who had been hoisted
by his friends through the roof of the tent into the bright spring
morning—was attacked more than twenty years later by an
enemy against whose terrors, unlike those of solitude or a snow-

quake, he had no defence. A form of multiple sclerosis was diagnosed in 1953 when he was forty-nine. His courage and quiet cheerfulness, though he never surrendered them, were useless in a losing battle that lasted nearly six years.

The disease usually strikes young people, seldom anyone over forty. Its cause is poorly understood. An unknown agent attacks the covering sheath of nerve fibres, forming hard patches of tissue in the brain and spinal cord, between the size of a pinhead and a pea, that interrupt the flow of nervous impulses. Early symptoms—disturbed vision, tremors, unsteadiness in the use of limbs and other neurological signs—may come and go. Permanent paralysis sets in later and in the last stages almost the entire nervous system can be affected, with varying loss of control and mental damage.

Such was the agony of August's last years. His eyes, his limbs, his brain were destroyed in turn as if by the creeping cold that had failed before. Whether there was any link, beyond a strange analogy, between his privations on the ice cap and this second ordeal is improbable but not impossible. The similarities were bizarre, the differences fatal.

Nothing could stop his activities. Until near the end he continued to make plans for the future, for the next journey, for the time when he would be well again, just as on the ice cap he had planned what he was going to do after being relieved. He went to lectures at the Royal Geographical Society and attended the annual dinner of the Arctic Club, which always started with a special donation from himself—a plate of Essex oysters. Early in 1955 ('somewhat crippled with neuritis,' he wrote in his under-stated, elliptical way, reminiscent of the ice-cap diary) he went on a cruise to Australia, though he had to be pushed up the liner's gangway in a wheelchair. At Melbourne, summoning his old gaiety, he sent the tail of a kangaroo, shot by his eldest son, to the ship's galley to be cooked for a dinner party. Later that summer he went on one more voyage in *Duet*, the furthest ever, to the Mediterranean.

No longer able to sail his own yacht, he engaged a professional skipper, a veteran sailor from Tollesbury in Essex. August stayed below in the cabin, writing the log and inspiring his crew of friends and family by his old meticulous sense of seamanship and navigation; also by something greater. Sometimes he was carried up on deck and propped in a corner of the cockpit. It was a sad decline but nobody on board, at the sight of this man's contempt for his own tragedy, could be too cast down.

They sailed from West Mersea in mid-July and within a week, to avenge her failure six years earlier, *Duet* had rounded Finisterre. Thence to Vigo, Lisbon, Gibraltar, Malaga, Cartagena and, on August's fifty-first birthday, to Palma de Mallorca. On board for part of the cruise were the friends who in their youth had sailed with him on his first voyage abroad after leaving Cambridge. The style was rather different now—the Portuguese ambassador gave advice on his country's harbours and the White Ensign of the Royal Yacht Squadron brought the compliments of an admiral at Gibraltar—but the spirit was more or less the same and the men who had once waved empty beer bottles at a passing steamer in a storm could still share August's undimmed delight in a hard sea passage, a fresh landfall and an unknown port. For him, though in agony of mind and body, nothing could kill the fun of sailing in *Duet*, a pleasure spiced by having his four sons on board. The boys went off to see a bullfight, the skipper lent a hand in the galley and developed a famous line in pancakes, a waterspout played for them one day, a Moorish castle loomed under a full moon, a midnight gale turned a sheltered island anchorage into a place of dragging anchors and sleeplessness, the canvas filled, the ropes stretched, the water sang and frothed and slapped along *Duet*'s white hull as she sailed the ancient sea—an altogether fitting cruise.

Taking his chance before the disease went too far—and perhaps reminded in his growing isolation of the great dinner-party he had planned at the ice-cap station—August arranged a reunion for members of the British Arctic Air Route Expedition, with a few extra polar men and the captain of the *Quest*. It was held at *The Prospect of Whitby* pub in an upper room overlooking the

Thames near the dock from which they had sailed for Greenland, though the host was by now so helplessly paralysed that he had to be carried upstairs by his friends. The ship's flag with the emblem of a winged polar bear was hoisted on the terrace beside the river, old sledging flags decorated the table and August brought the tattered bits of Union Jack that had flown above him on the ice cap. With an elaborate seven-course menu translated into Eskimo and including a very superior version of pemmican soup, with toasts to the Queen of England and the Kings of Norway and Denmark and the memory of Gino Watkins and much else drunk in plenty of good wine, with wry talk of modern airlines flying over the Arctic route that they had once explored—with August 'in tremendous form' as one of the guests remembered twenty years later—the evening went as happily as he could have wished.

At home at Spencers, with the disease gaining control, he slowly surrendered the command of his life—as he had already done with his yacht—and let the professionals take over. Through the window he watched the flag flying from *Duet*'s old mast which had been stepped on the lawn. His last gesture of independence, an act of defiance as much as of reconciliation, was to dictate his memoirs to his nurse who copied them down in longhand. 'There is no reason why I should write a book,' he said in the preface. 'I have always felt there were too many, but some of my friends have persuaded me. I expect I shall be thought to be shooting a line . . . Anyway, here goes.' It was called *Man the Ropes*, from the verse of Masefield's that had hung in the expedition hut in Greenland, and was published in 1957.

The book was a disappointment to some of his friends and family. He wasn't himself any more, they said; he was already too ill when he dictated it; its tone was too flippant, too lightweight, too unworthy. Certainly he hurried over anything that was in danger of becoming pompous or dogmatic and dismissed his own achievements in the briefest way. From *Man the Ropes* nobody would get more than half a picture of his career. Yet there is more of the man himself in it than in many more ponderous autobiographies. His laconic prose, his throw-away style, his oblique view of life, his distaste for sustaining anything serious too long, his preference for the flash of a detail rather than the sweep of a theme—even the addition of some ingenuous poems which hardly bear scrutiny—all illustrate a character that remained sensitive, humble, unpredictable and lively almost to the end. The book carries the voice of its author talking quietly from his bed about the things he liked to think about; no heroics, no grand attitudes, no sententious afterthoughts. No wonder it annoyed people who wanted something more substantial to do justice to their old friend, something more monumental to remember him by. But what they got instead was truer to August Courtauld.

The sclerosis crept on. Such was its cruelty that his personality was altered, his behaviour distorted. No frostbite could match this evil. Praising his fortitude and Mollie's devotion in appalling circumstances, his doctor wrote of August's 'wretched and humiliating end'. He attempted things he could no longer do, to the extra strain of his family. And he did strange uncouth things too, unthinkable for the 'normal man' he once was, as the ice closed in on him and his mind froze. Without control of his body he lost the use of memory, intelligence and judgement. Any schizoid tendency was enhanced in a lacerating form of a grim disease. He was no longer the husband that Mollie could recognize and she watched him turn against her, away from those he loved most, and trail with his nurse to yet more doctors and clinics and dubious cures in a futile search for help.

In the last months he lay waiting, as he had once before, for the relief that would surely come. He often said he would live to be a hundred, but he must have known he was dying, though he never said so; his reserve at least remained intact, like his fearlessness. At New Year 1959 a twenty-first birthday party was held at Spencers for one of the children. Beyond reach of any social comfort, August listened in his room to the celebrations, sucking at the pipe that he could no longer fill. Perhaps he remembered that distant New Year on the ice cap. Perhaps this was all too familiar—the loneliness, the cramp, the awful besieging cold, the winter that would one day end. Perhaps nobody could have borne it so well as he, fortified by having been through it all before. Perhaps, as last time, he was confident (or so one hopes) in the certainty of his rescue.

Early in 1959 he was moved to hospital in London, where his multitude of friends visited him and where he died on 3 March, aged fifty-four. In a codicil to his will he had written, 'I wish my funeral to be as simple as possible and if it is convenient I wish to be buried at sea from my boat *Duet*. The ensign should be lowered to half-mast until my remains are disposed of and then should be hauled close-up while the boat returns to harbour.' But *Duet* was still laid up for the winter. Instead he was buried off the Essex coast from the lifeboat that he had presented in memory of his mother. Some years later another lifeboat—given by his brother Peter, launched by his sister Betty, consecrated by his own clergyman son Christopher—was named *Augustine Courtauld*.

Index